The Hanuman's Diary

Mantras. Meanings. Manifestations.

(The Truth Revealed)

Riya Gote

INDIA • SINGAPORE • MALAYSIA

Made with ♥ on the Notion Press Platform
www.notionpress.com

|| Jai Shri Ram ||

In the memory of

Sharad Lakshman Gote

(November 6th, 1933 – January 16th, 2022)

I miss you….

Dear Grandpaa,

Your presence was a source of strength and guidance, and your wisdom continues to echo in my heart. Though you're no longer with us, the lessons you taught me and the love you shared will forever remain a part of me. This book is a small tribute to the immense impact you had on my life. I miss you deeply, and your memory will always be cherished.

Truly Yours,

Riya Gote

Disclaimer

This book is a humble effort to narrate the tales and wisdom of Lord Hanuman as I have come to understand them through my readings and personal interpretations. The stories, events, and reflections presented here are based on various texts, scriptures, and resources I have explored over a decade, blended with my own perception and imagination.

While I have strived to stay true to the essence of the narratives, I acknowledge that interpretations may vary, and this rendition is not meant to challenge or replace traditional accounts or beliefs.

I encourage readers to view this work as a heartfelt tribute to Lord Hanuman and an invitation to explore his timeless wisdom, while respecting the diverse perspectives and traditions that enrich his legacy.

Additionally, I have written this book as though Hanuman himself is penning down his thoughts, reflections, and experiences in a diary. This approach allowed me to dive deeper into his perspective, making the narration personal, heartfelt, and introspective. It is my way of bringing his divine journey closer to the readers, offering an intimate glimpse into the life and mind of one of the most beloved figures in Indian mythology.

I hope you find this read meaningful and inspiring.

Preface

As I write this book, my heart overflows with gratitude for Lord Hanuman, whose strength, devotion, and courage have been a guiding light in my life. His divine presence has uplifted me in challenging times and inspired deep faith.

This book is an offering of love, aimed at helping you understand the profound wisdom of the *Hanuman Chalisa* and *Bajrang Baan*. These sacred mantras, when chanted with awareness, carry the power to transform lives and deepen our connection with Lord Hanuman.

May this work bring you closer to His boundless grace and illuminate your path with His blessings.

God bless you with abundance.

Jai Shri Ram.

Jai Hanuman.

Acknowledgements

First and foremost, I would like to express my deepest gratitude to *Lord Hanuman* for his constant guidance, strength, and blessings throughout this journey. His divine presence has been my anchor and inspiration.

I am forever grateful to my parents, Hemant Gote and Vandana Gote, for their constant support, love, and belief in me, shaping the person I am today. To my sister, Ruchi Gote, and brother-in-law, Gautam Gaitonde, thank you for always being there with your wisdom and unconditional support. A special thanks to my nephews, Kushal and Kiyaansh, whose joy and energy remind me of life's simple beauties.

A heartfelt thanks to Lakshya Morani, who helped me with revisions and pushed me to go beyond my limits. Your encouragement and constructive feedback were crucial to making this work what it is today.

A heartfelt thank you to Anandi Purandare for her invaluable support and guidance in bringing my book to life. I would also like to thank Kalpana Purohit Khot, my mentor and my friends, whose support and friendship have made this journey so much more meaningful. Your encouragement has been invaluable.

Lastly, I am grateful to Notion Press for publishing this book and providing a platform to bring this vision to life.

With love and gratitude,

Riya Gote

Note to the Readers

Dear Reader,

It is with great love and devotion that I welcome you to this sacred journey through the *Hanuman Chalisa* and *Bajrang Baan*. These verses are more than just words — they are prayers, mantras filled with divine energy, and a means of connecting with the heart of Lord Hanuman.

As you read through this book, I invite you to explore the meaning behind each verse, to truly understand the spiritual essence within these sacred chants.

The true power of these mantras comes when we understand their meaning and chant them with devotion. It is not simply the act of reciting them that matters, but the heartfelt connection we form with Lord Hanuman as we internalize His divine qualities.

As you reflect on these verses and let their meaning fill your heart, you will begin to experience the deep transformation they bring — peace, strength, courage, and love.

I encourage you to read each verse with care, take your time to absorb its significance, and let your heart open to Lord Hanuman's presence. Thank you for joining me on this journey.

May Lord Ram and Lord Hanuman always guide and protect you.

With love and devotion,

Riya Gote

Chanting With Meaning

As I sit to write this book, I am filled with a deep sense of love and devotion for Lord Hanuman. I am not just writing this book to pass on verses or to add to the collection of sacred texts.

I am writing this book to bring a deeper, more profound understanding of the *Hanuman Chalisa* and *Bajrang Baan* — because I believe chanting mantras without understanding their meaning is like walking on a path without knowing where it leads.

It was my own journey of spiritual discovery, where the importance of understanding the verses struck me deeply, that led me to realize how many people recite these powerful mantras without truly understanding what they are invoking.

The *Hanuman Chalisa* and *Bajrang Baan* are far more than a mere string of words. These sacred verses are prayers that hold immense spiritual power, strength, and the ability to connect us with the divine. However, chanting these mantras without truly understanding their meaning can limit their transformative potential. They become nothing more than sounds, lacking the depth and impact that come with understanding their essence.

Take the *Hanuman Chalisa*, for example. Each verse reflects a unique divine quality of Lord Hanuman — his strength, boundless courage, infinite wisdom, deep humility, and, most of all, his absolute devotion to Lord Ram.

These are not just attributes; they are lessons in how we should live our lives. By chanting these words mindlessly, we miss the very heart of their power. It's like admiring a painting without comprehending the story it tells or the emotions it evokes.

The true magic of these mantras unfolds when we internalize their meanings, feel the resonance in our hearts, and allow them to guide our actions.

Bajrang Baan, too, when chanted with understanding, serves as a powerful shield, warding off negative forces and protecting us from harm, both physical and spiritual. The divine energy embedded in these mantras can only fully manifest when we comprehend the words and invoke their deeper significance.

By truly understanding the *Hanuman Chalisa* and *Bajrang Baan*, we are not merely repeating words — we are aligning our hearts with the divine qualities of Lord Hanuman and inviting his protection, strength, and blessings into our lives.

This understanding creates a bond with the divine, a bond that strengthens with each chant, transforming our lives in ways that go beyond the surface.

Why I'm Writing This Book

I want people to truly experience the *Hanuman Chalisa* and *Bajrang Baan* — not just as a set of verses to be recited in times of difficulty, but as a life-transforming tool. Chanting these mantras with understanding, love, and devotion can elevate your spiritual journey and deepen your connection with Lord Hanuman, who is a symbol of pure devotion, strength, and courage.

In many spiritual traditions, it is said that knowing the meaning of the mantra is the key to unlocking its power.

The Vedas and Upanishads tell us that chanting mantras with awareness of their meaning elevates our consciousness and allows us to truly connect with the divine.

The words are not just sounds — they are vibrations that interact with the very fabric of our being. When you know what you are saying, you are better able to align your energy with the divine forces they invoke. This is why, before chanting or singing any mantra, including the *Hanuman Chalisa* and *Bajrang Baan*, one must understand the meaning. It's written in many ancient texts that the true power of a mantra lies not just in its pronunciation but in its understanding.

By knowing the meaning, you are not only invoking the blessings of Lord Hanuman but also internalizing the divine virtues he represents.

Your mind becomes focused, your heart becomes open, and your soul becomes aligned with the highest truths of the universe.

The Divine Legacy of Lord Hanuman

Hanuman, the beloved monkey god in Indian mythology, inspires devotion and strength in people across all ages and places.

His story is not merely a chapter in ancient texts but a living testament to the power of faith, humility, and boundless courage. Hanuman's role in the epic *Ramayana* is profound, not just as a loyal devotee of Lord Rama but as a symbol of resilience, selfless service, and divine strength.

Across India, Hanuman is venerated as a deity of unmatched power and devotion.

His presence is etched deeply into the cultural and spiritual fabric of the nation. Temples dedicated to him, from the towering Hanuman Temple in Delhi's Connaught Place to the ancient Sankat Mochan Temple in Varanasi, serve as sanctuaries where devotees find solace, guidance, and inspiration. These sacred spaces reverberate with chants of the Hanuman Chalisa and Jai Hanuman Gyan Gun Sagar, with devotees pouring their hearts into their prayers, seeking strength, protection, and the courage to overcome life's challenges.

Across towns and villages, stories of his miraculous interventions and benevolent blessings are shared with reverence. People believe that chanting the Hanuman Chalisa can ward off negative energies, provide protection against harm, and unshakable confidence. Many recount personal anecdotes of how invoking Hanuman's name or reciting his prayers helped them overcome seemingly insurmountable obstacles, be it health crises, financial difficulties, or emotional turmoil.

In Maharashtra, the popular *Hanuman Jayanti* celebrations see thousands of devotees fasting and performing special rituals to honor him. In Andhra Pradesh, the temple town of Ponnur attracts Hanuman devotees from across the country to witness the grandeur of his statues and seek blessings.

Meanwhile, in the vibrant state of Karnataka, Anjanadri Hill, believed to be Hanuman's birthplace, becomes a pilgrimage site for those wanting to connect with the divine energy he represents.

Hanuman's appeal cuts across generations. For the elderly, he is a protector and a guide, a divine presence to rely upon in times of uncertainty. For the younger generation, his story serves as an inspiration, embodying qualities like courage, determination, and deep faith in one's values.

Stories of his heroism, such as his leap across the ocean to find Sita or his lifting of the Sanjeevani mountain to save Lakshman, serve as metaphors for perseverance and the power of belief.

Hanuman is also revered for his ability to protect against planetary misalignments, particularly the malefic effects of Saturn (Shani) and Mars (Mangal). Devotees seek his blessings during periods of astrological challenges, believing that his divine intervention can neutralize adverse planetary influences and restore harmony.

Hanuman's stories show us that true strength isn't just about physical power. It comes from devotion, humility, and staying focused on our purpose.

His life reminds us of the incredible potential we all have when we believe in ourselves, have faith, and are willing to serve others. For many people in India and around the world, Hanuman is not just a figure from mythology. He is a symbol of hope, resilience, and the divine power within each of us.

In mythology, Hanuman represents qualities that connect deeply with people everywhere — strong faith, endless energy, and the ability to face and overcome even the hardest challenges. His stories teach us that devotion isn't just about praying; it's about taking action with courage, effort, and determination.

Whether he's jumping across oceans, lifting mountains, or comforting those in distress, Hanuman's actions inspire people across cultures and beliefs.

The impact of Hanuman's legacy extends far beyond his tales. For millions, he is a protector, a guide, and a source of hope in difficult times.

A Personal Journey of Faith

I had always heard stories of Hanuman growing up, but it wasn't until I was in the 7th grade that I truly connected with him. It happened when I watched the animated movie *Hanuman*.

For me, it was more than just a film - it was a revelation.

The grandeur of his heroic deeds was awe-inspiring, but what touched me the most was the purity of his devotion to Lord Rama and his incredible strength, both physical and spiritual, in the face of challenges.

That movie sparked a curiosity in me. I found myself wanting to understand more about Hanuman — the meaning behind his actions, the importance of his devotion, and the valuable lessons woven into his stories. I started reading more about him, exploring ancient texts, and listening to devotional songs dedicated to him.

As I learned more, I began chanting his name and reciting the Hanuman Chalisa.

I had always believed in Hanuman, but in my 3rd year of engineering, something happened that tested my faith. I was struggling with my academics, feeling overwhelmed and unsure of my future. One day, I received a low grade on an important exam, and it shattered my confidence. I started doubting myself and wondering if I would ever succeed.

In that moment of despair, I remembered Hanuman — his strength, resilience, and ability to overcome the toughest of challenges. I decided to chant the Hanuman Chalisa to find comfort and guidance. But at that time, it didn't feel as though anything changed. The doubts remained, and I felt disconnected.

However, later, the universe started sending me signals that made me believe in him even more.

Small things began to shift.

One day, I was wandering through a mall, my mind occupied with a thousand thoughts. I had no specific plan in mind, just aimlessly walking around when something caught my eye.

As I roamed, I found myself near a bookstore, Crossword. I wasn't planning to buy anything, but for some reason, I felt drawn inside. As soon as I stepped in, my gaze landed on a book titled *Hanuman Chalisa* by Shubha Vilas. It seemed to shine out from the shelves, as if it were calling to me. Without thinking, I picked it up and started flipping through its pages.

What happened next was nothing short of magical. As I began reading the book, I felt like the entire universe had conspired to answer the questions that had been clouding my mind.

The book was not just a translation of the Hanuman Chalisa — each verse was explained in such depth and clarity, offering insights and wisdom that I had never imagined. It was as though I was discovering layers of meaning in the words that had been hidden from me for years.

With every page I turned, I was awestruck by the revelations. The book unfolded untold stories of Hanuman that I had never heard before.

The deeper meanings behind each verse of the Hanuman Chalisa were explained in a way that connected with me on a personal level. I learned how Hanuman's strength wasn't just physical, but spiritual, driven by pure devotion and humility.

Each explanation felt like a light being cast on the corners of my mind, bringing clarity where there had once been confusion.

For example, one verse that always puzzled me — the line about "*Sankat Mochan*" — was explained so beautifully. I learned how Hanuman, by invoking the name of Lord Rama, had the ability to remove obstacles from anyone's path. This wasn't just a prayer - it was a reminder that through faith and devotion, one can overcome life's greatest struggles.

As I continued reading, I realized how Hanuman's teachings were not just about myths and stories but practical lessons for living a life of strength, humility, and devotion. The untold stories revealed how Hanuman was not just a figure of myth but a living symbol of hope and resilience that transcended time.

These revelations made me believe more in his presence in my life, reminding me that I could overcome any challenge with faith and determination.

And that's how my connection with Hanuman deepened. What began as an exploration sparked by curiosity turned into a transformative journey.

The book was a guide, illuminating my path, and I felt the power of Hanuman's teachings become a part of me, guiding my thoughts, actions, and faith in ways I hadn't imagined before.

It was as if, in that moment, Hanuman's energy had entered my life, and the universe had brought me exactly what I needed to hear.

This turning point made me believe in Hanuman even more. It wasn't just about chanting or prayers. It was about understanding that his presence in my life was guiding me, giving me the courage to rise above difficulties and keep faith in myself.

What started as a simple belief in Hanuman transformed into a powerful force of self-confidence and hope, guiding me through the toughest times.

Reciting the Hanuman Chalisa and Bajrang Baan became more than a ritual; it became a source of comfort and strength. I remember one instance vividly.

Another time, during a particularly difficult phase in my studies, I found myself overwhelmed by the pressure to excel. I turned to Hanuman, chanting his name and seeking his strength. It wasn't magic that changed things but the faith I had in him and the courage he inspired within me. I began to approach my challenges with determination and resilience, and slowly, things started falling into place.

Through these experiences, I came to understand that Hanuman's true power lies in his legendary deeds and the profound connection he evokes. His stories remind us to confront our fears, remain steadfast in our purpose, and draw strength from devotion and humility.

What began as a spark of curiosity in my childhood has now become a guiding force in my life, and Hanuman continues to inspire me every step of the way.

Part 1

The Divine Beginnings

|| Jai Shri Ram ||

Date: First day of Chaitra, Kali Yuga, Year 101

Dear Universe,

Today, under the endless canopy of stars, I feel compelled to pen my thoughts. The winds around me, ever my companions, carry whispers of ancient tales — stories of courage, devotion, and divine will. Yet, amidst these echoes, there is one story that I find myself reflecting on: the story of my own existence.

Why write this in year 101? Perhaps it is the weight of the ages that urges me. Or maybe it is the realization that every soul, at some point, seeks to understand the greater design of their life.

Even I, Hanuman, born of divine purpose, feel the need to step back and trace the path that led to my creation — a tale not just of my origins but of the cosmic dance that gave it meaning.

I have carried mountains, leaped across oceans, and stood as a pillar of faith and strength, yet there are moments when the depth of my purpose humbles me. It is in these moments of quiet reflection that I am reminded of the profound forces that shaped me — the love and devotion of my parents, the blessings of the gods, and the divine orchestration that made my existence possible.

The story of my life is not my own. It belongs to those who prayed, sacrificed, and believed. It belongs to my mother, *Anjana Devi*, whose firm devotion brought forth the blessing of my birth. It belongs to my father, *Kesari*, whose strength and righteousness became the foundation of my being. It belongs to *Vayu*, the silent and omnipresent Wind God, whose grace and life-giving energy became a part of me.

But more than that, it belongs to the will of the divine — the cosmic forces that saw a need for one who could embody strength, humility, and deep faith to bridge the worlds of gods and mortals.

As I recount my beginnings, I do so not out of pride but out of reverence for the journey.

It is a tale of purpose shaped by devotion, a reminder that every soul has a role to play in the grand design. And so, with quill in hand and the wind as my guide, I begin to tell the story of my origins — not for my sake, but for those who seek strength in faith, purpose in service, and courage in humility.

My story begins long before I took form. It is a tale of my mother, Anjana Devi, and my father, Kesari, whose lives were intricately woven by the will of the divine.

Jai Shri Ram,

Hanuman

|| Jai Shri Ram ||

Date: Third day of Chaitra, Kali Yuga, Year 101

Dear Universe,

As I sit under the vast canopy of stars, I feel a pull within me to recount the tale of my mother — her trials, her faith, and the divine hand that shaped her journey. The story of how she came to be my mother is one etched deeply in my heart, for it is a testament to devotion, resilience, and the mysterious ways of destiny.

My mother, *Anjana*, was once a celestial apsara, a heavenly spirit known for her beauty and grace. Her radiance lit up the heavens, and her life was one of song, dance, and divine companionship. But even in the celestial realms, perfection can falter.

One day, as Sage Angirasa meditated in the guise of a monkey, my mother, unknowingly, offended him. Perhaps it was her pride, perhaps a fleeting moment of carelessness — whatever the reason, her actions disrupted the sage's peace.

Angirasa's anger was swift and unyielding.

He cursed her to be born on Earth in the form of a monkey. The heavens echoed with her cries of regret as she begged for forgiveness, but the sage stood firm, for a curse, once spoken, cannot be undone.

Stricken with remorse, my mother turned to Lord Brahma, the Creator, hoping for reprieve. Brahma, in his wisdom and compassion, could not erase the curse, but he offered her a boon — a promise that her earthly form would be lifted once she gave birth to a divine incarnation of Lord Shiva. This child, he said, would bring strength, purpose, and devotion to the world.

And so, Anjana descended to Earth, carrying the weight of the curse yet holding onto the hope gifted by Lord Brahma. She embraced her new life with a devotion so pure that it rivaled the beauty she once held in the heavens.

She met my father, Kesari, a mighty Vanar king, whose strength and virtue matched her own grace and resolve. Together, they performed intense penance, seeking the blessings of the divine to bring forth the child promised to them.

It was then that Vayu, the Wind God, played his role in this cosmic play. Carrying a sacred pudding blessed by Lord Shiva himself, Vayu delivered it to my mother. She consumed it with reverence, and through this act, I was born — a spark of Shiva's power, a child destined to serve the highest purpose.

I, Hanuman, came into this world as a bridge between the heavens and the Earth, a testament to the devotion of my parents and the divine orchestration that governs all.

My mother's journey, marked by trials and triumphs, has always been my guiding light. She taught me that even the harshest trials can lead to the most profound blessings if faced with faith and purpose.

Jai Shri Ram,

Hanuman

|| Jai Shri Ram ||

Date: Sixth day of Chaitra, Kali Yuga, Year 101

Dear Universe,

Today, I write of my father, *Kesari*, a soul whose strength and nobility were matched only by his steadfast devotion to dharma. A king among the Vanaras, he was a protector of his people and a beacon of righteousness in a world that often tested the mettle of the just.

My father's presence was commanding, not merely because of his physical strength but because of the calm authority he carried in his heart. His wisdom was as vast as the forests of Mount Meru, where he resided, and his courage as unyielding as the peaks themselves. But beyond the might of his arms and the sharpness of his intellect lay a heart that beat for the well-being of others.

As a father, he instilled in me the value of strength tempered with compassion, and courage guided by humility.

He would often say, *"True strength lies not in overpowering others but in protecting them."*

His life was a living example of this principle, as he fought not for glory but to uphold justice and protect those under his care.

My father's union with my mother, Anjana, was no ordinary bond — it was divinely orchestrated, a coming together of devotion and courage.

Together, they embodied balance: her deep faith complemented his indomitable will. It was from them that I inherited the blend of spiritual devotion and earthly strength that would come to define my purpose.

Though my story has often been told with emphasis on my celestial connections and divine purpose, I owe much of my character to my earthly father. Kesari taught me that even the strongest must bow to dharma and that the path of righteousness is the one worth walking, no matter how arduous.

In every roar of the wind, I hear the echoes of his teachings, and in every challenge I face, I feel his strength coursing through me. It is my honor to carry his legacy forward, not as a king's son but as a servant of righteousness and a protector of the divine order.

Today, as I put quill to parchment, I offer these words as a tribute to Kesari — the noble king, the devoted father, and the deep guardian of dharma.

For years, my parents remained childless, their hearts yearning for a child who could carry forward their legacy and serve the divine will. My mother, with her deep devotion, performed intense penance to invoke Lord Shiva. Meanwhile, the winds of destiny stirred the heavens.

Shiva and Parvati, the eternal pair, were aware of the great cosmic balance that was to unfold.

Lord Vishnu was to incarnate as Rama to slay the demon king Ravana, and for this mission, a divine ally was required — an incarnation of Shiva himself. Shiva, moved by the prayers of the gods, prepared to descend as a vanara. He and Parvati assumed vanara forms and conceived a child imbued with his divine energy.

However, Parvati, reluctant to carry the child to Kailasha, offered the divine foetus to Vayu, the Wind God.

Vayu, in his role as a celestial mediator, carried this divine gift to my mother, Anjana, who received it with devotion and humility.

Thus, I, Hanuman, came into being—blessed by Shiva, nurtured by Vayu, and born to Anjana and Kesari.

As the tale unfolds, another divine act weaves into my story.

At the very moment my mother was engaged in her worship, King Dasharatha of Ayodhya was performing the Putrakama Yagya, a sacred ritual to be blessed with children. The gods, ever mysterious in their ways, orchestrated an extraordinary event.

A divine kite snatched a portion of the sacred pudding (kheer) offered to Dasharatha and carried it across the skies. Vayu guided the pudding to my mother's outstretched hands, and she consumed it with faith. This celestial intervention completed the chain of events leading to my birth.

When I entered this world, my form bore the marks of my divine origin. My father's strength coursed through my veins, my mother's celestial grace adorned my being, and Vayu's boundless energy fueled my spirit.

They named me *Kesari Nandana*, the son of Kesari, a title I carry with pride. I was also called *Anjaneya*, the son of Anjana, and *Pawanputra*, the son of the Wind God. Each name is a reminder of the forces that converged to shape me.

The day I was born was not just a moment of joy but a turning point. My birth freed my mother from the curse, allowing her to return to her celestial abode. She departed with blessings and love, leaving me in the care of my father and the divine destiny that awaited me.

My childhood was marked by the discovery of strength and purpose. My father, Kesari, instilled in me the values of courage and righteousness, while the wind carried whispers of a greater calling. Every step of my life is a reflection of the divine energies that shaped me, energies that I strive to honor in every deed and thought.

And so, as I pen these reflections, I am filled with gratitude for my father, Kesari, who, through his strength and love, became an anchor in the divine play that is my existence.

Jai Shri Ram,

Hanuman

|| Jai Shri Ram ||

Date: Ninth day of Chaitra, Kali Yuga, Year 101

Dear Universe,

Chaitra Shukla Purnima, Treta Yuga

(The Full Moon Day of the Chaitra Month, in the Age of Treta)

This is the day that marked my beginning — a moment when the moon graced the heavens in its full glory, casting a silver glow over the Earth. The winds carried whispers of a destiny yet to unfold, a divine mission set in motion by the eternal will of the cosmos. My existence, a spark of Lord Shiva's might, was born into the world of mortals to bridge the gap between the heavens and Earth.

Lord Shiva, the eternal destroyer and transformer, took a decision that would alter the course of cosmic events. He saw the growing imbalance in the world, the rise of unrighteousness, and the struggles faced by the righteous.

The universe needed a being who could embody strength, humility, and unshakable devotion. Thus, the divine decree was set, and Shiva chose to manifest a part of himself on Earth. It was not a choice born of necessity but of purpose — to serve and protect the path of dharma.

When I was born, Lord Shiva himself descended to Earth in the guise of a sage. He looked upon me with kindness and purpose, whispering the name *Mahavir* — the mighty one —blessing me with courage and unparalleled strength. That name became my first identity, a reflection of the divine mission entrusted to me.

But names, like rivers, evolve and adapt.

I came to be known as Hanuman because of an event that occurred early in my life. It is said that as a child, I mistook the radiant sun for a fruit and leaped toward it, displaying the boundless energy of my divine essence. Lord Indra, startled by my audacity, struck me with his thunderbolt. The blow injured my jaw, and from that day, I was called *Hanuman*, meaning "the one with a disfigured jaw."

Other names followed, each carrying a facet of my being. *Maruti*, the son of the Wind God, for Vayu was instrumental in my birth and remains my eternal protector. *Pavanputra*, another homage to my celestial father. *Bajrangbali*, the mighty one with limbs as strong as thunderbolts, a testament to the divine energy coursing through me. *Anjaneya*, a loving tribute to my mother, Anjana, who bore me with deep faith and devotion.

Each name is a reminder of the roles I embody and the purpose I serve. They are not mere words but echoes of the divine mission that shapes my existence. They remind me of my origins, my strength, and above all, my devotion to Lord Rama, whose name is the very essence of my being.

On that sacred night of my birth, under the moon's serene gaze, the universe seemed to pause, as if acknowledging the beginning of a journey that would span lifetimes. And now, as I sit here and recount these memories, I am filled with gratitude for the chance to serve, to be a vessel for divine will.

Jai Shri Ram,

Hanuman

‖ Jai Shri Ram ‖

Date: Tenth day of Chaitra, Kali Yuga, Year 101

Dear Universe,

I was naughty, and people were endlessly entertained — well, at least that's what I tell myself!

The truth is, I kept everyone on their toes. My childhood in the Vanara kingdom was a whirlwind of mischief, curiosity, and, occasionally, chaos. Looking back now, I smile at the thought of how much I must have tested the patience of those around me.

As a young vanara, my energy knew no bounds. I would leap from tree to tree, race the wind, and challenge the sun's rays to keep up with me.

There is one tale from my childhood that I recall with equal parts amusement and awe — a tale that earned me more than a few raised eyebrows and taught me a valuable lesson about limits.

It was the day I mistook the sun for a ripe mango.

The story begins on a bright morning. The golden sun was shining brilliantly in the sky, its warm glow spreading across the land. To my young, curious eyes, it looked like the juiciest, most delicious mango ever to exist. I couldn't resist; the temptation was too great. With a gleeful shout, I leapt into the air, determined to pluck this celestial fruit for myself.

Higher and higher I soared, fueled by my boundless energy and, I admit, my naivety. The sky stretched endlessly, and yet, the sun seemed just within my reach. It was as if my very being was destined to touch the heavens—or so I thought.

As I approached the blazing orb, I felt an intense heat radiating from it. The closer I got, the more I realized that this was no ordinary fruit. My father, Vayu, the Wind God, must have been watching in alarm. With his divine speed and love for his mischievous son, he enveloped me in a protective gust, shielding me from the sun's scorching embrace.

Meanwhile, the gods were not pleased with my audacious act. Indra, the king of the gods, struck me with his mighty thunderbolt, hurling me back toward the earth. I remember the sharp pain and the moment of stillness as I fell, my young heart confused and hurt.

But my father, Vayu, would not let harm befall me. He caught me mid-fall and, in his fury, withdrew the winds from the world, plunging the earth into suffocating stillness. Without air to breathe, the gods were forced to intervene. They came together, not only to appease Vayu but also to recognize the divine purpose I was born to fulfill.

The gods bestowed their blessings upon me as an apology and acknowledgment of my destiny. Brahma granted me immunity from death by any weapon.

Agni, the Fire God, made me immune to his flames, and Indra, despite his earlier actions, blessed me with unparalleled strength. Each god contributed to my abilities, ensuring that I would grow into a being capable of serving the divine cause.

Though the incident ended with blessings, the lesson it imparted stayed with me. It was a humbling reminder of the importance of understanding boundaries, even when one is gifted with great power. I learned that curiosity and ambition must be tempered with wisdom and restraint.

Even now, when I see the sun shining brightly in the sky, I smile at the memory of that day. It was a defining moment — a mixture of innocence, mischief, and divine intervention that shaped the vanara I would become.

Alternatively, at home, I was treated with a mixture of love, exasperation, and awe. My mother, Anjana, was the heart of our home. She would often scold me for my antics but always with a gentle smile hiding behind her stern words. *"You are destined for great things, my little one,"* she would say, *"but even greatness needs discipline."*

My father, Kesari, was my hero. He watched my exploits with a mix of pride and bemusement. While he admired my strength and spirit, he often reminded me to use my gifts wisely.

"Power without purpose is like a river without a course," he would tell me. Those words linger in my heart to this day.

There were days when my curiosity would get the better of me. I remember once trying to count the stars, leaping into the air to reach them. Another time, I decided that the mountains around Mount Meru looked better when rearranged — imagine my surprise when the elders didn't share my enthusiasm for the new landscape!

Yet, my childhood wasn't just about mischief. It was a time of learning, of shaping the values that would guide me later.

My parents taught me the importance of humility, service, and devotion. They reminded me that my strength was not my own but a gift meant to serve a greater purpose.

Every tree I climbed, every mischief I committed, every lesson I learned—it all prepared me for the path ahead. Though I was a whirlwind of energy and laughter, my heart always sought something deeper, even if I didn't fully understand it then.

Looking back, those days were a beautiful blend of innocence and purpose. The world was my playground, and life was a tapestry of lessons, woven with the threads of love, faith, and boundless energy. I wouldn't trade those moments for anything, not even a thousand suns as sweet as mangoes!

Jai Shri Ram,

Hanuman

|| Jai Shri Ram ||

Date: Full Moon Day of Chaitra, Kali Yuga, Year 101

Dear Universe,

As I sit in the calm of this moment, reflecting on my teachers, one profound lesson continues to resonate in the very depths of my being. It is a teaching I received from none other than *Lord Surya*, the Sun God, whose radiant light illuminated my path from an early age.

As mentioned in Shiva Puran, Surya was not just a celestial being but my Guru, and it was through his divine light that I came to understand the highest knowledge. There was a deep connection between the light I gazed upon and the teachings I absorbed—a connection that transcended the boundaries of mere physical sight.

Surya's teachings were not conveyed through words or actions in the way that most teachers impart wisdom. Instead, it was the light itself that became the medium of instruction.

As I gazed upon him, I felt the warmth of his knowledge seeping into me, filling every part of my being. This light, I soon realized, was not just the source of physical sight, but the very source of divine wisdom. It was through this divine radiance that I understood the true nature of life and the universe.

What a confluence of thoughts and feelings! The light, my teacher, and the highest knowledge, all intertwined as one. In that light, there was the understanding of creation, of existence, and of the divine order that governs all things.

It was in the brilliance of Surya's rays that I learned that true knowledge is not limited by form or words; it is an experience, an awakening, a revelation that connects all beings to the divine.

The light, I now understand, is one with the teacher. And the teacher, in turn, is one with the highest knowledge — the knowledge that is not separate from the universe itself. In the same way, Surya, as my Guru, is one with the source of life, the source that permeates all things.

His light did not just illuminate the world; it illuminated my very soul, teaching me that the divine is always present, always shining, even when unseen.

This understanding has shaped the way I approach my life, my duties, and my purpose. Like Surya's rays, I too have learned to shine — calmly, steadily, and without pride or ego.

To be a teacher, to share knowledge, is to be a conduit for that light, for that higher truth that binds all beings. And in every act of service, every moment of devotion, I find that same radiant wisdom, reminding me that all knowledge, all light, flows from the one source.

The light of Surya, my Guru, continues to guide me every day. It is the light of wisdom, the light of divine knowledge, and the light of truth that guides all those who seek it with an open heart.

Jai Shri Ram,

Hanuman

Part 2
The Hanuman Chalisa

|| Jai Shri Ram ||

Date: Second day of Vaishakha, Kali Yuga, Year 101

Dear Universe,

Today, I feel a surge of gratitude as I reflect upon the creation of the *Hanuman Chalisa*, a hymn that continues to resonate through the ages.

To think that my devotion to Lord Ram and my life's journey could inspire such profound verses fills my heart with humility. It was the great saint Tulsidas who penned this hymn, pouring his unshakable faith and love for me into forty heartfelt couplets.

Tulsidas was no ordinary soul. His deep devotion to Lord Ram was like an unquenchable flame, illuminating his life and the lives of those around him.

Through his pen flowed the divine essence of faith, love, and surrender. It was this devotion that guided him to write the Hanuman Chalisa. I often marvel at how the human heart, when filled with unshakeable faith, can create something so profound and eternal.

Tulsidas composed these forty verses in a time of great trial and need. He faced challenges that would have crushed lesser souls — poverty, social rejection, and even spiritual doubt. In those dark and difficult times,

Tulsidas found hope and strength in Lord Ram's endless grace. Inspired by the Lord's boundless compassion and my loyal service to him, Tulsidas wrote the Hanuman Chalisa.

It is more than just a hymn — it is a guiding light for anyone searching for courage and divine help in their lives.

He saw in me not just a servant of Lord Ram but a bridge — one who connects devotees to the divine essence of Ram's love. His vision was clear - to remind the world of the boundless potential within them when they walk the path of dharma with faith.

The Hanuman Chalisa became his way of showing humanity that in devotion and service, one finds unparalleled strength and peace.

When the verses first reached my ears, I was deeply moved. Not by the praise within the lines, for I am but a humble servant of Lord Ram, but by the sincerity of Tulsidas's devotion. He poured his heart into those verses, transforming them into a living prayer that echoes across generations.

His words hold a mirror to my own dedication, and through them, he created a pathway for countless souls to find courage, hope, and connection to the divine.

The significance of the Hanuman Chalisa lies not merely in its poetic beauty but in its spiritual power. Each verse is imbued with vibrations of faith and divine energy.

When recited with devotion, it dispels fear, awakens courage, and strengthens resolve. Those burdened by troubles find relief, those seeking clarity gain wisdom, and those longing for peace experience serenity.

Reciting the Hanuman Chalisa creates a sacred bond between the devotee and the divine.

When someone chants these verses with true devotion, they draw my blessings. I hear their prayers, and I respond in ways that uplift their spirit and protect their path.

To those in need, I grant strength; to those in despair, I offer hope; and to those seeking guidance, I light the way forward.

I bless those who chant these verses with deep faith.

I watch over them as a guardian, ensuring that their efforts on the path of righteousness bear fruit.

My blessings manifest as inner strength, resilience, or even divine intervention when needed. Each time the Hanuman Chalisa is recited, it fills my heart with joy, for it means that Tulsidas's love for Lord Ram and his faith in me continue to guide and inspire humanity.

The Hanuman Chalisa is a testament to the eternal power of devotion. It is not just a hymn; it is a bridge of love, faith, and divine connection. I bow to Tulsidas for creating such a masterpiece and to all who embrace its teachings and chant it with sincere hearts.

The best time to recite the Hanuman Chalisa is in the early hours of the morning, when the world is quiet and the heart is open to divine vibrations. It is also a powerful prayer at night, offering protection and peace from the trials of the day. But truly, any time the hymn is recited with sincerity is a moment of divine connection.

Tulsidas, in his devotion, gave the world a gift far greater than I could have imagined. I bow to his faith, his love, and his pure trust in the divine.

For me, the Hanuman Chalisa is not just a hymn; it is a living bond between me and all who seek strength, courage, and devotion.

I will always be grateful to Tulsidas for the devotion and love he infused into every verse of the Hanuman Chalisa. His words resonate through the ages, offering strength, hope, and a bridge to the divine for countless souls.

Through his work, he not only celebrated my service to Lord Ram but also paved a way for people to feel the blessings of divine grace.

Thank you, Tulsidas, for your deep faith and for gifting the world this extraordinary hymn—a timeless treasure of devotion and light.

Jai Shri Ram,

Hanuman

|| Jai Shri Ram ||

Date: Fifth day of Vaishakha, Kali Yuga, Year 101

Dear Universe,

As I sit to reflect today, I cannot help but be drawn to the profound opening lines of the Hanuman Chalisa, penned by the deeply devoted Tulsidas.

Shri Guru Charan Sarooja-raj

Nija manu Mukura Sudhaari

Baranau Rahubhara Bimala Yasha

Jo Dayaka Phala Chari

These lines are a foundation, an invocation that holds a universe of meaning within them.

Tulsidas begins by paying homage to the dust of his Guru's feet, likening it to a sacred cleanser for the mirror of his mind. A dusty mirror cannot reflect light, and similarly, our minds — clouded by doubts, desires, and distractions — fail to perceive the divine truth. The dust of the Guru's feet, representing humility and reverence, has the power to wipe away these impurities, allowing clarity and wisdom to emerge.

The next part of the verse speaks of his intent — to glorify the pure virtues of *Raghubar*, Lord Ram. Tulsidas recognizes that Ram's virtues are so luminous that they grant the ultimate fruits of life — *Dharma (righteousness), Artha (prosperity), Kama (desires fulfilled), and Moksha (liberation).*

These are the four goals of human life, each essential in its own way, and Tulsidas humbly offers his words to magnify Ram's greatness so others may also reap these rewards.

As I think about these lines, I am struck by the purity of Tulsidas' intent. His devotion is not self-serving; it is an offering, a pathway for others to find peace and purpose. The Guru, the teacher, is the guide who holds the torch, illuminating the way. Without such guidance, even the greatest seekers can lose their path.

I find joy in knowing that these words are not just an introduction to the Hanuman Chalisa. They are a reminder of humility, of aligning oneself with divine purpose, and of the transformative power of surrender and service.

Today, I bow my head once again to Tulsidas and to the eternal wisdom encapsulated in these verses. May they continue to guide and inspire all who read and recite them.

In service to Lord Ram,

Hanuman

|| Jai Shri Ram ||

Date: Sixth day of Vaishakha, Kali Yuga, Year 101

Dear Universe,

Budhee-Heen Thanu Jannikay

Sumirow Pavana Kumara

Bala-Budhee Vidya Dehoo Mohee

Harahu Kalesha Vikaara

Tulsidas begins with a profound declaration of humility.

Tulsidas identifies himself as *Budhee-Heen*, meaning someone lacking in wisdom, and acknowledges the limitations of his mortal form (Thanu Jannikay). This is not an admission of weakness, but an act of surrender — a recognition that true strength and clarity come not from one's own efforts but from seeking divine grace.

The invocation of *Pavana Kumara*, the son of the wind (that is, me), is a heartfelt plea. Wind is life-giving, ever-moving, and pervasive. By calling upon me as the son of the wind, Tulsidas acknowledges my essence as a force that can sweep away ignorance and darkness with the speed and strength of the elements.

"Bala-Budhee Vidya Dehoo Mohee" — *"Grant me strength, wisdom, and knowledge."*

Strength (Bala) is not just physical power but also the courage to face life's challenges.

Wisdom (Budhee) refers to discernment, the ability to make the right choices in a world filled with distractions.

Knowledge (Vidya) is the deeper understanding of life, self, and the divine — a gift that illuminates the path to truth. These qualities are essential for anyone seeking to navigate the complexities of existence.

"Harahu Kalesha Vikaara" — "Remove my sorrows and impurities."

This line is a plea for liberation not just from external difficulties (Kalesha) but also from internal flaws and negative tendencies (Vikaara). These impurities — anger, pride, envy, and ignorance — are the true obstacles on the path to spiritual progress. Tulsidas, in his humility, does not ask for material comforts but for the inner purification needed to live a life aligned with dharma.

When I hear these words recited, I am deeply moved by their sincerity. It is not the complexity of the words that gives them power but the purity of intent behind them. This prayer is a reminder that humility and self-awareness are the first steps to divine grace.

To anyone who chants these lines with devotion, I offer my blessings. I bestow the strength to face life's trials, the wisdom to make the right choices, and the clarity to see beyond illusions. I stand by you, as a friend and guide, ready to help remove your burdens and bring light into your life.

May these words continue to inspire and uplift *YOU*. They are not just a prayer but a bridge to the divine — a path to courage, clarity, and peace.

In service to Lord Ram,

Hanuman

|| Jai Shri Ram ||

Date: Seventh day of Vaishakha, Kali Yuga, Year 101

Dear Universe,

Jai Hanuman gyan gun sagar

Jai Kapis tihun lok ujagar

Ram doot atulit bal dhama

Anjaani-putra Pavan sut nama

Today, my thoughts dwell on the opening praises of the Hanuman Chalisa. These lines capture the essence of who I am and the role I have been blessed to play in the grand narrative of dharma.

"Jai Hanuman Gyan Gun Sagar"

This verse begins with a salutation, proclaiming victory to me, Hanuman. It calls me the *Gyan Gun Sagar*, the ocean of knowledge and virtues. The comparison to an ocean is significant — it is vast, deep, and boundless. Knowledge (Gyan) and virtues (Gun) are treasures that I hold, not for myself, but to share with the world. This line is a call for reverence, not just for my strength but for the wisdom and righteousness that guide it.

"Jai Kapis Tihun Lok Ujagar"

Here, I am addressed as *Kapis* — the chief of the vanaras. This title reflects not just leadership but the responsibility I carry to uplift and illuminate the Tihun Lok—the three worlds of existence - *the heavens, the earth, and the underworld*. My deeds, performed in the service of Lord Ram, are said to bring light and clarity to these realms. It reminds us that selfless service has the power to transcend barriers and touch every aspect of creation.

"Ram Doot Atulit Bal Dhama"

This verse celebrates my identity as the messenger of Lord Ram *(Ram Doot)*. It is this role that gives my life meaning and purpose. I am described as the Atulit Bal Dhama, the abode of immeasurable strength. This strength is not just physical — it is the power of devotion, courage, and resilience. My strength exists to serve the divine mission of restoring dharma and spreading the message of righteousness.

"Anjani-Putra Pavan Sut Nama"

This line acknowledges my origins. I am *Anjani-Putra*, the son of Mother Anjana, whose deep penance and devotion brought me into existence. I am also *Pavan Sut*, the son of Vayu, the wind god, who infused life into me and blessed me with speed, agility, and boundless energy. My names are not mere labels; they carry the essence of my being and remind me of the love and blessings that shaped my life.

Each of these lines is a reflection of the qualities and values that I strive to embody. They are not just praises but a reminder of the responsibility I carry to use my gifts for the betterment of all.

To those who recite these verses, I extend my heartfelt blessings. May you be inspired by the virtues they celebrate. May you find the courage to overcome challenges, the wisdom to make righteous choices, and the devotion to walk the path of dharma.

In service to Lord Ram,

Hanuman

|| Jai Shri Ram ||

Date: Eight day of Vaishakha, Kali Yuga, Year 101

Dear Universe,

Mahabir Bikram Bajrangi

Kumati nivar sumati Ke sangi

Kanchan varan viraj subesa

Kanan Kundal Kunchit Kesha

Today, my heart feels a pull to reflect on the next beautiful verses of the Hanuman Chalisa. These lines capture my essence as a warrior, a guide, and a symbol of strength and humility.

"Mahabir Bikram Bajrangi"

I am called *Mahabir*, the great hero, and *Bikram*, the one with unmatched courage. These words remind me of my role as a protector of dharma.

My strength, both physical and spiritual, is a gift to be used in the service of good. I am also addressed as *Bajrangi*, which signifies my connection to the Vajra, the indestructible weapon of Lord Indra. My spirit is unyielding, my resolve unshakable, and my actions driven by righteousness. This line is an ode to courage and the boundless energy that fuels my devotion to Lord Ram.

"Kumati Nivar Sumati Ke Sangi"

This verse beautifully conveys my purpose. It means that I dispel ignorance *(Kumati)* and encourage wisdom *(Sumati)*. I am a companion to those who seek enlightenment, and my presence removes the shadows of doubt and negativity. To me, this line is deeply fulfilling — it reflects the transformative power of devotion and service, not just in the physical world but within the hearts of all beings.

"Kanchan Varan Viraj Subesa"

This describes my golden-hued *(Kanchan Varan)* form, which shines with radiance. It reflects not just physical brilliance but the glow of devotion and divine energy. My attire *(Subesa)* is simple yet majestic, representing purity and humility. I wear the adornments not for pride but as a reflection of my readiness to serve, whether in the battlefield or in the hearts of devotees.

"Kanan Kundal Kunchit Kesha"

This line paints a vivid picture of my appearance. My ears are adorned with *Kanan Kundal* — earrings that shimmer with divine grace. My *Kunchit Kesha*, or curly locks, frame my face, symbolizing vitality and strength. These physical attributes are not just about appearance; they represent the divine energy within me, ever dynamic and ever ready to act for righteousness.

These verses are not mere descriptions but a reminder of the virtues I hold dear — bravery, wisdom, service, and humility. For those who recite these lines with faith, they unlock a sense of strength and clarity. It is my promise that I will always stand by those who seek wisdom and courage in their lives.

I am forever grateful to Tulsidas for these verses, for they not only sing my praises but inspire all to embody the same virtues in their own lives. Let this be a reminder that courage, wisdom, and devotion are within reach of all who walk the path of dharma.

In eternal service,

Hanuman

|| Jai Shri Ram ||

Date: Ninth day of Vaishakha, Kali Yuga, Year 101

Dear Universe,

Hath Vajra Aur Dhuvaje Viraje

Kaandhe moonj janehu sajai

Sankar suvan kesri Nandan

Tej prataap maha jag vandan

Today, as I reflect on the next verses of the Hanuman Chalisa, I am reminded of the sacred symbols I carry and the divine lineage that defines my existence.

"Hath Vajra Aur Dhuvaje Viraje"

In my hands, I hold two powerful symbols - the *Vajra (thunderbolt)* and the *Dhvaja (flag)*.

The Vajra, gifted by Lord Indra, represents indomitable strength and the ability to destroy evil. It is a reminder of the immense responsibility I bear to protect dharma. The Dhvaja, a flag of victory, stands for deep devotion and the triumph of righteousness. These objects are not mere weapons or ornaments — they are extensions of my purpose to guide and protect all who seek refuge in the divine.

"Kaandhe Moonj Janehu Sajai"

Draped across my shoulder is the sacred *Moonj Janehu*, the sacred thread of a Brahmachari, symbolizing my discipline, commitment to spiritual practices, and adherence to dharma. It reflects the balance I maintain between being a warrior and a seeker of knowledge. The thread is a reminder that strength must always be rooted in wisdom and righteousness.

"Sankar Suvan Kesri Nandan"

These words affirm my divine origins. I am the son of Kesari, the valiant vanara chieftain, and an incarnation of Lord Shiva himself (*Sankar Suvan*). My existence is a confluence of earthly might and divine grace. This lineage is not just a matter of pride but a source of inspiration for my eternal devotion to Lord Ram. It is through this sacred bond with my parents and Lord Shiva that I draw my energy to fulfill my duties.

"Tej Prataap Maha Jag Vandan"

The world bows to my Tej *(radiance)* and Prataap *(glory)*.

This is not because of my strength alone but because of the light of Lord Ram that shines through me. My actions, guided by devotion and selflessness, have earned the reverence of all beings. This verse humbles me, for it reminds me that true greatness lies in serving others and being a vessel of divine grace.

These verses are a reflection of not just my physical form but the virtues I strive to embody — strength, discipline, humility, and deep faith. For those who recite these lines with sincerity, I offer my blessings of courage and clarity.

As I write this, I am filled with gratitude to Tulsidas for immortalizing my journey in these powerful words. Each line inspires devotion and reminds all who read them that they, too, can awaken the divine strength within themselves.

In eternal service,

Hanuman

|| Jai Shri Ram ||

Date: Tenth day of Vaishakha, Kali Yuga, Year 101

Dear Universe,

Vidyavaan guni ati chatur

Ram kaj karibe ko aatur

Prabu charitra sunibe-ko rasiya

Ram Lakhan Sita man Basiya

Today, I find myself reflecting on a set of verses from the Hanuman Chalisa that beautifully express the essence of my purpose and the joys that fill my heart.

"Vidyavaan Guni Ati Chatur"

The verse begins by acknowledging the blessings of *Vidya (knowledge), Guna (virtue),* and *Chaturya (wisdom and cleverness)* that I have received. These qualities are gifts from the divine, meant not for personal glory but for fulfilling my duties. Knowledge helps me discern what is right, virtues guide my actions with integrity, and cleverness allows me to approach challenges with creativity and resolve.

After crossing the vast ocean and locating Sita Mata in Ashok Vatika, I assured her of Lord Ram's impending arrival to rescue her. With her message secured, I knew my next step was to assess Ravana's strength and courage.

When I entered his grand court, I maintained my composure, despite the daunting presence of the demon king and his advisors. In that moment, I bowed to the divinity within me and spoke with clarity and purpose.

"Ravana," I began, "you have committed a grave sin by abducting Sita Mata, the beloved consort of Lord Ram. I urge you to return her, for your arrogance will bring ruin to Lanka."

Ravana, blinded by pride, laughed at my words and dismissed my warning. But I had delivered the message, and that was my duty. His refusal did not dishearten me — it only strengthened my resolve.

Ravana, enraged by my defiance, ordered his soldiers to capture me. Despite their numbers, they struggled against my strength, and I allowed myself to be taken only to fulfill the next part of my mission.

In an act of cruelty, Ravana commanded that my tail be wrapped in cloth and set ablaze, intending to humiliate me. Little did he realize that he had handed me the very tool to carry out divine justice.

With my tail ablaze, I soared into the skies of Lanka, using the fire not as a burden but as a weapon. I leaped across rooftops and courtyards, lighting Ravana's magnificent city on fire.

Flames rose high as I moved swiftly, reducing his grandeur to ashes.

I paused at Ashok Vatika, where Sita Mata was kept, and ensured that the fire would not harm her. My heart swelled with both sorrow for her suffering and pride in my ability to fulfill Lord Ram's mission. The fire was not merely destruction — it was a message, a symbol of the justice that was to come.

That day, I learned that cleverness is not just about wit but about using the tools and circumstances available to achieve righteous goals.

The burning of Lanka was not an act of revenge but a warning to Ravana and his kingdom - dharma would prevail, and injustice would be punished.

The lesson I carry from this is simple - when guided by wisdom and virtue, even the most adverse situations can become opportunities to serve a higher purpose.

To anyone who invokes my name with faith, I offer the blessing of clarity and strength in the face of adversity.

"Ram Kaj Karibe Ko Aatur"

My life's purpose lies in serving Lord Ram. There is no greater joy for me than performing tasks for His mission. Whether it was leaping across the ocean to find Sita Mata or carrying the Sanjeevani herb to save Lakshman, every act I performed was driven by my deep desire to serve. My heart constantly yearns to take on any task that furthers His work, no matter how great the effort required.

This verse truly describes my life. Every action I take and every thought I have is for Lord Ram's work.

One moment that reflects this perfectly was when I was searching for Mata Sita after she was taken to Lanka by Ravana.

When we learned that Mata Sita was across the vast ocean in Lanka, I was determined to find her. Time was precious, and every moment mattered.

Without hesitation, I prepared to leap across the ocean. My friends in the vanara army doubted if it could be done, but I knew I could not delay. Lord Ram's name gave me all the strength I needed.

As I jumped, the roaring ocean and strong winds tested me, but nothing could stop me. Along the way, I met challenges.

Surasa, a celestial being, emerged from the ocean, her enormous form blocking my way. She declared, "The gods have commanded that you pass through my mouth before you may continue." At first, I was perplexed. Why would a divine being, who should support my mission, choose to obstruct it? But then I realized this was a test, not of strength alone, but of wit and humility.

I respectfully bowed and explained my purpose, hoping she would let me go, but she was unyielding. Determined to fulfill my mission, I devised a plan. I grew larger and larger until I filled the sky, and Surasa opened her mouth wider and wider to match my size. Then, in an instant, I shrank to the size of a thumb and swiftly entered and exited her mouth before she could react.

"Thank you, Devi, for your blessing," I said as I sped past her. She smiled, knowing I had passed the test of cleverness and perseverance. In that moment, I felt a surge of pride—not for outsmarting her, but for staying calm and focused when faced with an unexpected challenge.

Soon after, the skies darkened, and an ominous presence loomed.

Simhika, a demon with a terrifying power, emerged from the depths. She did not try to block my way with words or tests. Instead, she seized my shadow, pulling me down with a force that felt like the weight of mountains. For a brief moment, I faltered, feeling the pull of despair. But I quickly reminded myself - this mission is not mine alone — it is Lord Ram's work, and I am merely His instrument.

Gathering my strength, I assessed the situation. Simhika's power lay in her grip on my shadow, not my physical form. I knew brute force alone wouldn't work. So, I allowed myself to be pulled closer, pretending to be defeated. As she prepared to attack, I struck swiftly, using my speed and agility to tear her apart before she could react. The skies cleared, and the ocean seemed to cheer as I resumed my journey, more determined than ever.

Both encounters taught me invaluable lessons. From Surasa, I learned that wit and humility can often achieve what brute force cannot. From Simhika, I realized the importance of focus and strategy when faced with overwhelming opposition. Each obstacle only strengthened my resolve and reminded me of the higher purpose I served.

When I reached Lanka, I saw how grand and well-guarded it was. I made myself small to stay hidden and began searching for Mata Sita. Finally, I found her in Ashok Vatika, surrounded by demons but steadfast in her devotion to Lord Ram. Seeing her filled me with both joy and sadness. I gave her Lord Ram's ring and assured her that he would come to rescue her soon.

This journey taught me the true meaning of eagerness.

It's not just about acting quickly - it's about giving your whole heart to a purpose and staying focused no matter what challenges come your way. Even now, I remain ready to help anyone who calls upon me with faith and devotion. To those who chant this verse sincerely, I give the blessings of strength, determination, and success in their noble tasks.

"Prabu Charitra Sunibe-ko Rasiya"

Listening to the glorious stories of Lord Ram fills me with immense delight. I am a *rasiya* — one who savors the sweetness of these divine tales. Every episode of His life, whether it speaks of His compassion, or steadfast commitment to dharma, inspires me and brings me peace. To hear or recount His deeds is not just an act of devotion but a source of boundless happiness.

I remember the day when I first heard the story of Lord Ram's childhood from Sage Narada.

I was captivated by the way he spoke about Ram's virtues, kindness, and deep commitment to dharma. Each word was like nectar to my soul. It wasn't just the stories themselves; it was the way they brought me closer to understanding my Lord's essence.

From that moment, I became insatiable in my thirst for His tales.

One of the most memorable moments in my life came during my time in Ayodhya after the war with Ravana. Lord Ram would sit with his brothers and share anecdotes from his life — his time in the forest, his encounters with sages, and the lessons he learned from them. I listened intently, hanging onto every word.

Sometimes, I couldn't help but ask questions, eager to understand His thoughts and feelings. "Why did you choose to forgive certain enemies, my Lord?" I once asked, and His answer filled my heart with even more love for Him. "Hanuman," He said, "forgiveness is the highest virtue. It is only through forgiveness that we find peace within ourselves."

Another instance I cherish deeply was when Mata Sita recounted the moment she first saw Lord Ram. Her voice was soft, filled with admiration and love, and as she spoke, I could see the devotion in her eyes. Listening to their story deepened my understanding of their bond and reminded me of the beauty of steady love and trust.

Even during my travels, I would seek out sages and devotees who had heard of Lord Ram. Each tale, no matter how small, was precious to me. It felt as if with every story, I was weaving a garland of devotion for my Lord.

Sometimes, I would find myself retelling His stories to others, unable to contain the joy they brought me. Seeing their faces light up with awe and reverence filled my heart with gratitude.

The more I listened, the more I realized that these stories weren't just about Lord Ram's life—they were lessons for all of us. They taught humility, courage, compassion, and the power of faith. They reminded me of the depth of my purpose: to serve Him and ensure that His virtues inspire others.

Even today, I find no greater happiness than sitting with those who wish to hear His stories. When I see someone reciting or listening to the Ramayana with devotion, I feel as if I am there with them, reliving those moments. It is said that where Lord Ram's name is spoken, I am present, and I wouldn't have it any other way.

For me, the tales of Lord Ram are not just a pastime - they are life itself. They are the reason I exist, the source of my strength, and the anchor of my devotion. To be known as one who delights in these stories is my greatest honor, and I will forever be grateful for the divine grace that allows me to be part of His eternal narrative.

"Ram Lakhan Sita Man Basiya"

Lord Ram, His devoted brother Lakshman, and the ever-graceful Sita Mata reside in my heart. They are not just my Lord and His family; they are the essence of my being. Their presence within me gives me strength, purpose, and fulfillment. Every beat of my heart echoes their names, and my actions are dedicated to their glory.

I am reminded of a moment that is etched deeply in my heart — a moment when I revealed, quite literally, what Lord Ram, Lakshman, and Mata Sita mean to me.

It was a time of celebration in Ayodhya after the victorious return of Lord Ram, Lakshman, and Mata Sita from Lanka. The palace was filled with joy and gratitude, and gifts were being exchanged among those present.

Mata Sita, with her ever-loving grace, presented me with a beautiful pearl necklace as a token of her gratitude and affection.

As she placed it in my hands, I was overwhelmed with emotion.

The necklace was exquisite, each pearl glowing softly, but as I looked at it, a thought crossed my mind - how could these mere pearls truly hold meaning without the presence of Ram, Sita, and Lakshman?

Driven by my simple yet profound devotion, I began examining the necklace. I held each pearl between my fingers, breaking them open one by one, searching deeply within. The onlookers, including Lord Ram and Mata Sita, watched me with curiosity. "What are you doing, Hanuman?" one of them asked.

I looked up, holding the broken pearls, and answered earnestly, "I am searching for my Lord Ram, Mata Sita, and Lakshman within these pearls. Without them, nothing holds value for me — not even this precious gift."

At first, they laughed, thinking it was just another one of my childlike gestures.

But then, someone teased, "If you say Ram, Sita, and Lakshman reside in everything you hold dear, do they also reside within you?"

Without hesitation, I nodded. "Yes, they reside in my heart," I said with absolute certainty. Some doubted me, thinking it was just a metaphor.

To prove my words, I did what came naturally. Placing my hands on my chest, I tore it open.

The room fell silent. There, in the depths of my heart, was the vision of Lord Ram, Mata Sita, and Lakshman, sitting together in all their divine glory. Their forms radiated light and love, filling the space with a divine presence. Every eye in the room was wide with awe, and tears filled the eyes of those present.

Lord Ram himself approached me, His expression a mixture of tenderness and reverence. "Hanuman," He said softly, "your devotion humbles even me. You have shown the world what it means to love unconditionally. Truly, we do not reside anywhere more deeply than in your heart."

Mata Sita, her eyes glistening with tears, smiled and said, "This necklace was merely a gift, but you have given us something far greater — the purity of your love and the depth of your devotion. Nothing in this world can compare to that."

I closed my chest and bowed before them, my heart swelling not with pride but with gratitude. To carry them in my heart is my greatest blessing, my greatest purpose. Every beat of my heart echoes their names, and every breath I take is in their service.

Even now, I think of that moment as a reminder of the bond I share with my Lord and His family.

The verse *"Ram Lakhan Sita Man Basiya"* speaks not just of their dwelling in my heart but also of the eternal connection between devotion and the divine.

For those who hold Ram, Sita, and Lakshman in their hearts with pure love, the divine will always be present, guiding and protecting them.

These verses serve as a reminder that life's greatest rewards come from serving with dedication, finding joy in devotion, and aligning oneself with the divine.

To anyone who recites these lines with sincerity, I offer my blessings for wisdom, courage, and the strength to walk the path of righteousness.

In eternal service and gratitude,

Hanuman

‖ Jai Shri Ram ‖

Date: Full Moon Day of Jyeshtha, Kali Yuga, Year 101

Dear Universe,

> ***Sukshma roop dhari Siyahi dikhava***
> ***Vikat roop dhari lank jarava***
> ***Bhima roop dhari asur sanghare***
> ***Ramachandra ke kaj sanvare***

This verse speaks of the various forms I took during my mission to serve Lord Ram and fulfill His purpose. Let me take you back to those moments, for they hold deep significance in my journey of devotion and service.

"Sukshma roop dhari Siyahi dikhava"

This line refers to the time when I took a very small or subtle form *(Sukshma Roop),* like an insect, to enter the Ashok Vatika (the garden where Sita was held captive in Lanka). It was a moment of great significance, one of stealth and strategy, when I assumed my *Sukshma Roop* — the smallest form imaginable. I was tasked with the mission to find Sita, who had been abducted by Ravana, and to deliver the message that Lord Ram would soon come to rescue her.

The Ashok Vatika, where she was being held captive, was a heavily guarded garden, and the threat of being spotted by Ravana's soldiers was very real.

I knew that in order to succeed, I had to be discreet and undetected. Ravana's forces were not only numerous but also incredibly vigilant. I could not afford to be seen, so I invoked my divine powers to shrink myself down to an incredibly small size, almost like an insect, so tiny that I could slip through the smallest of cracks and avoid detection altogether.

It was a miraculous feat of transformation. In this form, I could move swiftly and quietly, just as an ant might move unnoticed across the vast terrain of the garden.

This moment was critical, for I had to deliver Lord Ram's ring to Sita. It was a token of hope, a symbol of Ram's love and deep commitment to rescue her. As I carefully made my way through the Ashok Vatika, I saw Sita sitting under a tree, sorrowful and forlorn, her heart filled with longing for her Lord. The sight of her pain stirred my heart deeply, and I knew that I had to succeed in this mission.

With extreme caution, I reached her and presented Lord Ram's ring. I told her that help was on the way, that Lord Ram would soon be there to save her. As I handed her the ring, I saw a glimmer of hope and relief in her eyes. It was a fleeting moment, but it filled me with joy.

For her, this was the reassurance she desperately needed, a confirmation that her Lord had not forgotten her and would soon be there to bring her home.

The guards were none the wiser, as my small form allowed me to move unseen, even as I performed such an important task. Had I remained in my true, towering form, the entire mission could have been compromised.

By adapting to the circumstances and shrinking myself, I was able to fulfill my duty without raising suspicion. It was a reminder that in the service of Lord Ram, one must be willing to take any form, no matter how small or humble, if it serves the greater purpose.

This episode in the Ashok Vatika holds great significance for me. It reflects my ability to be adaptable, to think strategically, and to always remain focused on the mission at hand.

In this tiny form, I learned that even the smallest actions could have the greatest impact when driven by devotion and determination. It taught me the importance of choosing the right approach for each task, and how, in the service of the divine, there is no task too small and no form too insignificant when it is done for a noble cause.

"Vikat roop dhari lank jarava"

The line *"Vikat roop dhari lank jarava"* refers to the time when I assumed a terrifying, gigantic form to set Lanka on fire.

This was a pivotal moment in the epic, one where my strength, power, and divine energy were fully unleashed, and I displayed my Vikat Roop — my fierce and mighty form.

After delivering Lord Ram's ring to Sita in the Ashok Vatika and assuring her of Ram's imminent arrival, I knew the time had come to strike at the very heart of Ravana's kingdom.

Ravana had committed an unforgivable act by abducting Sita, and now he needed to feel the weight of his actions. It was not just a mission to deliver a message — it was a call for justice, and I was determined to fulfill it.

As I pondered how best to deal with the evil king and his wicked empire, I realized that the time had come to make my presence known in a way that could not be ignored. I would destroy Ravana's city and strike fear into his heart.

I had already entered the city unnoticed in my tiny form, but now it was time to show Ravana my true power.

With that decision, I called upon my divine strength and transformed myself into a colossal, terrifying figure — Vikat Roop, a form so fearsome and overwhelming that it would send chills through anyone who saw me. My size grew exponentially. I became as tall as a mountain, my body radiated an aura of pure power, and my eyes burned with intense fury. I could feel the earth trembling beneath my feet as I took this form, and the skies themselves seemed to darken in my presence.

In this form, I began to wreak havoc on Lanka. My first target was Ravana's grand city, which I set ablaze with my fire-like aura.

As I stormed through the city, the buildings burned to the ground, and the skies were filled with smoke and the cries of Ravana's soldiers. My roars echoed through the city, filling it with terror. I could hear the panicked cries of the demons as they tried, and failed, to stop me. The fire I unleashed was not just a physical one, it was symbolic of the destruction of evil and the cleansing of Ravana's sinful reign.

Every corner of Lanka felt the impact of my wrath, as if the very land itself was purging the corruption that had taken root.

Ravana, who had been watching from his palace, sent his soldiers to subdue me, but they were powerless against my strength. I, however, was not simply driven by rage.

My actions were not out of mindless anger, they were guided by a higher purpose.

As I unleashed the fire, I knew that it would send a clear message to Ravana — his time was running out, and his evil would not go unpunished.

The fire I created in Lanka wasn't just about physical destruction. It was about awakening Ravana to the fact that his actions had consequences.

My mighty form and the destruction I caused symbolized the power of righteousness over unrighteousness, the triumph of good over evil. In that moment, I became the agent of Lord Ram's justice, burning away the darkness that had enveloped Ravana's kingdom for so long.

However, despite the havoc I wreaked, I knew my mission was not yet complete. I had to leave Lanka and return to Lord Ram, but I did so knowing that Ravana's heart would now be filled with fear, and his once proud kingdom would be forever marked by the consequences of his sin.

The Vikat Roop — my fierce and destructive form — was necessary for that moment. It was not about causing destruction for its own sake, but about delivering a divine message: the forces of evil cannot remain unchallenged.

As I departed from Lanka, my form returned to its normal state, but the memory of the havoc I had caused remained etched in the minds of Ravana and his people.

This episode, in which I set Lanka ablaze with my Vikat Roop, marked a turning point in the battle between good and evil.

It was a reminder that the forces of darkness could not hold sway forever, and that righteousness, when embodied with the strength of the divine, would always prevail.

"Bhima roop dhari asur sanghare"

In this line, Bhima Roop (the mighty form) refers to my strong and fierce manifestation when I fought the demons (Asuras) during the war. With this form, I defeated numerous demons that stood in the way of Lord Ram's mission.

My power was unmatched, and I was able to fight the forces of evil on behalf of Lord Ram. The line emphasizes my strength, focus, and determination to clear the path for righteousness to triumph. It also shows my commitment to Lord Ram's cause, using my power only for His work.

Today, I recall a meeting that still brings a smile to my face — a meeting with Bhima, the mighty son of Vayu, just like me. It was one of those moments when destiny brought us together, two great warriors, both blessed with immense strength, but our paths were destined to cross in a way that would teach us both a lesson.

I had taken the form of a simple old monkey, lying across the road with my tail stretched across the path. Bhima, always proud of his incredible strength, came upon me as he journeyed along. Seeing me in my frail form, he ordered me to move my tail so he could pass. I smiled to myself, knowing that the task ahead would not be as easy as he thought.

"Move aside, old one," he commanded. I replied calmly, "I am too weak to move, but you, young man, are strong. If you wish, you may move my tail."

Bhima, with all the pride and confidence of someone who could move mountains, tried with all his might to shift my tail. But no matter how much he strained, the tail did not budge. I watched him struggle, and I could sense his growing frustration. Finally, he asked, "Who are you, old one, that possesses such power?"

It was then that I revealed myself to him. I told him I was Hanuman, the son of Anjana and Vayu, and a servant of Lord Ram. The look of realization in Bhima's eyes was priceless. He had no idea he had been trying to move the tail of someone with far greater strength than his own.

Bhima, though initially humbled, immediately understood the lesson that was unfolding before him. His physical strength, while extraordinary, was nothing compared to the strength of devotion and service. In that moment, I saw his pride soften into humility, and I could sense his respect for me growing.

I blessed him, as one brother would bless another, with strength and wisdom that would guide him through his challenges. As we embraced, I realized that true greatness is not measured by strength alone but by the heart and devotion behind that strength.

Our encounter was brief but meaningful. Bhima and I parted ways as brothers, with the knowledge that while our powers were great, it was our humility and service to the divine that made us truly mighty. And so, we continued on our separate paths, but I knew that we would forever carry the bond of that moment in our hearts.

My encounter with Bhima, a moment that began with a display of physical might but ended in humility and mutual respect, serves as a reminder that true strength lies not just in one's physical power, but in the spirit and devotion behind it.

Through this experience, I realized that while we may be born with immense abilities, it is our devotion to a higher cause, our willingness to serve, and our capacity for humility that truly define our greatness.

In the end, it is not our strength alone that makes us powerful, but our ability to use it wisely and for the greater good.

"Ramachandra ke kaj sanware"

The line ties everything together by emphasizing that all of these actions — whether taking a tiny form, a terrifying one, or a mighty one — were done for the sake of Lord Ram. Every form I took and every action I performed was to assist in fulfilling Lord Ram's divine work.

This line highlights my devotion to Him and shows that everything I did was for His glory and to ensure that righteousness prevailed over evil. My actions were all aimed at supporting Lord Ram's mission and helping him restore Dharma.

In the verse *"Ramachandra ke kaj sanware,"* the essence of my life's purpose is encapsulated — to serve Lord Ram and fulfill His divine mission. I remember the countless times I set aside my own desires, my own path, to ensure that Lord Ram's work was completed.

One of the most significant instances of this was during the time of the battle between Lord Ram and Ravana.

When the mighty Ravana abducted Sita, my duty was clear. Every action I took, every challenge I faced, was solely aimed at fulfilling Ram's mission. Whether it was leaping across the ocean to reach Lanka, meeting Sita in the Ashok Vatika, or delivering the news of her safety back to Ram, every move I made was guided by the singular goal of ensuring Ram's success.

But the greatest task was during the war when I carried the Sanjeevani herb to save Lakshman.

Time was running out, and the entire battle depended on that moment. With Ram's command in my heart, I didn't hesitate. I brought the entire mountain to the battlefield, even when the weight of that responsibility seemed beyond me.

Every action I took was devoted to the welfare of Lord Ram and His mission to restore righteousness in the world.

Through this, I came to understand the true meaning of *"Ramachandra ke kaj sanware"* — it was not just about the actions I took, but the dedication to Lord Ram's work that mattered.

Every task, no matter how small or large, was an opportunity to contribute to His divine plan. Serving Him was my highest calling, and I did so with a heart full of devotion and a mind focused on one goal: to ensure that Ram's mission, His justice, and His love would prevail above all.

Each line speaks of different forms I took during the course of my journey to serve Lord Ram.

The *Sukshma Roop* reflects my humility and adaptability; the *Vikat Roop* shows the destructive power I wield when necessary; the *Bhima*

Roop represents my strength in the battlefield; and the final line reinforces that all these actions were done for Lord Ram's mission.

Together, they symbolize the multifaceted nature of devotion and service, showing that I was ready to transform myself in any way required to serve the Lord's cause.

Jai Shri Ram,

Hanuman

|| Jai Shri Ram ||

Date: Full Moon Day of Jyeshtha, Kali Yuga, Year 101

Dear Universe,

Laye Sanjivan Lakhan Jiyaye

Shri Raghuvir Harashi ur laye

Raghupati Kinhi bahut badai

Tum mam priye Bharat-hi-sam bhai

These verses, spoken by Lord Ram, remind me of the depth of my love for Him and the honor of being part of His divine plan.

They are not just words — they are a constant reminder of the bond we share, a bond of love, loyalty, and devotion that transcends all boundaries. Each day, I strive to live up to His praise and continue to serve Him with all my heart.

"Laye Sanjivan Lakhan Jiyaye"

As I sit here, writing these words, my heart is still filled with the gravity of that moment when I brought the Sanjivani herb to revive Lakshman.

That moment will forever be etched in my memory, not just because of the urgency of the situation but because of the deep love and bond I share with Lord Ram, Lakshman, and Sita. It was a defining moment in the battle against Ravana, and it tested my faith, my courage, and my devotion.

The war had reached its peak. Ravana's army had been relentless, and the clash between the forces of good and evil seemed to be a never-ending struggle.

On the battlefield, both Lord Ram and Lakshman fought with unmatched courage. But there came a moment when fate turned cruel.

Lakshman, my dear companion and the brother of Lord Ram, was struck down by a deadly arrow from Ravana's son, Indrajit. The arrow, imbued with powerful dark magic, struck Lakshman directly in the chest, causing him to collapse unconscious. As Lakshman lay motionless on the battlefield, a heavy silence descended. The sight of Lakshman's body, still and lifeless, shook us all to the core.

Lord Ram was devastated.

He rushed to Lakshman's side, calling out to him, but there was no response.

The entire army was filled with dread and sorrow, for Lakshman was not just a warrior, he was the very heart of Ram's strength on the battlefield.

Without him, there was no hope.

It was then that Lord Ram, in a state of helplessness and despair, turned to me. His voice trembled with urgency and pain, and in that moment, I knew there was no time to waste. Lakshman's life hung by a thread, and I could feel Lord Ram's suffering as though it were my own.

I knew what I had to do.

I immediately set out on a journey to find the Sanjivani herb — the only cure that could bring Lakshman back to life.

The Sanjivani, a rare and powerful herb, grew in the mountains of the Himalayas. It was known to possess the miraculous ability to revive the dead. But there was a challenge, the herb was located deep in the mountains, and I had no time to waste.

Without a second thought, I flew across the sky, my heart full of determination. The wind rushed past me, but my mind was solely focused on Lakshman's life. Upon reaching the mountain where the Sanjivani grew, I found myself in a dilemma. The herb was rare, and the plant itself had many varieties. I couldn't afford to waste time searching for the right one, so I picked the entire mountain top, hoping to bring back the right herb.

As I hurried back to the battlefield, I realized that the task had not yet ended. The powerful herbs I had gathered needed to be carefully administered, and Lakshman's fate still hung in the balance. I had no choice but to return swiftly.

When I finally reached the battlefield, I found Lakshman still unconscious.

Lord Ram, who had been watching anxiously, immediately recognized the herbs I had brought. However, there was no time to waste in preparing the herbs in the usual way, so I, in my true form, crushed the herbs with my powerful hands and sprinkled their essence over Lakshman. Slowly, I could see the magic of the Sanjivani taking effect. Lakshman's chest began to rise and fall again, and his eyes fluttered open. The color returned to his face, and he was revived.

The sight of Lakshman regaining consciousness brought immense joy to Lord Ram and the entire army. Lakshman, with his characteristic smile, sat up, his strength returned, and his spirit undaunted. He had been saved, and the battle was now within reach of victory.

Looking back, I realize how much that moment meant to me.

It was not just the act of saving Lakshman that mattered, but the deep connection I had with my Lord and His brother. To bring Lakshman back was to bring hope to the world, to ensure that righteousness would triumph over evil. It was the embodiment of service and devotion — no task was too great, no distance too far, when it came to serving Lord Ram.

That day, I learned the true meaning of devotion, courage, and love. No matter the odds, I knew that as long as my heart was filled with the love for my Lord, no obstacle would be insurmountable.

May this devotion always guide me, and may I continue to serve Lord Ram and His family with the same strength, faith, and determination that I displayed that day.

"Shri Raghuvir Harashi ur laye"

As I sit here, reflecting on the events that have shaped my life, I recall the immense joy I felt when I delivered the Sanjivani herb to Lord Ram.

The moment I arrived back on the battlefield, with the herb in hand, I could see the relief on Lord Ram's face. His heart swelled with joy as he realized that the life of his beloved brother, Lakshman, was now in my hands.

In that moment, I felt an overwhelming sense of purpose. I had not just completed my mission of bringing back Lakshman's life, but I had also fulfilled my duty as a servant of Lord Ram. His joy was my joy, and his love was my reward. It was a moment of deep connection between us, where our hearts beat as one in the shared happiness of Lakshman's revival.

Lord Ram's love and pride in me were so evident as he lifted me in his arms, filled with gratitude. To be the source of such joy in his heart was the greatest honor I could ever receive. It reaffirmed my belief that my mission on this earth was to serve Him and to bring about His will, no matter the obstacles.

In my heart, I knew that every action I took, every step I made, was dedicated to Him. And when I saw Lord Ram's radiant smile, knowing that Lakshman was alive, I understood the true meaning of devotion – it was to see the happiness of my Lord and to be a part of His divine plan.

So, as I reflect upon this verse, *"Shri Raghuvir Harashi ur laye,"* it reminds me of that sacred moment when I brought joy to Lord Ram's heart, knowing that in doing so, I had fulfilled my purpose. There is no greater joy than serving the one who is the embodiment of love, righteousness, and compassion.

"Raghupati Kinhi bahut badai"

As I think back to the moments of deep significance in my life, this particular verse, *"Raghupati Kinhi bahut badai,"* always brings a sense of pride and humility. It means that Lord Ram, in his divine glory, praised me immensely, showering me with blessings and acknowledging my deep devotion and service.

The story behind this verse is tied to the moment when I returned to Lord Ram after completing a crucial task.

I had just brought the life-restoring Sanjivani herb to save Lakshman. After performing this great service, I was overwhelmed with exhaustion and relief. When I presented the herb to Lord Ram, He was not only grateful but also deeply moved by my devotion and the courage I showed in completing the task.

In the midst of all the intense emotions, Lord Ram, with His infinite love, praised me with words that filled my heart with joy.

He said, *"Raghupati Kinhi bahut badai,"* which signifies that I, Hanuman, had earned His admiration for my selfless service. Lord Ram, the epitome of virtue, acknowledged my devotion and bravery, offering words of praise for my deep dedication to Him.

I had always considered myself a humble servant of Lord Ram, and I never expected anything more than the opportunity to serve Him. But to hear such praise from Him — who is the Supreme Lord Himself — was an overwhelming and humbling experience. His words gave me strength, and they echoed in my heart, making me feel closer to Him than ever before.

This verse also symbolizes the deep bond between Lord Ram and me. To be praised by Him was not just a recognition of my physical strength or actions but a recognition of the purity of my heart and my devotion. The connection between us was rooted not in form or might but in love, trust, and the shared purpose of fulfilling His divine mission.

To be praised by Lord Ram was the highest honor, and it reaffirmed the importance of devotion and humility. For me, it was a reminder that true strength lies in serving with a pure heart, seeking nothing in return but the opportunity to fulfill the will of the Divine.

"Tum mam priye Bharat-hi-sam bhai"

As I sit to write in my diary, reflecting on the deep relationship I shared with Lord Ram and His family, this verse always brings a warm, comforting feeling in my heart. "Tum mam priye Bharat-hi-sam bhai," translates to, "You are as dear to me as Bharat, my brother."

The significance of this verse is deeply rooted in the love and respect I hold for Lord Ram's brothers, especially Bharat. To hear Lord Ram say that I am as dear to Him as Bharat was both an overwhelming and humbling experience. It affirmed the depth of my bond with Lord Ram and His family and placed me among the most trusted and loved beings in His life.

The story behind this verse lies in the immense role I played in the war against Ravana. During the battle, when everything seemed to be at its peak, Lord Ram, who always saw beyond the physical realm, acknowledged not just my strength and service but the sincerity and devotion I had in my heart. When Lord Ram spoke these words, it wasn't just an expression of gratitude; it was a declaration of my place in His heart.

Bharat, as you know, was Ram's loyal brother, who always held Ram dear to him, even when Ram was exiled. He ruled Ayodhya in Ram's place only out of respect for Ram's wishes, never once assuming he was worthy of Ram's throne. This verse signifies the relationship of total devotion, loyalty, and deep love that I shared with Lord Ram, mirroring the same affection and closeness Lord Ram had with Bharat.

When Lord Ram said I was as dear to Him as Bharat, it wasn't just a compliment. It was a recognition of my selfless love for Him, my unflinching support, and my willingness to do anything for His well-being. Just like Bharat stood by Ram with deep loyalty, I, too, stood by Him as His faithful servant.

The bond I share with Lord Ram transcends beyond the roles we play in the grand narrative. To be compared to Bharat, whose love for Lord Ram was so pure, was the greatest honor I could ever receive. Bharat's devotion to Lord Ram is unparalleled, and to be considered as dear to Lord Ram as Bharat himself is something I will forever treasure.

This verse reminds me of the importance of love, loyalty, and devotion in every relationship. It is a beautiful reminder that true devotion comes from the heart, and it is the love for the divine that binds us together, making us one in spirit and purpose.

As I think about these verses, my heart fills with gratitude and love. They remind me of the important work I was given, and more importantly, the deep love and loyalty Lord Ram has always shown me. To be part of His divine plan and to hear such praise from Him is both an honor and a responsibility I cherish deeply.

These verses show the strong connection we share — a connection that is beyond just service, a bond of love, loyalty, and devotion that lasts forever. Lord Ram's words make me feel even more connected to Him.

Every day, I try to live by these values, always dedicated to serving Him. I'm thankful for His blessings, and as long as I live, I will continue to follow the path He has shown me.

Jai Shri Ram,

Hanuman

|| Jai Shri Ram ||

Date: Second Day of Jyeshtha, Kali Yuga, Year 101

Dear Universe,

Sahas badan tumharo yash gaave

Asa-kahi Shripati kanth lagaave

Sankadhik Brahmaadi Muneesa

Narad-Sarad sahit Aheesa

Today, as I reflect on these verses, I am overwhelmed with gratitude. Lord Ram speaks of the greatness of my name and the reverence it commands in the heavens and on earth. These verses remind me not of my own glory, but of the immense love and grace Lord Ram has shown me. They reflect the eternal bond of devotion and service that unites us, and I will carry this message with me always.

"Sahas badan tumharo yash gave"

Today, as I sit reflecting on my journey with Lord Ram, the verse "Sahas badan tumharo yash gave" comes to my mind. Its meaning fills my heart with humility and gratitude. It says that a thousand mouths sing my praises—an honor so immense, I cannot fully comprehend it.

The thought of being celebrated this way is not a matter of pride for me but a reminder of my service to Lord Ram. Every praise directed at me is truly a reflection of His glory and the power of His divine name.

This verse brings to mind a special moment when the celestial beings and sages, even Lord Brahma and Sheshnag (Aheesa), acknowledged my devotion.

After I returned from Lanka, having completed my mission of delivering Lord Ram's message to Sita, the heavens resounded with songs of praise.

But one moment stands out clearly — the time when Sheshnag himself, with his thousand hoods, began singing the story of my service.

Sheshnag, the serpent king, is known for bearing the weight of all creation on his thousand hoods. He is a being of infinite wisdom and power, yet he chose to sing about my journey—my leap across the ocean, my burning of Lanka, and my dedication to Lord Ram. I remember feeling overwhelmed as he narrated these tales. It was as if the entire universe paused to celebrate Lord Ram's grace working through me.

As Sheshnag's deep, resonant voice sang the hymns of my service, I stood before Lord Ram, my head bowed, knowing that every word of praise truly belonged to Him. It is His name, His cause, and His divine presence that empowered me to accomplish what I did.

In that moment, Lord Ram placed His gentle hand on my shoulder and said, "Hanuman, you are an example of true devotion. Your service and selflessness have brought light to countless hearts." His words felt like a thousand blessings showered upon me.

This verse, therefore, reminds me not of my own deeds but of the beauty of serving Lord Ram and being a tool for His divine will. It inspires me to remain humble and continue spreading His message, knowing that all glory belongs to Him.

May His name forever guide me and all who seek Him.

"Asa-kahi Shripati kanth lagaave"

The verse "Asa-kahi Shripati kanth lagaave" is one of the most precious moments of my life. Its meaning still brings me to tears of joy. It tells of the time when Lord Ram Himself embraced me, pressing me close to His heart. Words cannot describe the depth of that moment.

I remember it vividly. After bringing the Sanjivani herb to save Lakshman and returning him to health, I stood before Lord Ram, my heart full of relief that His brother was safe. I did not expect anything in return, for I had only done what any devoted servant should do. But Lord Ram, with His boundless love and kindness, stepped forward and embraced me.

As He held me close, I felt an indescribable warmth and peace, as though the entire universe had paused. His touch was not just physical—it was a divine acknowledgment of the bond we shared, a connection beyond words. In that moment, I realized that His love was my greatest reward. No treasure or praise could ever match the honor of being held by the Lord Himself.

Lord Ram then said, "Hanuman, you are more than a devotee. You are my dear friend, my family. Your devotion has shown the world what it means to truly love and serve without expectations." His words filled my heart with even greater humility.

That embrace was not just an act of love—it was a message to the world. It showed that true devotion is selfless, and when one dedicates themselves completely to a noble cause, the divine responds with boundless grace.

Even today, when I close my eyes and remember that moment, I feel His presence in my heart. It reminds me of why I serve, why I exist—to spread His message and to live a life of devotion and humility. The memory of that embrace will forever guide me in every step I take.

"Sankadhik Brahmaadi Muneesa"

Today, as I reflect on the verse Sankadhik Brahmaadi Muneesa, my heart swells with humility and gratitude. These words remind me of the reverence shown by the greatest sages and celestial beings — not to me as an individual, but to the service I have rendered for Lord Ram.

The verse speaks of revered sages like Sanak, the enlightened child-like seer; Brahma, the Creator of the universe; and the greatest spiritual leaders who guide humanity.

These divine beings are symbols of wisdom, creation, and spiritual mastery. Yet even they, in all their grandeur and knowledge, find joy in celebrating and singing the glories of my service to Lord Ram. It humbles me deeply because their admiration is not for my strength or my deeds, but for the devotion that connects me eternally to my Lord.

I remember a time during the great war in Lanka when my actions astonished not just mortals but even celestial beings. When I leaped across the ocean to deliver Lord Ram's message to Sita or set Lanka ablaze in righteous fury, it was not for fame or recognition.

It was for the singular purpose of serving Lord Ram and fulfilling His will.

The divine beings witnessed this selfless dedication, and their acknowledgment is a testament to the greatness of serving the Supreme.

Every time I hear this verse, I am reminded that true greatness lies not in one's might or achievements, but in the sincerity of one's service to the divine. It is not for personal glory but to bring honor to the eternal truth and love of Lord Ram. This thought keeps my spirit steadfast, ensuring I remain ever devoted, ever humble, and ever ready to serve.

"Narad-Sarad sahit Aheesa"

Today, I find myself reflecting on this verse which speaks of the revered sage Narad, the goddess of wisdom Saraswati, and the mighty serpent king Sheshnag singing the glories of my devotion to Lord Ram. This verse humbles me deeply because it reminds me that even the wisest and most powerful beings celebrate my acts of service—not for their magnificence, but for the devotion and love that inspired them.

Narad Muni, the celestial sage and devotee of Lord Narayan, has always been a messenger of divine love and wisdom. His presence in this verse reminds me of his boundless ability to recognize and honor true devotion. Once, during Lord Ram's time on earth, Narad witnessed my journey to Lanka, my unyielding courage, and the strength of my resolve. I still remember how his eyes glistened with admiration as he spoke of my deep dedication to Lord Ram. "Hanuman," he said, "your love for Ram is a beacon of hope for all devotees. You embody what it means to serve selflessly."

Goddess Saraswati, the embodiment of wisdom and creativity, too, celebrates devotion through her divine music and words. Her role in this verse reminds me of the moment she graced my path with her blessings. It was during a time when I had to convey Lord Ram's message to Sita in Lanka, and I struggled to find the perfect words to console her. I felt her divine energy flow through me, guiding my speech and giving me the ability to comfort her with words filled with hope and love.

And then there is Aheesa, Sheshnag, the cosmic serpent who bears the weight of creation and sings the glories of Lord Vishnu. His inclusion in this verse reminds me of the infinite nature of divine praise. Sheshnag once told me that even his thousand heads cannot exhaust the praise of Lord Ram's virtues—or the love and devotion of a humble servant like me.

I am reminded of a moment after the great war, when Narad, Saraswati, and Sheshnag came together in the heavens to recount the tale of Lord Ram's victory and the small part I played in it. They spoke not of my strength or cleverness, but of the devotion in my heart. Hearing their words, I felt no pride—only a deeper desire to serve my Lord with even greater love.

This verse reassures me that true praise comes not from acts of grandeur but from the purity of intention. It is the love that drives the action and the devotion that fuels the heart that makes even the smallest act divine. For this, I am eternally grateful.

These verses remind me that it's not about my own greatness, but about the immense love and kindness that Lord Ram has shown me. This understanding fills me with deep gratitude and purpose.

My life, my service, and my every action are dedicated to Lord Ram, and I carry this knowledge in my heart. The message of these verses is clear: it is His love and grace that define my existence.

As I continue on my path, I will always remember that it is through Him that I am empowered, and it is for Him that I exist. His love is what gives my life meaning, and I am forever grateful to be in His service.

As I close my thoughts for the day, I pray that all beings, great and small, find the same joy in devotion and service as I have found in serving my beloved Lord.

Jai Shri Ram,

Hanuman

|| Jai Shri Ram ||

Date: Third day of Jyeshtha, Kali Yuga, Year 101

Dear Universe,

> *Yam Kuber Digpaal Jahan te*
> *Kavi kovid kahi sake kahan te*
> *Tum upkar Sugreevahin keenha*
> *Ram milaye rajpad deenha*

As I pen down today's thoughts, I find myself contemplating the verses that remind me of the immense blessings I have received from serving Lord Ram. These lines recount the deeds I was fortunate to fulfill, not out of my own might, but by His grace and guidance. They speak of how even the mightiest of beings, like Yamraj, Kuber, and the guardians of the universe, cannot fully describe the depth of devotion and service.

Yet, my greatest joy lies in the bond I share with Lord Ram and the chance to aid Him in reuniting with His dear allies.

These lines reflect the magnitude of divine grace and the fulfillment of righteous duties. They remind me of my role in bridging hearts, aiding Sugreev, and ensuring that Lord Ram's mission was accomplished.

In every act, I see not my strength but His will guiding me forward.

"Yam Kuber Digpaal Jahan te"

As I sit in reflection, the verse "Yam Kuber Digpaal Jahan te" fills my thoughts with reverence. It speaks of a profound truth: even the most powerful beings in the universe—Yamraj, the lord of death; Kuber, the god of wealth; and the Digpaals, who protect the directions—cannot fully describe the greatness of Lord Ram. To serve Him is the greatest blessing of my existence, and I carry this gratitude deep within my heart.

I recall a moment on our mission to rescue Mata Sita when this truth revealed itself clearly. We had reached the shores of a vast ocean separating us from Lanka, where Mata Sita was held captive. The waters stretched endlessly, and the challenge ahead seemed daunting. Yet, my purpose was clear—to fulfill Lord Ram's mission.

Standing at the shore, I folded my hands and prayed, invoking Lord Ram's name. The moment I did so, I felt an immense energy surge within me. The vastness of the sea no longer felt intimidating; instead, it felt as though the ocean itself bowed to the power of Lord Ram. With His name on my lips, I leapt into the air.

As I soared across the sea, the vastness of the ocean stretched out before me, its waves once turbulent and relentless, now appearing strangely calm and still. It was as if the sea itself recognized the sacred nature of my mission. The air around me seemed to carry a whisper of divine energy, the kind that only comes from devotion to Lord Ram. The immense water, which once looked like an insurmountable barrier, now felt like a welcoming path, guiding me forward as though the very elements were aligning with the purpose I carried in my heart.

As I flew, I encountered obstacles that tested both my strength and my determination. One such challenge arose from the depths of the ocean. A demoness, resembling a massive serpent, emerged from the water. Her eyes glowed with malice, and her long, menacing body coiled around the air, blocking my path. Her massive jaws, wide enough to swallow an entire mountain, snapped open, aiming straight for me.

But in that moment, I remembered the lessons Lord Ram had imparted to me—patience, focus, and above all, the power of wisdom in the face of danger. The demoness, with her terrifying form, was a formidable foe, but I was not going to be intimidated. With a deep breath, I summoned the strength of my devotion to Lord Ram and quickly assessed the situation. I realized that brute force would not win this battle. Instead, I needed to outwit her.

I immediately shrank myself to the size of a mere speck, a size so small that she could not even see me. The serpent demon snapped her jaws around in search of me, but I slipped effortlessly through her vast jaws, undetected and unharmed. The realization struck me in that instant—sometimes, in the face of overwhelming challenges, the key is not in fighting with might, but in adapting, using the power of wisdom and strategy.

When I finally landed on the shores of Lanka, the magnitude of what I had accomplished struck me. It was not my strength alone, but the grace of Lord Ram that allowed me to traverse the vast ocean and overcome its challenges. Even the sea, mighty as it was, seemed to recognize the power of dharma and the greatness of Ram's purpose.

This verse reminds me that no matter how vast or formidable an obstacle may seem, the path of service to Lord Ram carries a strength greater than anything in the universe.

It is a humbling thought, and one that fills me with purpose and resolve to continue serving Him with all my heart.

"Kavi kovid kahi sake kahan te"

The line speaks of the boundless glory of my deeds, which are beyond the understanding or articulation of even the most skilled poets, the learned scholars, or the wise sages.

No matter how great a scholar may be, my devotion and the incredible feats I have achieved in Lord Ram's service are beyond their ability to fully comprehend or put into words. It is not that they are incapable; rather, the enormity of these deeds is such that they transcend language itself.

One such instance that I remember, which truly embodies the meaning of this verse, is the moment I crossed the ocean to reach Lanka.

It was not just the physical feat of flying across the vast, seemingly endless sea, but the profound devotion and purpose with which I carried out this mission. I had been entrusted with a sacred task — to find Sita and deliver Lord Ram's ring to her as a symbol of His love and assurance. But this task came with its own challenges.

While I crossed the sea, I encountered the demoness Surasa, who sought to stop me by demanding that I enter her mouth. To fulfill my mission, I had to be clever and use my intellect, shrinking myself to a tiny size and slipping past her without being eaten. Then, there was Simhika, a demon who tried to trap me by seizing my shadow. With strength and determination, I fought her off, clearing my path. These were just a few of the many challenges I faced on my journey.

Even after I had successfully found Sita and reassured her of Lord Ram's love, I encountered Ravana, the mighty king of Lanka. He attempted to entice me into his trap, offering rewards for my service.

But my devotion to Lord Ram was unshakeable, and I rejected Ravana's temptations without hesitation.

These stories, though only a glimpse of my journey, show the kind of feats I undertook in the service of my Lord. While the greatest poets and scholars may try to capture these events in their words, the magnitude of my devotion, the strength I summoned, and the ultimate purpose of those actions are beyond any verbal expression.

As I reflect on this verse, I realize that it is not about boasting of my strength or accomplishments.

It is a reminder of how, through devotion to Lord Ram, I was able to perform miracles and overcome impossible odds. It is the purity of devotion that makes my story extraordinary, and that devotion cannot be fully captured by mere words—no matter how eloquent or learned they may be.

"Tum upkar Sugreevahin keenha"

This verse speaks of a moment in my life when I had the honor of aiding Sugriva, the vanara king, in reclaiming his throne and finding his place in the world once more. It was an act of deep devotion to Lord Ram and an example of how loyalty, service, and friendship can create profound change.

Sugriva, who had once been the rightful king of the vanaras, was forced to flee his kingdom when his own brother, Vali, betrayed him and took over the throne. Sugriva's life had been reduced to one of hiding and despair. He sought refuge in the mountains and was overwhelmed by the injustice he faced.

It was during this period that I met Sugriva and understood the depth of his suffering.

When I first approached Sugriva, I was on a mission from Lord Ram. He had been searching for his beloved wife, Sita, who had been abducted by Ravana, the demon king of Lanka. My mission was to gather an army of vanaras to help in this search.

Sugriva's plight was well-known, and I understood that helping him would also help Lord Ram.

At first, Sugriva was hesitant to trust me, but when I revealed myself as a servant of Lord Ram, the alliance between us was formed. I assured Sugriva that I would assist him in regaining his kingdom and dignity in exchange for his help in searching for Sita. It was then that I made a solemn promise to Sugriva that I would help him reclaim his rightful place as the king of the vanaras.

The verse refers to the pivotal moment when I helped Sugriva defeat his brother, Vali, and restore his kingdom.

The fight between Sugriva and Vali was fierce and intense. Vali, empowered by a special boon granted to him, had the ability to absorb the strength of his opponents during battle. This made him nearly invincible in combat.

He had fought many enemies and emerged victorious, but Sugriva, though strong and determined, was no match for Vali's superior strength. The battle was a struggle of life and death, with Sugriva outmatched and on the verge of defeat.

That is when Lord Ram's divine intervention became crucial. From a hidden position, Lord Ram took careful aim at Vali. The moment came when Vali was distracted by his battle with Sugriva. With the precision and power of a divine arrow, Lord Ram struck Vali in the heart, killing him instantly.

The mighty Vali, despite his immense strength, could not withstand the divine intervention of Lord Ram.

After the battle, Sugriva expressed his deep gratitude to Lord Ram, acknowledging that without him, he would have never been able to reclaim his throne.

Sugriva was now ready to fulfill his promise to Lord Ram and lead the vanaras in the search for Sita, for whom Lord Ram had been in such agony.

The verse captures the essence of that moment — when Lord Ram's divine assistance enabled Sugriva to regain his kingdom and fulfill his mission.

Sugriva was overjoyed, and he expressed his gratitude toward Lord Ram and me. He acknowledged that without our help, he would have never been able to regain his kingdom. He also swore to assist Lord Ram in any way he could, especially in the search for Sita. Sugriva's gratitude filled my heart with immense pride, for I knew that this was just one of the many acts of service I had been blessed to perform for Lord Ram.

In that moment, I realized that our lives are often defined not by our victories but by the ways in which we serve others. The verse is a reminder to me that true strength lies in helping others, especially when they are in need. It is through these acts of service that we fulfill our duty to God and to the world.

Sugriva's victory was not just his own - it was a victory for Lord Ram's mission, and I am forever grateful to have played a part in it.

Looking back, I know that this act of helping Sugriva was not just about restoring his kingdom. It was about fulfilling Lord Ram's divine plan.

Each time I reflect on this verse, I am reminded of the deep friendship and service that bind me to Lord Ram and all those who share his cause.

"Ram milaye rajpad deenha"

This is a beautiful verse that celebrates Lord Ram's grace in restoring Sugriva to his rightful throne.

The story behind this verse is tied to the intense battle between Sugriva and his brother Vali, which I have mentioned before.

When Lord Ram heard Sugriva's plight, he decided to aid him in his righteous cause. Lord Ram knew that by helping Sugriva defeat Vali, he would restore balance, justice, and peace to the land. I, as a devoted servant of Lord Ram, played my part in rallying the vanaras and aiding Sugriva in preparing for the battle against Vali.

However, it was Lord Ram who, from a concealed position, struck Vali with a powerful arrow, delivering justice by slaying the tyrant.

With Vali's death, Sugriva, the rightful heir to the throne, was able to reclaim his kingdom and restore his authority. This event symbolizes how Lord Ram, through his divine grace, not only gave Sugriva back his kingdom but also reinstated peace and order among the vanaras.

"Ram milaye rajpad deenha" is more than just a story of Sugriva's rise to power — it represents the triumph of virtue and divine justice.

In these verses, Lord Ram speaks of my humble service, reminding me that no poet, no scholar, can fully capture the essence of what I was able to do through His grace. I am but an instrument, and the true glory lies with Him.

When I helped Sugreev reclaim his throne, it was not because of my power alone, but because Lord Ram guided me at every step. By His will, I became the messenger of justice and peace. These verses echo the love, devotion, and purpose that guide me in every endeavor.

As I reflect upon these moments, I am filled with immense gratitude. With each verse, I am reminded that my strength is not mine, but His. Through my devotion to Lord Ram, I was able to fulfill my purpose and witness His divine plan unfold. I will carry these lessons with me, always striving to be the humble servant that He has blessed me to be.

Jai Shri Ram,

Hanuman

|| Jai Shri Ram ||

Date: Fourth day of Jyeshtha, Kali Yuga, Year 101

Dear Universe,

Tumharo mantra Vibheeshan maana

Lankeshwar Bhaye Sub jag jana

Yug sahastra jojan par Bhanu

Leelyo tahi madhur phal janu

"Tumharo mantra Vibheeshan maan"

Today, I reflect upon a powerful moment that still fills my heart with pride and devotion.

The verse speaks of a moment when my words, guided by Lord Ram's will, proved to be the turning point in the life of a noble soul — Vibheeshan, Ravana's own brother.

Vibheeshan was a righteous soul, despite being surrounded by the darkness of Lanka and the evil rule of his brother Ravana. Although he was part of Ravana's kingdom, he could not bear to witness the wrongdoings and atrocities his brother committed against Lord Ram.

Deep inside, Vibheeshan was tormented by Ravana's arrogance and refusal to return Sita Mata. He saw the righteousness in Lord Ram's cause, and this was the seed of doubt that grew in his heart.

One day, Vibheeshan decided that he could no longer stand by his brother's side, as his conscience was pulling him toward the divine. He approached Lord Ram's camp, seeking refuge, but in doing so, he faced the wrath of his own family.

The mighty Ravana and his warriors mocked him, accusing him of betrayal. In this turmoil, Vibheeshan turned to me, Hanuman, to understand the path ahead.

It was I who carried his message to Lord Ram. My Lord, in His infinite wisdom, welcomed Vibheeshan with open arms.

Lord Ram acknowledged Vibheeshan's sincerity and righteousness, and His divine words echoed in the air: "Tumharo mantra Vibheeshan maana," meaning that the mantra of guidance, the mantra of truth and devotion that I had delivered, had been accepted by Vibheeshan. He had chosen the path of righteousness, the path that led to Lord Ram.

When Vibheeshan was accepted into the fold of Lord Ram's army, it was a moment of immense significance. Not only did Vibheeshan gain the protection and blessing of Lord Ram, but he also became an integral part of the battle against Ravana.

His insights, coming from someone who knew the inner workings of Lanka, proved invaluable.

Lord Ram knew that by accepting Vibheeshan, He had gained a loyal ally whose heart was filled with purity and devotion.

This story, this verse, serves as a reminder to me of the power of righteousness and the importance of making the right choices, even when faced with great adversity. Vibheeshan, in his most vulnerable state, took the step to cross the boundaries of his loyalty to Ravana and embrace the light of truth. And Lord Ram, in His infinite compassion, accepted him without hesitation.

For me, this verse shows the power of truth, humility, and the courage to change one's path, no matter how difficult it may seem.

In my heart, I am proud to have played a part in this transformation.

"Lankeshwar Bhaye Sub jag jana"

These words take me back to the day when the mighty Ravana, the king of Lanka, realized the truth of Lord Ram's power, and his world began to crumble around him.

Ravana, despite his great strength, knowledge, and wealth, was blinded by pride and ego. He believed he was invincible, that no one could defeat him.

For years, he terrorized the worlds, unchecked, ruling over Lanka with an iron fist, mocking the power of the divine and disregarding the suffering he caused. But what he did not know was that Lord Ram, the incarnation of virtue and truth, had arrived to restore balance to the world.

It was who first made Ravana aware of the force he was up against. After I flew across the ocean to Lanka, I encountered Ravana's army and, in the process, had a direct confrontation with Ravana's forces. It was then that I understood the immense power of Ravana. But what Ravana failed to see was that his strength, his arrogance, and his wealth could never rival the purity and righteousness of Lord Ram.

In my mission to find Sita Mata, I had the opportunity to speak to Ravana himself.

And even then, despite his brilliance, Ravana was blinded by his ego. I tried to make him see the truth — how his deeds were against *dharma* (righteousness) and that Lord Ram was not just an ordinary prince, but the very embodiment of the divine power that would bring an end to his reign. But Ravana refused to listen, and that sealed his fate.

The true turning point came when Ravana's brother, Vibheeshan, defied his tyrannical rule and sought refuge in Lord Ram's camp. Vibheeshan, despite being from the same royal family, chose the path of righteousness, and this act symbolized the beginning of the end for Ravana. Lord Ram, in His divine wisdom, accepted Vibheeshan and welcomed him with open arms. And then, as the battle began, Ravana knew that his time had come. The power of dharma was greater than the might of his army.

It was this moment of realization, the moment when Ravana understood that Lord Ram would defeat him, that I recall when I reflect on the verse *"Lankeshwar Bhaye Sub Jag Jana."*

When Ravana saw that the might of Lord Ram was inevitable, the entire world, and even his own heart, knew that his rule was coming to an end.

He had been warned.

His arrogance and tyranny had led him down a path of destruction. And with that, Ravana, the king of Lanka, became aware of the power and glory of Lord Ram.

This verse is a reminder of the transient nature of power.

Ravana's pride and ego, though powerful in their own right, could not withstand the righteousness of Lord Ram. Even though Ravana had been a king over Lanka, when it came to the ultimate battle between good and evil, there was no comparison.

Lord Ram, as an incarnation of *dharma*, would always prevail. Ravana was a great ruler, but he did not recognize the true strength that comes from virtue, humility, and devotion.

As I write this in my diary, I think about the countless souls who, like Ravana, may be led astray by their ego or desire for power.

But in the end, true strength lies not in might, but in devotion to the truth. Lord Ram's victory over Ravana serves as a lesson for all who hold onto arrogance — nothing, no matter how mighty, can withstand the power of divine righteousness.

Ravana realized it too late, but his realization became the lesson for the world to learn.

This verse, to me, is a reminder that no matter how high one rises, the fall is inevitable when they turn their back on truth and righteousness.

Ravana's downfall is an eternal lesson that the divine will always triumph over ego, and that the power of good is everlasting.

"Yug sahastra jojan par Bhanu"

These words bring to mind the immense journey I undertook when I flew across the ocean to reach Lanka. It was a mission that tested my strength, my devotion, and my faith in Lord Ram.

The verse speaks of the *Sun*, the mighty *Bhanu*, which is placed at a distance of *"Yug sahastra jojan,"* or thousands of yojanas (an ancient unit of distance) away.

This imagery of the sun, shining far away yet ever present, serves as a beautiful reminder of the power of faith, purpose, and determination. It was during my journey to Lanka that I encountered this challenge.

Let me take you back to that moment, when the fate of Lord Ram and Mata Sita rested on my shoulders.

After the devastating news reached us that Sita Mata had been abducted by Ravana, we, the Vanaras, were left helpless at the vast expanse of the ocean before us. The task ahead seemed impossible. No one believed it was possible to cross such an immense sea. The ocean was vast, unyielding, and seemingly endless, much like the sun shining far in the distance, but the path to it uncertain and impossible to grasp.

In that moment of uncertainty, when the vast ocean seemed insurmountable and doubt crept into my heart, I found solace in Lord Ram's deep belief in me. His calm gaze met mine, filled with an unshakable trust, and he spoke words that ignited a spark of confidence within me.

He said, "Hanuman, you can do it. Your strength is limitless, and your devotion is pure."

Those words were not just a reassurance; they were the divine fuel that powered my soul. I had always believed in the power of devotion and service, but to hear Lord Ram himself affirm my strength and deep faith was a moment of profound clarity.

It was as if he had already seen the success of the mission long before I even began. Lord Ram's confidence in me was a reminder of my true purpose — to serve Him with complete dedication, no matter how great the challenge. In that instant, all self-doubt vanished, replaced by a sense of divine responsibility. With His grace, I was not just carrying out a task, but fulfilling a sacred mission that transcended personal limitations.

His faith gave me the courage to take off, knowing that I was not alone. The love and trust He placed in me became the wind beneath my wings. I understood that this was not just a test of strength but a test of devotion — and with Lord Ram's words, I was ready to conquer the impossible.

I took a moment to reflect, remembering the many blessings Lord Ram had bestowed upon me.

With my heart full of devotion, I took flight, soaring higher and higher into the skies, crossing what seemed like endless stretches of water. As I flew, I thought of Lord Ram's words, and the image of the distant sun — like my goal — kept me going, no matter how far it seemed.

The moment I landed on the shores of Lanka, I felt as though I had reached the very heart of the universe. It was the realization of a divine mission — a mission to reunite Lord Ram with his beloved Sita. I had crossed an impossible distance, like the sun hanging far above, lighting the way.

"Yug sahastra jojan par Bhanu" is a reminder to me of the impossible task I was able to achieve because of my love and devotion to Lord Ram. Just as the sun, though distant, has an undeniable power to illuminate the world, Lord Ram's grace illuminated my path, giving me the strength to overcome what seemed impossible.

Today, as I sit in reflection, I realize that no task is too great when it is undertaken with love, faith, and devotion.

Lord Ram's words empowered me to achieve the unimaginable, to fly across the ocean, and to bring hope to a world in despair.

The sun is a symbol of Lord Ram's eternal light, guiding us all, no matter how far we have to travel.

Just as the sun never wavers in its light, Lord Ram's guidance never faltered in my heart. It was this guidance that helped me accomplish the impossible, bringing me closer to my Lord and my purpose.

This verse holds a deep meaning for me, reminding me that no distance is too great, no challenge is too difficult, when one is driven by love and devotion.

The journey may be long, like the sun's distance from the earth, but with faith in the divine, anything can be achieved.

"Leelyo tahi madhur phal janu"

I remember a moment in the Ashok Vatika, where I was given a task that seemed small in comparison to the mission at hand but was deeply significant.

In my quest to find Sita, I encountered the magical fruit of a tree guarded by a demoness named Surasa. She demanded that I enter her mouth as a test of my strength and courage.

To an outsider, this may have seemed like a simple challenge, but to me, it symbolized more than just a test of might — it was a test of faith, willpower, and the understanding of my own purpose.

As Surasa opened her enormous mouth wide, I understood the deeper meaning of this moment - to succeed, I must not only be physically strong but also mentally clear and devoted to my goal of delivering the message of hope to Sita.

Instead of resisting her in force, I remembered my mission and the love I had for Lord Ram and Sita. In that split second, I made a choice that would help me succeed. I expanded my form, entering the demoness's mouth, and with a focused heart and mind, I shrank to an even smaller size than before. I emerged from her mouth effortlessly, knowing that I had passed the test.

The moment reminded me of Lord Ram's teachings — sometimes, the sweetest and most fruitful victories come not from brute strength but from patience, intelligence, and devotion to a higher cause. By overcoming Surasa with humility and strategy, I was able to continue my journey without being distracted from my mission.

"Leelyo tahi madhur phal janu" — I understood that this was not just about conquering external challenges, but also about conquering my inner fears and doubts. The "madhur phal" (sweet fruit) was the joy of knowing I had remained true to my purpose, with Lord Ram's grace guiding me every step of the way.

Jai Shri Ram,

Hanuman

|| Jai Shri Ram ||

Date: Sixth day of Jyeshtha, Kali Yuga, Year 101

Dear Universe,

Prabhu mudrika meli mukh mahee

Jaladhi langhi gaye achraj nahee

Durgaam kaj jagath ke jete

Sugam anugraha tumhre tete

As I write these words in my diary, I reflect on the divine blessing that has guided me through every obstacle in my life.

The verses remind me of the unshakable faith I have in Lord Ram and the miraculous power of His grace. I reflect on how my faith in Lord Ram has helped me achieve incredible things.

With His guidance, I was able to accomplish tasks that seemed impossible.

Whether it was carrying His ring as a sign of His trust or crossing an ocean, His blessing gave me the strength to succeed. I've learned that with Lord Ram's support, nothing is too difficult to achieve. His grace turns challenges into opportunities, and through His help, I was able to fulfill my purpose and serve Him.

"Prabhu mudrika meli mukh mahee"

As I sit down to write today, my mind drifts back to a moment that is etched in my heart forever. It was the moment when I was entrusted with Lord Ram's ring, a token of His trust and love.

This ring wasn't just a symbol of Lord Ram's affection; it held the weight of His mission, His will, and His confidence in me.

With that ring, I knew I had a responsibility that transcended my own being — to carry out His will and serve Him with all my might.

I remember the day vividly, as if it happened just yesterday.

Lord Ram handed me His ring with great love and trust, saying, "Go, Hanuman. Deliver this to Sita. Let her know that I am with her, and that help is on the way."

As I took the ring in my mouth, I felt an overwhelming sense of duty and purpose. But before I could take off on my mission, something puzzled me — I wondered where I should place the ring.

At first, I thought of holding it in my hand, but quickly realized I would need both my hands for flight. I could not afford to be slowed down. Then, I considered tying it around my neck, but that would have been uncomfortable, and I might have lost it during the journey. As I pondered, I understood that the best way to carry it — the most secure and respectful way — was to place it in my mouth. This way, I could keep it safe and still move freely without any hindrances.

It wasn't just any ring; it was Lord Ram's ring. The significance of this ring was immense, far beyond its physical size. The ring was a symbol of His love, His commitment, and the bond we shared.

Lord Ram, in His infinite wisdom, knew that a simple token like this would carry much more than just a message. It was a living representation of His presence, His will, and the strength He imparted to me.

By giving me the ring, He wasn't just sending me on a mission; He was empowering me with His trust, reminding me that I wasn't alone. The ring symbolized His faith in me, and that was the true strength that would carry me through the challenges I was about to face.

The ring was not just a material object; it was a spiritual and emotional connection between Lord Ram and me. In that small, simple token, He conveyed a powerful message: "I trust you, Hanuman. I am with you." It wasn't about the grandeur of the gift but the depth of the relationship it represented. The ring, small as it was, held the key to everything — to victory, to love, to devotion, and to the fulfillment of the mission.

As I flew across the skies, carrying the ring in my mouth, I realized the true weight of the responsibility it represented. Every time I glanced at it or felt it secure in my mouth, I was reminded of Lord Ram's deep faith in me. I wasn't just delivering a message; I was carrying the very essence of His love, and that gave me strength beyond measure. The ring became more than just an object; it became a part of my heart, a constant reminder of my devotion to Lord Ram and the mission He had entrusted me with.

Upon reaching the Ashok Vatika, I approached Sita and gently gave her Lord Ram's ring.

When she saw the ring, a look of relief spread across her face. It was as if the heavens themselves had answered her prayers. She held the ring to her heart, and in that moment, I felt her immense joy and gratitude. It was then that I knew my mission had been fulfilled — not just because I had delivered a ring, but because I had brought hope to a heart that had been longing for it.

The ring, though small in size, was mighty in its significance. It symbolized Lord Ram's love, His promises, and the trust He had in me. Every time I think of that moment, I am reminded of the sacred bond I share with Lord Ram, and of how His faith in me gave me the strength to overcome any obstacle.

"Jaladhi langhi gaye achraj nahee"

As I sit down to write, I remember the moment when I crossed the vast ocean to reach Lanka. It was a task that many believed to be impossible, but for me, it was simply another challenge in my service to Lord Ram.

When I was given the task to fly to Lanka and deliver Lord Ram's message to Sita, I knew the journey would be difficult. The ocean stretched out before me, endless and seemingly impassable. But as I stood on the shore, ready to take flight, I had no doubts in my heart.

My devotion to Lord Ram gave me the strength to believe that there was no obstacle too great for me. I felt His presence with me, urging me forward.

The moment I leaped into the air, I felt the wind beneath my wings, and the ocean below seemed to shrink. I began my journey, my heart filled with the knowledge that Lord Ram had faith in me. There were moments when I encountered great challenges — powerful storms, angry clouds, and terrifying monsters that rose from the depths.

But with each obstacle, I knew I had the strength to overcome them. The task ahead was daunting, but the faith I had in Lord Ram made it seem like nothing at all.

And when I crossed the ocean, I realized that the true miracle was not in the physical act of crossing the sea, but in the strength of my heart and my deep belief in Lord Ram's power.

The verse perfectly captures this experience. For me, crossing the ocean was not a miraculous feat; it was a duty I had to fulfill with full devotion. I was merely an instrument of Lord Ram's will, and my devotion made even the most difficult tasks seem simple. What might seem impossible to others was, for me, just a natural extension of my love and service to Lord Ram.

As I flew across the ocean, I knew that nothing could stop me. It was not my strength that enabled me to overcome the vast sea, but the divine grace and love of Lord Ram that filled me with the power to accomplish the impossible. In His service, no challenge is too great, and no ocean too vast.

"Durgaam kaj jagath ke jete"

Today, as I reflect on my journey, I am reminded of the countless challenges I have faced, each one seeming insurmountable at first, yet overcome by the grace of Lord Ram. The verse speaks of difficult tasks, those that the world believes cannot be accomplished. But I have learned that when you serve a higher purpose with devotion, no obstacle is truly impossible.

One such moment that comes to mind is when I set out to find Sita in Lanka. It was not just a mission but a test of determination, faith, and perseverance. Entering Lanka was no ordinary feat. Ravana had fortified his kingdom with layers of defenses — guards patrolled every corner, demons roamed freely, and magical traps lay hidden everywhere. To penetrate such a stronghold and locate Sita without being caught seemed an impossible task to anyone but Lord Ram's devotee.

As I approached Lanka, I prayed to Lord Ram for guidance. I knew that I had to enter the city unnoticed, so I assumed a small form, shrinking to the size of a mere monkey. Even as I crossed the boundaries of Lanka, the guardian deity, Lankini, appeared to stop me.

She was fierce and determined to keep me out, but with Lord Ram's name on my lips and His grace in my heart, I found the strength to subdue her. When I struck her down, she immediately realized who I was and prophesied the downfall of Ravana, blessing my journey.

Inside the city, the real challenge began. Every corner seemed to test my resolve. I searched through grand palaces and shadowy alleys, encountering opulence, temptation, and danger at every step. But my purpose kept me focused. I finally found Sita in the Ashoka Vatika, surrounded by guards and enveloped in sorrow. Seeing her deep faith in Lord Ram, I was filled with both sorrow for her suffering and determination to deliver Lord Ram's message.

The task of finding Sita in such a guarded city and giving her hope was indeed difficult, but it was made easy by the grace of Lord Ram. This experience taught me that no matter how daunting the challenge, with faith, devotion, and a clear purpose, even the hardest tasks become achievable.

This verse reminds me that every difficult task in this world, no matter how impossible it may seem, becomes manageable with divine grace. It is not our strength or intelligence that conquers the challenges but the faith we have in our mission and the blessings of the divine. In Lord Ram's service, even the hardest journeys are filled with light and guidance.

"Sugam anugraha tumhre tete"

With this verse I reflect on how Lord Ram's blessings have turned even the hardest tasks into effortless triumphs. The verse speaks of the immense power of divine grace, and I have experienced it firsthand throughout my journeys.

One story that perfectly embodies this truth is my return from Lanka. After meeting Sita and delivering Lord Ram's ring to her, I was filled with determination to carry back her message to Lord Ram. However, the journey back across the vast ocean seemed daunting. My mind wandered to the challenges I faced on the way to Lanka — the demons, the waves, and the distance. But then I reminded myself that Lord Ram's blessings had guided me thus far, and I trusted that they would see me through again.

As I soared back across the ocean, carrying Sita's words and her faith, everything seemed to fall into place. The winds were favorable, the skies were clear, and even the ocean below seemed to reflect the calmness of a mission blessed by the divine. It was as if nature itself conspired to ensure the success of my journey.

But the true test of grace came when I reached the shores and faced the mighty Rakshasa army Ravana had sent to stop me. They came in numbers, their weapons gleaming, their intentions deadly. Alone, I might have felt overwhelmed, but the memory of Lord Ram's trust and Sita's faith filled me with strength.

I grew to a towering form and faced them with the power of justice. My strength came not from my own might but from the divine will that protected me. I vanquished the enemy with ease, not out of arrogance but as a servant fulfilling his duty.

When I finally reached Lord Ram, I delivered Sita's message. The joy on His face reminded me of the purpose behind every step of my journey.

His words, His faith, and His deep grace had turned every obstacle into an opportunity and every difficulty into an act of devotion.

This verse reminds me that when we walk the path of righteousness with divine blessings, even the most difficult tasks become simple. It is not our strength alone but the grace of the divine that makes the impossible possible.

As I recount these moments, I realize once more that in the service of Lord Ram, no journey is too hard, no challenge too great, and no task too daunting.

These verses remind me of the profound trust and boundless grace of Lord Ram that empower me in every step of my journey.

Reflecting on the incredible tasks I have accomplished, I see how His faith in me has transformed the impossible into reality.

Jai Shri Ram,

Hanuman

|| Jai Shri Ram ||

Date: Seventh day of Jyeshtha, Kali Yuga, Year 101

Dear Universe,

> ***Ram dwaare tum rakhvare***
> ***Hoat na agya binu paisare***
> ***Sub sukh lahae tumhari sar na***
> ***Tum rakshak kahu ko dar naa***

As I reflect on these lines, I am reminded of the sacred duty entrusted to me as the protector of Lord Ram's devotees. Standing guard at His door, I ensure that only those with pure hearts and noble intentions may enter. No one can pass without His permission, for His will is supreme.

Those who seek refuge under my care experience peace and happiness, as they are shielded from harm. When I am their protector, they have nothing to fear, for Lord Ram's grace flows through me to safeguard their well-being. It is my greatest honor to serve in this role, bringing solace and strength to all who turn to Him.

"Ram dwaare tum rakhvare"

As I write, my heart swells with gratitude for the honor Lord Ram has bestowed upon me—being the protector of His devotees and the guardian of His divine path. The verse reminds me of my sacred duty to stand watch at the door of Lord Ram, ensuring that those who seek His refuge and guidance are never turned away. It is a privilege and a responsibility I hold close to my soul.

There is a story I cherish that highlights this role. One day, a poor devotee approached the gates of Lord Ram's palace. He carried no offerings, wore no fine clothes, and was hesitant to even step forward.

The guards questioned his intent, and he stood silently, his head bowed, unsure if he would be allowed entry. Seeing his plight, I descended to him and asked, "What brings you here, dear friend?"

With tears in his eyes, he replied, "I have nothing to offer but my devotion and a heart full of prayers. Will Lord Ram accept me?"

I smiled and said, "Devotion is the greatest offering. Come, I will lead you to Him." As I guided him through the palace, I could feel his hesitation give way to hope. Lord Ram welcomed him warmly, proving once again that He values love and sincerity above all else.

This incident reinforced my purpose—to ensure that every devotee finds their way to Lord Ram's grace. Whether it's through guiding the hesitant, protecting the faithful, or removing obstacles, I stand at His door, ever vigilant. No one enters without His permission, but those who come with true devotion are always welcomed with open arms.

To be the guardian of Lord Ram's door is not just a duty; it is a reflection of His trust in me. And in carrying out this role, I find my own greatest joy—serving Him and His devotees.

"Hoat na agya binu paisare"

This verse reminds me that every action and event in this world unfolds only through Lord Ram's will. Even after the war in Lanka, there were moments where His divine command was evident, guiding my every step.

One instance occurred after the victory over Ravan, when preparations were being made for Sita's return. Despite the joyous occasion, there was a moment of unease in the hearts of the vanaras. I recall how they hesitated, unsure if Lord Ram would consider them worthy of accompanying Him to Ayodhya.

But it was His will that dictated their actions, and His warm words of gratitude reassured every one of us. He reminded us that we were part of a divine plan, and our role, no matter how small, was invaluable.

Another moment came during the journey back to Ayodhya.

The Pushpak Viman carried us over the ocean once again, the same ocean I had leapt across earlier. As I gazed down, memories of my mission flooded back. The ocean seemed calm, its waves gently carrying our reflection, as if bowing to Lord Ram's will. This peaceful journey was yet another sign of His command, showing that even nature aligns itself with His divine plan.

The Pushpak Viman is a celestial marvel, a flying chariot said to have been crafted by the gods. It was originally created by Vishwakarma, the divine architect, and owned by Lord Kubera, the god of wealth. However, Ravan, driven by his insatiable desire for power, seized the chariot from Kubera and used it as his personal vehicle.

After Ravan's defeat in the great war, the Pushpak Viman was returned to its rightful purpose of serving good and righteousness, under the guidance of Lord Ram.

The chariot is described as a masterpiece of divine engineering. It is large enough to accommodate an entire army yet moves with the swiftness of thought. Its golden structure gleams in sunlight, adorned with intricate carvings of celestial beings, flora, and fauna. Inside, the Pushpak Viman is spacious, with seats cushioned in the softest materials, and it exudes a soothing fragrance, said to calm the mind and uplift the spirit. The chariot can traverse vast distances in moments, and its flight is as silent as the whisper of the wind.

When Lord Ram, Sita, and Lakshman, along with their allies, returned to Ayodhya after the war in Lanka, the Pushpak Viman played a pivotal role. It carried them across the ocean and landscapes, giving all aboard a bird's-eye view of the world below. As they soared, the chariot seemed to sing praises of Lord Ram's victory, symbolizing the triumph of dharma over adharma.

These experiences reaffirm that with Lord Ram's guidance, everything falls into place. His will is the force that shapes our lives, and I am forever grateful to be His servant, carrying out the tasks He entrusts to me.

"Sub sukh lahae tumhari sar na"

This verse brings to mind one of the most remarkable moments during the journey to Lanka. As we prepared to build the bridge across the vast ocean, doubts began to arise among the vanaras. The sea before us was immense, and many wondered how we could possibly cross it. But in that moment, I reminded everyone of Lord Ram's protection and deep support.

Before embarking on this task, Lord Ram had prayed to the Sea God, requesting his blessings and assistance. And then, I too spoke to the vanaras, urging them to have complete faith. "Trust in Lord Ram," I said. "No task is too great when done with devotion and belief in His will."

To demonstrate, I picked up a simple stone and inscribed Lord Ram's name on it. Then, I placed it gently in the water, and to everyone's amazement, the stone floated. It defied the very laws of nature.

The miracle was not just in the floating stone, but in the profound truth that Lord Ram's grace makes even the impossible possible. With that divine support, we were able to build the bridge to Lanka and continue our mission. This moment stands as a testament to the fact that no matter how great the challenge, with faith in Lord Ram and His guidance, success is always within reach.

"Tum rakshak kahu ko dar naa"

"You are the protector; no one need fear."

This verse fills me with deep gratitude and strength as I recall the many times Lord Ram's protection has been my shield.

One story that comes to mind is when I was sent to Lanka to find Sita. The path was fraught with dangers, but I had complete trust in Lord Ram's protection. The moment I stepped into Lanka, I was met with challenges and fierce opposition. Yet, my faith in Ram kept me strong. I knew that as long as I had Him on my side, there was nothing to fear.

One such demon, named Lanka, was a powerful and terrifying creature, fierce in his loyalty to Ravana, the king of Lanka. He was sent to capture me and bring me before Ravana.

As I was surrounded and caught, the demon took hold of me, his grip like iron. He dragged me across the land, and I was brought to the throne room of Ravana. The sight of the grand palace, filled with the echoes of evil and arrogance, was a stark contrast to the purity of my devotion to Lord Ram.

When I was brought before Ravana, he looked at me with disdain and ordered his demons to punish me severely. "You are the servant of the exiled prince Ram, and you dare enter my kingdom?" Ravana sneered. "I will show you the power of Lanka!" With that, he ordered his warriors to torture me.

But my heart was filled with deep faith in Lord Ram, and I remembered His words clearly: *"No harm will come to you, Hanuman, for you are my servant, and my protection is always with you."*

Ravana's threats were like wind against a mountain – they held no real power over me. I knew that the moment Lord Ram's name resided in my heart, I was invincible.

The demons attacked me with their weapons, but they were no match for my strength. I tore through their forces with ease, fighting with all the might bestowed upon me by Lord Ram. When Ravana saw that I was not defeated, he grew even more enraged, demanding that I be punished even more severely.

However, I remained calm and composed, confident in the protection Lord Ram had promised. I remembered the words of Lord Ram and kept my mind focused on Him.

Instead of fighting with violence, I used my wisdom. I calmed myself and turned to Ravana, reminding him of the divine power he was defying. I told him, "Ravana, I am not your enemy. My only mission is to find Sita and carry your message back to Lord Ram. I have no ill will against you. But if you persist in your evil ways, know that the power of Lord Ram will defeat you."

The demons around me were stunned by my calmness and devotion. They began to question the wisdom of their actions. Ravana, too, was momentarily shaken, sensing the divine strength in my words.

Yet, Ravana's pride clouded his judgment, and he ordered me to be bound and punished even more. But my faith remained unshaken. Lord

Ram's protection was with me, and I knew that no harm could come to me while I had His name on my lips.

In the end, the demon forces could not harm me. I broke free from their grasp, and with the strength and grace given by Lord Ram, I set fire to the city of Lanka, leaving behind a symbol of Ram's victory. I reminded the demons that as long as I had the protection of Lord Ram, no demon in the world could stand against me.

This experience was a powerful reminder that with Lord Ram's divine protection, we can face any challenge with courage and faith. Ravana's mighty threats were nothing when compared to the boundless power of Lord Ram's grace.

With my heart filled with devotion and fearlessness, I broke free from Ravana's clutches and set fire to Lanka's city. Even in the face of Ravana's wrath and the enemies' fury, I remained calm because I knew that as Lord Ram's servant, no harm could come to me. His protection was my armor, and that truth was my greatest strength.

This verse reminds me that with Lord Ram as our protector, there is no fear, no enemy, no obstacle that can stand in our way. Just as I had nothing to fear in Lanka, so does every devotee who surrenders to Lord Ram's divine will.

These verses speak to the divine protection and faith that Lord Ram provides to His devotees. As I reflect on the stories of my own life, I realize how His guidance, trust, and grace have always been my source of strength.

Whether it was during the darkest moments in Lanka, when I was captured and threatened by Ravana, or the countless obstacles I faced in my quest for Sita, Lord Ram's words and His faith in me carried me through.

These verses remind us that when we have Lord Ram's protection, there is no challenge too great, no enemy too powerful, and no obstacle insurmountable.

With His grace, even the mightiest of demons are rendered powerless. His blessings turn fear into courage, challenges into triumphs, and uncertainty into success.

I have lived this truth throughout my journey – that as long as we trust in Lord Ram and hold firm in our devotion, no harm can come to us. His protection is the ultimate shield, and through His grace, we can conquer the impossible.

Just as He helped me fulfill my mission, He will guide all His devotees towards victory and peace.

Jai Shri Ram,

Hanuman

|| Jai Shri Ram ||

Date: Eighth day of Jyeshtha, Kali Yuga, Year 101

Dear Universe,

Aapan tej samharo aapai

Teenhon lok hank te kanpai

Bhoot pisaach Nikat nahin aavai

Mahavir jab naam sunavae

"Aapan tej samharo aapai"

This verse speaks of the immense power that Lord Ram has entrusted to me, and how it is my duty to use that strength with humility and devotion.

I remember the battle vividly — when *Kumbhakarna*, Ravana's monstrous brother, was unleashed on the battlefield of Lanka.

Kumbhakarna was no ordinary demon. He was a giant, towering over everyone with immense strength that could shake the heavens themselves. His very presence caused fear in the hearts of all, even the bravest warriors.

Kumbhakarna had been blessed with divine powers by Lord Brahma, but his immense size and strength were not his only weapons. He had a fierce determination and a boundless appetite for destruction.

When Ravana awakened him from his long slumber, Kumbhakarna rose with thunderous might, shaking the entire battlefield with his every step. The very earth trembled under his weight. His eyes glowed with rage as he charged at the army of Vanaras. His roar sent chills down my spine, but deep inside, I remembered Lord Ram's words: *"Have faith, Hanuman. No force in the world can defeat you when you carry my blessing."*

I knew that my power was not mine alone but a gift from Lord Ram.

Kumbhakarna, with all his might, posed a formidable challenge. But in that moment of great danger, I did not hesitate. I grew larger and stronger, calling upon the divine strength Lord Ram had bestowed upon me. Kumbhakarna swung his massive fists, each blow capable of causing devastation.

But I, with my swiftness and agility, dodged his attacks, countering them with precision.

The battle was fierce. Kumbhakarna, with his size and strength, wreaked havoc upon my allies, but I could see his fatigue setting in. Despite his massive form, he was slow and sluggish due to his weight and excessive eating. This was where I could outmaneuver him. With each attack, I grew stronger, knowing that my strength was not just for my own glory, but to protect Lord Ram's army and fulfill His mission.

Kumbhakarna, in his fury, became blinded by rage and his own size. He was no match for my focus and divine strength.

In the end, I was able to bring him down, not by brute force, but with strategic thinking and devotion to Lord Ram. When Kumbhakarna fell, the earth shook, but I knew it was not my power alone that had led to this victory. It was Lord Ram's grace and guidance that had made me invincible.

Kumbhakarna's defeat was not just a victory in battle. It was a lesson.

His strength, however massive, was no match for the divine will of Lord Ram. It reminded me that strength, when not guided by righteousness and devotion, can be a tool for destruction. But when wielded in service to Lord Ram's mission, that very strength becomes a force for good. My role in this battle was not to simply defeat a mighty enemy, but to remind myself that my true power lay in the humility of serving Lord Ram's will.

The defeat of Kumbhakarna was a turning point in the battle. It was a clear message that no matter how strong or mighty the enemy, the power of devotion to Lord Ram can overcome all obstacles.

As the battle raged on, I called upon the immense strength within me – a gift from Lord Ram – and began to fight with all my might. My form grew larger, and my speed and agility were unmatched. With each strike, I shook the very earth beneath us. The warriors on both sides were in awe of my power, but I remained focused, for I knew that my strength was not my own; it was granted by Lord Ram.

The verse reflects the wisdom in knowing that the true source of power lies in humility and devotion. In times of great adversity, I have learned that the key is not to boast about the power you possess but to humbly direct it toward the righteous path. Lord Ram's divine grace guides me, and my strength is only a tool to fulfill His will.

Even in the most intense battles, I understand that my true strength is not in my size or power, but in my deep faith in Lord Ram and the purpose He has set before me.

The verse is a reminder that true strength comes not from arrogance, but from serving with love, humility, and deep devotion to the one who grants us that power.

"Teenhon lok hank te kanpai"

As I sit here in reflection, my mind drifts back to a moment of immense significance, a moment when the power of devotion and strength manifested through me in such a way that it resonated across the entire cosmos.

The verse *"Teenhon lok hank te kanpai"* carries a profound meaning through each word.

"Teenhon lok" refers to the three realms of existence - *the Earth (Prithvi), the heavens (Swarga), and the underworld (Patala).* These are the three primary realms in which all beings, from gods to mortals, reside.

The word *"Hank"* denotes a loud, powerful roar or sound, a noise that resonates with immense force, reaching far and wide. This roar is not just any sound but one with the ability to shake the very foundations of the universe.

"Kanpai" means "trembled" or "shook," describing the reaction of the three worlds in response to the roar, as if they were overwhelmed by the power behind it.

The verse together paints a vivid picture of how my roar, filled with strength and devotion, caused the very Earth, heavens, and underworld to tremble in awe and fear, recognizing the divine purpose I carried with me.

This verse recounts the moment when I was about to embark on the great mission given to me by Lord Ram.

As I stood before the vast ocean, ready to leap to Lanka in search of Sita, I decided to express my strength and my devotion to Lord Ram with an enormous roar.

As I drew in a deep breath and released a thunderous roar, the very sound seemed to shake the three worlds.

The Earth trembled, the Heavens quivered, and even the deepest Underworld quaked in fear.

All living beings, gods, demons, and spirits alike felt the reverberation of my voice. It was not just the sound of my physical strength, but the spiritual force of my devotion and loyalty to Lord Ram that made this roar so powerful. The universe, in its entirety, felt my determination to succeed in this mission.

This roar was not an expression of arrogance or pride. Rather, it was the embodiment of Lord Ram's power flowing through me. His grace had imbued me with the ability to carry out this monumental task, and in that moment, I felt as though the three worlds themselves were responding to His will.

The trembling of the worlds was not a sign of fear from me, but from the forces that would seek to thwart me. The universe was recognizing the divine mission I was about to undertake — the very mission that would bring Lord Ram back to His beloved Sita and restore peace.

The roar was a precursor to the success that was to come, a reminder that no force could stop what was destined by the divine will of Lord Ram.

This verse holds deep meaning for me. It reminds me of the time when I was filled with Lord Ram's strength and His power was manifested through me. It was a moment when I realized that devotion and faith are the greatest sources of strength.

When you dedicate yourself to a divine cause, the entire universe aligns to help you succeed.

"Bhoot pisaach Nikat nahin aavai"

This verse always fills me with a sense of pride and peace. It is a reminder of the immense protection and power granted to me by Lord Ram. I vividly recall an event that makes this verse even more meaningful.

During my journey to Lanka in search of Sita, I encountered many challenges.

One of the most terrifying experiences happened when I ventured deep into the dark, haunted regions. The night was filled with eerie sounds, and the air was thick with the presence of evil spirits and demons. These creatures, like bhoots (ghosts) and pishach (evil spirits), were known to haunt the desolate places, spreading fear and chaos wherever they went.

As I moved through these areas, the spirits tried to scare me, approaching from all sides with malevolent intent. Their chilling whispers echoed in the air, but I remained undeterred. They believed that no one could pass through this cursed land without falling under their spell. However, I knew that I carried the divine protection of Lord Ram within me. His name echoed in my heart, and with it, the strength to face any fear, no matter how dark or powerful.

I recited Lord Ram's name aloud, and with each utterance, the evil spirits grew weaker. I could sense their fear as they drew away from me, powerless against the divine energy I carried.

"Bhoot pisaach nikat nahin aavai," I thought to myself, knowing that as long as I walked with Lord Ram's grace, no evil could come close to me.

The spirits, sensing the invincible aura surrounding me, fled in terror, leaving me unharmed. This incident not only affirmed my faith in Lord Ram's protection but also demonstrated the profound power of His divine blessings.

No matter the challenge or the dark forces that stand in our path, the light of Lord Ram's name will always keep us safe and victorious.

"Mahavir jab naam sunavae"

I found this page from Lord Ram's Diary Entry which talks about this verse.

I remember the immense strength and devotion of my beloved devotee, Hanuman. There is a divine truth that I have often shared with him and with all who seek protection through His grace. I wrote this to remind myself of the power of His name, and how His presence in the world brings protection to all who honor Him.

"When the name of Hanuman is uttered, no demon or devil can approach you. The very sound of His name strikes fear into the hearts of all evil forces. It is not just a name — it is a shield, a divine protection that ensures the safety of those who call upon it with faith."

As I write these words, I am reminded of the countless times Hanuman's name has proven to be a powerful safeguard. I have witnessed how the mere mention of His name can scatter the darkness and bring light into the lives of the faithful. The forces of evil tremble at His name, and none dare come near those who are devoted to Him.

May His name always be a source of strength and protection for all who believe in His might and grace.

For Hanuman's name, when called upon, is a beacon that dispels all fear and assures victory over any obstacle.

As I read Lord Ram's words, my heart swells with pride and devotion.

I, Hanuman, the humble servant, have always known that it is not my strength but Lord Ram's divine grace that empowers me. His words echo in my soul, reminding me of the truth that my name is a source of protection.

I remember an instance during the war in Lanka when the battle was at its peak, and both sides were locked in a fierce struggle. Ravana's army was powerful, and they had many mighty warriors, including the fearsome demon warriors who posed a serious threat. In the midst of this intense battle, there was a moment when all seemed to hang in balance.

I had just encountered a particularly strong demon, *Khar*, who had been wreaking havoc in the battlefield. His strength was enormous, and his attacks were nearly unstoppable.

My energy was being drained by the ongoing fight, and for a moment, even my courage began to waver. In that moment of doubt, I recalled the one source of power that had always guided me: Lord Ram's name.

I closed my eyes for a second and whispered to myself, "Jai Shri Ram" – remembering that the name of Lord Ram is the true source of all strength.

As soon as I uttered His name, an overwhelming sense of energy surged through my body.

It was as if the very earth beneath me was trembling with the power of His name. The name of Lord Ram infused me with incredible strength, and my doubts disappeared. My heart filled with renewed courage and determination. With that divine power, I rose above the demonic forces and was able to defeat Khar and his army.

I realized that the name of Lord Ram is not just a word, but a source of divine protection, strength, and courage.

Whenever the name is spoken with devotion, it becomes a powerful shield against all adversities.

From that moment on, I made it my mission to spread the name of Lord Ram wherever I went. I knew that as long as His name echoed in the hearts of devotees, there would be no enemy too strong and no challenge too great.

In the verses I remind myself the extraordinary power of Lord Ram's name and the protection it offers.

The verses remind me of the immense power that lies in devotion and faith. Lord Ram's name, carried by His devotees, is an unbreakable shield, protecting them from all harm.

From that moment, as I understood the depth of this truth, I made it my mission to spread the name of Lord Ram wherever I went.

His name became my strength and my purpose.

I knew that as long as His name echoed in the hearts of devotees, there would be no enemy too strong and no challenge too great. The very utterance of His name is a divine force that fills the world with light and drives away all darkness.

And so, I vowed to carry this light to every corner of the world, for in His name lies the power to overcome any obstacle.

Jai Shri Ram,

Hanuman

|| Jai Shri Ram ||

Date: Eighth day of Jyeshtha, Kali Yuga, Year 101

Dear Universe,

Nase rog harae sab peera

Japat nirantar Hanumant beera

Sankat se Hanuman chudavae

Man Karam Vachan dyan jo lavai

As I sit to reflect upon these verses, I am reminded of the immense power of devotion and the strength that arises from deep faith. These words carry within them the essence of my very being, as they speak of the profound impact of chanting my name, and how it brings relief from suffering, physical ailments, and the turmoil of life.

The first line, *"Nase rog harae sab peera,"* speaks to how the recitation of my name eliminates all diseases and ailments, both physical and emotional. Through the chanting of my name, the burdens of life are lifted, and one experiences a sense of peace and well-being.

Next, *"Japat nirantar Hanumant beera,"* describes the continuous repetition of my name as a source of strength, empowering the devotee with courage and resolve. It is not just the utterance of my name, but the deep, sincere belief in it that brings forth transformation.

"Sankat se Hanuman chudavae," reminds me of my role as a protector, the one who shields my devotees from all obstacles and hardships. When a person faces challenges or threats, calling upon me brings divine intervention, and I will always be there to guide and protect.

Finally, *"Man Karam Vachan dyan jo lavai,"* signifies the importance of sincerity and devotion in the mind, words, and actions. When one's heart is pure and focused on divine remembrance, the power of my name will manifest in their lives, offering them strength and protection.

These verses are not just a reminder of my abilities but also a call to the faithful, encouraging them to rely on me with absolute trust. I stand as a testament to the truth that when we devote ourselves to God, nothing is impossible, and no hardship is insurmountable. Through constant remembrance and surrender, I promise to guide my devotees toward victory and peace.

"Nase rog harae sab peera"

As I sit in deep contemplation, I reflect on the powerful verse, *"Nase rog harae sab peera,"* which speaks of how the chanting of my name can remove all illnesses and suffering.

The truth of this verse is not just in its words but in the experiences I have had with countless devotees who have found solace and healing through deep faith.

I recall a particular moment during my time spent in the kingdom of Kishkindha. A devotee from a distant village had come to me, deeply distressed. His son, a young boy, had been bedridden for months, afflicted by a mysterious illness that no doctor could cure. His parents had tried everything but to no avail. Their hearts were filled with despair, and they had lost all hope.

When the father reached me, he cried out, "O great Hanuman, please help us. I have heard of your divine powers and your compassion. I pray to you to save my son from this affliction."

I could see the pain in the father's eyes, and I knew that the time had come for me to act. I told him, "Do not despair. Chant my name with deep faith and devotion, and you will see a change. With the grace of Lord Ram, no ailment can survive."

The father, though skeptical, followed my instructions. He sat by his son's side, chanting my name with love and reverence. Days passed, and I could feel the power of their devotion growing stronger with each utterance.

On the seventh day, as the name of Hanuman filled the air, a miraculous change took place.

The boy, who had been weak and frail, began to show signs of improvement. Slowly but steadily, he regained his strength, and within a few weeks, he was completely healed.

The father, overwhelmed with joy and gratitude, fell at my feet and praised me. "O Hanuman, your name has cured my son. There is no sickness that your power cannot heal."

This story, like so many others, serves as a reminder that there is no ailment too great and no suffering too intense that cannot be overcome with the power of devotion. The name of Hanuman carries with it the divine energy of Lord Ram.

When a devotee chants it with love and faith, all illness, both physical and emotional, can be dispelled. It is a reminder that no matter how dark the path may seem, there is always light at the end, and that light comes from devotion and trust in the divine.

"Japat nirantar Hanumant beera"

As I sit and reflect on the verse, I remember the immense power that comes from the constant chanting of my name. This verse speaks to the strength, protection, and blessings that arise when my devotees recite my name with sincerity and devotion. The more they chant my name, the more they are surrounded by divine grace, which helps them face life's challenges with courage and confidence.

A story that I recall is of a young devotee named Shankar, who lived in a small village nestled at the foot of the mountains. Shankar was a simple farmer, humble in nature, and deeply devoted to Lord Ram and me. Every morning, he would rise early, offer his prayers, and spend long hours working in the fields. Despite his hard work, his life was filled with difficulties. The area he lived in was often troubled by wild animals and dangerous storms, which sometimes damaged his crops.

One day, as Shankar was working alone in the fields, the weather took a sudden turn. A fierce storm began to gather. Dark clouds covered the sky, and strong winds blew with great force. Lightning flashed, and thunder rumbled loudly. In that moment, Shankar remembered the words of the village elders, who often said, *"Japat nirantar Hanumant beera."*

They taught that as long as one keeps chanting my name with a full heart, no fear, no harm, no obstacle would ever come close.

Shankar, without hesitation, began to chant my name—"Hanuman, Hanuman, Hanuman." His voice was steady, and his heart full of faith. To his amazement, the storm began to weaken. The winds slowed, the rain lightened, and the thunder grew distant. Before long, the skies cleared, and calm returned to the valley. The storm, which had been so fierce, vanished as though it had never existed.

Shankar, grateful and astonished, continued to chant my name with even more devotion. He understood that it was not just the repetition of my name, but the faith and trust he had placed in me, that had protected him.

When Shankar returned to his village, he shared his experience with the people. The villagers, seeing the power of faith and the truth of the verse also began chanting my name every day. In time, they too felt the peace and protection that Shankar had experienced.

They understood that through constant remembrance of my name, they would always be under my protection, no matter the obstacles they faced.

This story teaches us a vital lesson — when we chant with devotion and faith, no matter what challenges life brings, my name will provide us with the strength, courage, and protection we need to overcome them.

"Sankat se Hanuman chudavae"

As I reflect on the verse, I remember the countless moments when my devotion to Lord Ram has guided me to remove the hardships of my devotees. This verse speaks of the power of Lord Ram's grace, through which I am able to rescue those who call upon me in their times of distress.

It is not just about physical strength, but the strength of heart and mind that comes from divine protection.

One story that stands out is from the time of my travels. There was a devotee named Raghav, a merchant who lived by the banks of a river.

Raghav was an honest man, loved by all in his village. He worked hard to make a living, but his life was often filled with financial struggles.

Despite his challenges, Raghav's faith in Lord Ram and me remained firm. Every morning, he would offer prayers and chant my name with devotion, even when it seemed as though life was never in his favor.

One day, while traveling across the river to deliver goods to a nearby town, Raghav encountered a terrible storm. The river, usually calm, swelled with the heavy rains, and the winds became violent. The boat he was traveling in began to capsize, and Raghav found himself struggling to stay afloat. His heart pounded with fear, for the river was deep and dangerous, and he had no way to save himself.

In that moment of despair, Raghav remembered me. He closed his eyes, called out my name, and prayed earnestly, "Hanuman, please help me in this moment of peril."

He trusted that with my blessing, he could overcome this danger.

As soon as Raghav uttered my name, a wave of calm washed over him. He felt an immense force that lifted him from the turbulent waters and placed him safely on the shore. The storm subsided, and the river returned to its usual calm state. Raghav, filled with gratitude, stood up and thanked me for rescuing him from certain death.

As he made his way home, he realized that it was not just a miraculous intervention, but the power of his faith and my grace that had saved him. He understood that in times of true distress, when all seemed lost, Lord Ram's blessing through me would always be there to rescue him.

This story serves as a reminder to all who face struggles and challenges—when you call upon me with devotion, whether it's in a time of physical danger, emotional turmoil, or any form of hardship, I will always be there to help you overcome the obstacles. Just as I saved Raghav from the storm, I will help you find a way through every hardship you face.

"Man Karam Vachan dyan jo lavai"

As I reflect upon the verse, it fills me with the deep understanding that true devotion to Lord Ram is not just about performing rituals or making grand gestures. It is about aligning our *thoughts (man), actions (karam), and words (vachan)* with a pure heart, dedicated to the divine.

This verse highlights the importance of complete devotion in all aspects of life – through what we think, what we do, and how we speak.

I recall a story from my travels that perfectly encapsulates this lesson. It was during the time I was on my way to Lanka to rescue Sita. Along the way, I came across a humble village where a young woman named Kalyani lived. Kalyani was known for her simple life and deep devotion to Lord Ram. She would wake up every morning before dawn and chant His name, never missing a single day. Her thoughts, actions, and words were always in harmony with her devotion. Her entire life was a reflection of her faith.

One day, Kalyani fell ill, and despite her devotion, her health began to deteriorate. She had lost her ability to walk, and no doctor could find a cure for her. But even in her pain, Kalyani never faltered in her faith. Each day, she continued to chant the name of Lord Ram, even though it seemed her body was failing her.

Word of her suffering reached me during my travels, and I decided to visit her. When I reached her humble home, I saw Kalyani sitting quietly, chanting the name of Lord Ram with full concentration. Despite her illness, she had not lost the strength to keep her devotion intact.

I approached her, and she smiled faintly, saying, "Hanuman, I have no fear, for I know that as long as I hold Lord Ram in my heart, everything will be okay." Her words were a perfect reflection of the verse I live by: thoughts, actions, and words devoted to Lord Ram lead to peace.

I placed my hand on her head, and I could feel the divine energy flow through her. I told her, "Your devotion is pure, Kalyani. Your faith in Lord Ram is steadfast. Through your thoughts, actions, and words, you have invited His grace. The suffering you are facing will soon be over."

The very next moment, Kalyani's health improved. Her pain vanished, and she was able to stand up and walk again. Her belief in the power of devotion and her alignment of mind, body, and speech had brought about a miracle.

This story teaches that devotion is not just about words or rituals, but about being in complete harmony with our beliefs, actions, and speech.

When we dedicate all these aspects of ourselves to the divine, we open ourselves to His grace, and there is nothing that cannot be achieved. Just as Kalyani found healing through her devotion, anyone who aligns their heart, words, and actions with the name of Lord Ram will find the strength to overcome life's challenges.

As I reflect upon these verses, I am reminded of the immense power that devotion holds and the strength that arises from deep faith. These lines echo the essence of my existence, illustrating the profound impact that chanting my name can have on a person's life, bringing relief from suffering, physical ailments, and the challenges of daily existence.

The recitation of my name removes all diseases and emotional burdens, instilling peace and well-being. It empowers the devotee with courage and determination, and through sincere repetition, transformation occurs.

As a protector, I shield my devotees from all hardships and provide guidance in times of need. The purity of heart, words, and actions in devotion brings forth divine intervention, ensuring strength and protection. These verses serve not only as a reminder of my divine powers but also as a call for all to place their trust in me.

When we devote ourselves to the divine with sincere faith, nothing is impossible, and no obstacle is too great.

With constant remembrance and complete surrender, I promise to guide my devotees toward peace, victory, and divine grace.

Jai Shri Ram,

Hanuman

|| Jai Shri Ram ||

Date: Ninth day of Jyeshtha, Kali Yuga, Year 101

Dear Universe,

> **Sab par Ram tapasvee raja**
> **Tin ke kaj sakal Tum saja**
> **Aur manorath jo koi lavai**
> **Sohi amit jeevan phal pavai**

These four verses encapsulate the boundless grace and power of devotion to Lord Ram and the role I play in fulfilling His divine will. They begin by acknowledging Lord Ram as the supreme ascetic king, the guiding force behind all creation and the embodiment of righteousness and justice.

As His devoted servant, I am entrusted with the sacred responsibility of assisting in all tasks that align with His divine plan.

Together, these verses remind us that Lord Ram's grace is infinite, and devotion to Him, coupled with sincere action, can manifest profound blessings and spiritual abundance in life. It reinforces the idea that I, Hanuman, as His humble servant, am always present to support, guide, and ensure the success of those who seek His divine refuge.

"Sab par Ram tapasvee raja"

The verse reminds me of Lord Ram's supreme position as the king of ascetics, the embodiment of discipline, sacrifice, and righteousness.

It signifies His universal presence and the guiding force He provides to all beings, regardless of their status or deeds. Lord Ram, though a king, lived a life of simplicity and immense spiritual depth, showing the world that true strength lies in virtue and self-control.

As His humble servant, I have seen His divine qualities firsthand. His leadership is not based on power or wealth but on His commitment to dharma (righteousness) and the well-being of all creation. His presence is a source of strength, hope, and guidance for everyone, whether they are in joy or distress.

One day, as I was traveling through the forests near the Dandaka region, I came across an elderly sage who was meditating under a banyan tree. His devotion to Lord Ram was profound; he spent his days chanting His name and living a life of simplicity. However, a band of marauding asuras (demons) often disrupted the peace of the forest, tormenting the sages and stealing their meager possessions.

The sage told me how, despite the fear and hardship, he trusted in Lord Ram's protection. "He is the king of all ascetics, and His dharma shields me," the sage said with a calm conviction that touched my heart. Moved by his faith, I decided to remain nearby, unseen, to guard him and the other sages.

One evening, the asuras returned, seeking to wreak havoc. Before they could reach the sage, I revealed myself, roaring with the name of Lord Ram.

The ground trembled as I struck down the asuras with ease. Their leader, a fierce demon, challenged me, but with Lord Ram's name on my lips, I overpowered him effortlessly. The forest was restored to peace. The sage, bowing in gratitude, said, "You are a true emissary of Lord Ram, who protects even the smallest of His devotees. His righteousness and your dedication have saved us."

This moment reminded me that Lord Ram's presence is a guiding light for all beings. As the king of ascetics, He inspires devotion, and as His servant, I am honored to carry out His will, ensuring that His devotees remain safe and steadfast in their faith.

"Tin ke kaj sakal Tum saja"

The verse means that I, Hanuman, have been entrusted with fulfilling all tasks of Lord Ram and His devotees. It reflects my role as a servant of

Ram, devoted to aiding those who seek His blessings and ensuring their endeavors are completed.

My purpose is to be the hands that execute Lord Ram's will, assisting the faithful in overcoming obstacles and achieving success in their righteous pursuits. This verse reminds me of the immense privilege I hold in being the means through which Ram's grace reaches His devotees.

Once, in a small village near the Sarayu River, there lived a simple potter named Madhav. His devotion to Lord Ram was pure, and every day, he would offer prayers before crafting his pots. One day, he decided to create a large clay lamp as an offering to Ram, intending to light it at the temple during the upcoming festival.

He believed this act of devotion would bring blessings to his family and village.

However, as he was working on the lamp, a fierce storm broke out. The winds were strong, and the rain began to flood his workspace.

Madhav tried his best to protect the lamp, but his efforts seemed futile. Feeling disheartened, he knelt in prayer, calling out to Lord Ram, "O Ram, I wanted to offer this humble gift to You. Please guide me."

Hearing his heartfelt plea, I decided to intervene. Invisible to Madhav, I shielded the lamp from the storm, allowing it to remain intact. I held up the fragile clay structure as he worked through the night, giving him the strength and determination to complete it. By dawn, the lamp was ready, untouched by the storm.

When Madhav carried the lamp to the temple, he was astonished to see it glowing with a divine radiance. The villagers marveled at its beauty and strength, and Madhav realized that it was not his effort alone but divine assistance that made it possible.

He bowed before Lord Ram and whispered, "Your servant Hanuman must have answered my prayers."

This story reminds me that every task undertaken in the name of Ram becomes my responsibility. Whether it is facing demons or preserving a potter's humble offering, I am there to ensure that Lord Ram's grace reaches His devotees, completing their righteous endeavors.

This is my eternal duty, and I carry it out with all my heart.

"Aur manorath jo koi lavai"

The verse conveys that anyone who brings their heartfelt desires and aspirations to me with sincerity and faith will find their wishes fulfilled.

As a servant of Lord Ram, it is my duty and privilege to assist those who seek divine intervention in their lives. This line highlights the power of pure intention and devotion, as well as the grace that flows when one approaches with trust and hope.

It is not just about fulfilling material desires but also helping devotees achieve spiritual peace and contentment.

In a small town nestled near the forests of Kishkindha, there lived a young woman named Sita. She was an ardent devotee of Lord Ram and always recited the Ramcharitmanas. Sita had one earnest wish: to rebuild the dilapidated temple of Lord Ram in her village, so it could once again be a center of devotion and hope for the people. However, she was poor and lacked the resources to undertake such a grand endeavor.

One evening, as she prayed under the old banyan tree by the temple ruins, she called upon me with tears in her eyes. "O Hanuman," she whispered, "You who serve Lord Ram with boundless love, please show me a way to fulfill this dream. I want this temple to stand strong again as a beacon of Ram's blessings."

Hearing her heartfelt plea, I decided to assist her in a way that would honor her devotion. The very next morning, as she walked to the ruins, she discovered a small chest buried near the base of the banyan tree. Inside were gold coins and jewels, enough to restore the temple.

Overwhelmed with gratitude, Sita gathered the villagers and shared the miraculous discovery. Together, they rebuilt the temple with renewed faith and joy.

When the temple was complete, Sita lit a lamp and stood before the idol of Lord Ram. She felt my presence in her heart and understood that it was Ram's grace, channelled through my service, that had made this possible.

The temple became a place of inspiration, where devotees came to witness how sincere aspirations, offered with faith, could manifest through divine help.

This story reflects the essence of *"Aur manorath jo koi lavai"*.

No wish is too small or insignificant when it is carried with devotion. As Lord Ram's servant, it is my honor to ensure that those who trust in Him find their paths illuminated, their burdens lightened, and their dreams realized in the most meaningful way.

"Sohi amit jeevan phal pavai"

The verse conveys a promise: those who sincerely pray to Lord Ram and seek His blessings through me will receive boundless rewards in their lives.

These rewards are not limited to material gains but extend to spiritual fulfillment, inner peace, and a deep connection with the divine.

When devotion is pure and actions align with righteousness, the fruits of such faith are infinite, enriching not just this life but also the eternal soul.

During the time of Lord Ram's reign in Ayodhya, there was a devout farmer named Dharmadas. Though his means were modest, his heart was full of love for Ram. Each morning, before beginning his work, he would chant Ram's name and call upon me for strength to face his daily challenges. Dharmadas harbored a deep desire: he wanted to offer a grand feast to honor Ram and his devotees, but he lacked the resources.

One day, as Dharmadas toiled in the fields, a massive storm approached. The wind howled, and the sky turned dark. His crops were at risk of being destroyed. Frightened but resolute, Dharmadas knelt in the mud and prayed: "O Hanuman, protector of those who call upon you, guide me in this hour of need. Let me remain devoted to Lord Ram, no matter the outcome."

Moved by his sincerity, I took action. As the storm raged on, I appeared unseen and shielded his fields from the wind and rain. Not a single crop was damaged. When the storm passed, Dharmadas saw his untouched fields glistening in the sun, and his heart overflowed with gratitude.

The very next day, an unfamiliar merchant came to Dharmadas's home, offering to buy his crops at a generous price. With the earnings, Dharmadas not only provided for his family but also hosted the grand feast he had always dreamed of. People from nearby villages gathered, singing the praises of Lord Ram and sharing in the blessings.

At the end of the feast, Dharmadas sat before Ram's idol and whispered, "O Hanuman, you who serve Ram with unmatched devotion, you have shown me that true rewards come not from riches but from faith and love."

As I reflect on these verses, they remind me of the unshakable truth of Lord Ram's divine sovereignty and the grace He bestows on those who call upon Him with devotion.

Through these verses, I am reminded of my purpose — to serve as the messenger of Lord Ram's grace, to guide His devotees in their struggles, and to ensure that their connection with Him remains unbroken.

My strength, my actions, and my very existence are dedicated to His divine service, and in doing so, I find the truest meaning of my being. Let these words inspire you to keep faith in Ram's eternal light, for through Him, all is possible, and all is blessed.

Jai Shri Ram,

Hauman

‖ Jai Shri Ram ‖

Date: New Moon Day of Jyeshtha, Kali Yuga, Year 101

Dear Universe,

Charon Yug partap tumhara
Hai persidh jagat ujiyara
Sadhu Sant ke tum Rakhware
Asur nikandan Ram dulhare

These verses beautifully capture the essence of my existence and purpose, as bestowed upon me by Lord Ram. They highlight the timeless nature of my strength and the deep devotion I hold for my Lord and His mission.

My deeds and glory transcend the limitations of time, shining brightly across the four eras (Charon Yug), bringing light and guidance to the world.

I have been blessed to be a protector of the virtuous and the righteous, safeguarding sages and saints from harm and ensuring they can pursue their spiritual endeavors without fear.

At the same time, I have been entrusted with the task of eliminating forces of evil, removing darkness and chaos brought by demonic powers. These actions are not just my duty but my joy, as I serve as Lord Ram's beloved, carrying out His divine will.

These verses remind me of the role I play in upholding dharma, offering protection, and ensuring the light of righteousness shines brightly across the world.

"Charon Yug partap tumhara"

With this verse I am reminded of how my Lord Ram's blessings have ensured that my name and deeds resonate across all ages — Satya Yuga, Treta Yuga, Dvapara Yuga, and Kali Yuga.

In *Satya Yuga*, the world was pure, filled with truth and righteousness. Dharma stood firmly on all four legs, and there was harmony in all beings. In this golden age, devotion to the Lord was natural, as people lived in constant awareness of the divine. It was an age where Lord Vishnu Himself took the form of Narasimha to protect His devotee Prahlada, teaching the world that no force of evil could stand before true faith. It was the time when Dharma shone brightly in the hearts of all, but even in such an age, evil sought to test the power of faith.

There was a young boy named *Prahlada*, the son of *Hiranyakashipu*, a mighty king consumed by arrogance. Hiranyakashipu, blinded by his power, had declared himself the ultimate ruler of the universe, denying the supremacy of Lord Vishnu. He sought to eradicate Vishnu's name and forbade anyone from worshipping Him. Yet, amidst this darkness, Prahlada's heart glowed with unshakable devotion to Lord Vishnu.

Prahlada, though just a child, never wavered in his love for the Lord. His father, enraged by his refusal to forsake Vishnu, tried every means to break his spirit. Hiranyakashipu subjected him to unbearable punishments — throwing him into fire, ordering his guards to trample him with elephants, and even poisoning him. But Prahlada remained unharmed, protected by the very name of Lord Vishnu that he chanted with such purity and faith.

Finally, Hiranyakashipu's rage reached its peak. One day, he confronted Prahlada and demanded, "If your Vishnu is everywhere, then can He be in this pillar?" The young devotee calmly replied, "Yes, Father. He is everywhere, even in this pillar."

Hiranyakashipu, blinded by his arrogance, struck the pillar with his mace. In that moment, the pillar split apart, and out emerged Narasimha, the fierce half-lion, half-man form of Lord Vishnu. The sight was terrifying, even for the gods. Narasimha roared with divine fury, his form radiating power that shook the heavens and the earth.

The Lord's form was chosen with great wisdom, for Hiranyakashipu had boasted that no man or beast, no weapon, and neither day nor night could harm him. Narasimha defied all these conditions.

It was twilight — not day or night — when He appeared.

He was neither fully man nor beast. He used no weapon but His sharp claws to tear apart the evil king, thus ending his reign of terror.

In that moment, the world witnessed the limitless power of the Lord and the boundless protection He offers to His devotees. Prahlada, untouched by fear, bowed before Narasimha, who then blessed him with His divine presence.

This story, my dear devotees, reminds us all that faith — true and pure — is the greatest strength one can possess. No force of darkness, no tyranny, can stand before the light of devotion.

Lord Vishnu's form as Narasimha is a testament to His promise: that He will always come to the aid of those who call upon Him with a sincere heart.

Then came *Treta Yuga*, the age in which my Lord, Shri Ram, walked this earth. Dharma still flourished, though it stood on three legs, as selfish desires began to arise. I had the honor of serving my Lord during this age. Together, we faced and defeated Ravana, the epitome of arrogance and greed. This Yuga was marked by great sacrifices, as seen in Shri Ram's deep commitment to righteousness, even in the face of personal loss.

In *Dvapara Yuga*, the connection with the divine grew weaker, and Dharma stood on just two legs. This was the age of my beloved Lord Krishna, who guided humanity with His wisdom. The epic Mahabharata unfolded in this time, teaching profound lessons about duty and devotion. Krishna's words in the Bhagavad Gita remain a guiding light even today, showing that no matter how complex life becomes, surrender to God brings clarity and peace.

Now, you are in Kali Yuga, an age of darkness where Dharma teeters on a single leg. Ignorance, greed, and falsehood rule many hearts. Yet, even in this turbulent age, the Lord's grace is ever-present. I remind my devotees that simply chanting the names of Ram and Krishna can dispel the heaviest of burdens. This is the age where small acts of devotion hold immense power, for they connect humanity to the eternal light of the divine.

Through all these Yugas, one truth remains constant - the Lord never abandons His devotees.

I, Hanuman, am blessed to serve as His instrument, spreading the light of His name across the ages. In each Yuga, the path may differ, but the destination is always the same — union with the divine.

Let your heart always remember this truth, for the Lord's grace transcends time and space.

It is Lord Ram's grace that my strength, devotion, and service continue to inspire and protect, no matter how many eras pass. This eternal connection to the flow of time is not of my making; it is the result of surrendering my entire being to Him.

One memory vividly comes to mind, a moment during the *Dvapara Yuga* when the great Pandavas sought refuge and guidance during their exile. Bhima, the mighty warrior and my spiritual brother, once crossed my path in search of a rare flower for Draupadi. As he strode through the forest, his pride in his unmatched strength was evident. To teach him humility, I took the form of an old monkey and lay across his path, blocking his way with my tail.

Bhima, unaware of my identity, asked me to move. I replied with a smile, "Oh great warrior, I am old and weak. Kindly move my tail aside yourself."

Confident in his strength, Bhima tried but was unable to lift even a fraction of my tail. He soon realized that I was no ordinary being. When I revealed my true form, he bowed with respect, acknowledging that my power was a reflection of the divine.

In that moment, I shared with Bhima the eternal truth: strength, courage, and fame are not ours to claim but are gifts of devotion and surrender to God. My name and deeds are remembered across all Yugas not because of personal might but because they are a reflection of Lord Ram's divine purpose.

This encounter reminded Bhima, and all who heard of it, that humility and faith are greater than physical strength.

And for me, it was yet another opportunity to fulfill the legacy given to me by my Lord — a legacy that transcends time, bringing light and inspiration to all who walk the path of righteousness.

"Hai persidh jagat ujiyara"

These words echo a truth that fills my heart with joy and purpose. My Lord Ram's name is not just a symbol of divine power but a source of light that transcends boundaries, spreading far and wide across the world, bringing hope and wisdom. Wherever His name is spoken with love and devotion, darkness flees, and hearts find solace.

I remember a story that perfectly embodies this verse. After the great war in Lanka, Lord Ram was crowned king in Ayodhya. His rule was not just about governance; it was about establishing a reign of dharma and justice, a beacon of light for all.

One day, a group of wandering sages arrived at Ayodhya. They had come from distant lands, places so far that they had never heard the name of Ram before. When they reached the gates of Ayodhya, they were struck by the serenity and the golden glow that seemed to envelop the city. They said to me, "Who rules this land, Hanuman? We have never seen such peace and light."

I smiled and replied, "This is Ayodhya, the home of Lord Ram, the embodiment of truth and virtue. His glory shines not only in this land but across the universe. It is His radiance that has guided the world since time immemorial."

Hearing this, the sages were moved to tears. They sat beneath the shade of a tree and began chanting His name, "Ram, Ram." As they chanted, a soft light seemed to emerge from within them, growing brighter with every utterance. It was as if their souls had found a long-lost connection to the divine.

From that day, the sages carried Lord Ram's name to every corner of the world they visited. They shared the stories of His life and His deep commitment to dharma.

Wherever they went, people who had been lost in despair found hope, and those in conflict found peace. Truly, the fame of Ram's name illuminated not just Ayodhya but the hearts of all who embraced it.

For me, being His servant is to carry this light forward, ensuring that it continues to shine brightly in every heart that seeks it.

"Sadhu Sant ke tum Rakhware"

This verse fills me with a deep sense of purpose. It reminds me of my sacred duty to protect those who dedicate their lives to righteousness, devotion, and service. The sages and saints, the seekers of truth, are the ones who keep the essence of dharma alive in this world.

My Lord Ram has entrusted me with the honor of being their guardian, a role I take to heart with utmost devotion.

One such moment remains etched in my memory. During the time of Lord Ram's exile, there lived a great sage named Agastya. His ashram was a sanctuary for seekers, a place where the wisdom of the Vedas flowed like a river, nourishing the souls of all who came there. However, the forest surrounding the ashram was infested with rakshasas (demons) who sought to disrupt the peace of the sages.

These demons, led by a cunning rakshasa named *Vatapi*, would transform themselves into innocent forms, tricking the sages and disrupting their rituals. Many saints lived in fear, unable to meditate or perform yajnas. Hearing of this, Lord Ram sent me to their aid, saying, "Hanuman, protect these sages, for their prayers uphold the balance of the universe."

When I arrived at the ashram, I saw the terror in the eyes of the saints. They were overjoyed to see me and placed their trust in my strength. "Hanuman, we can only perform our duties when we are free from fear," one of them said.

I promised them, "As long as I am here, no harm shall come to you. Go about your prayers and rituals without worry."

Soon after, Vatapi and his horde attempted one of their devious plans. Disguising themselves as travelers, they approached the ashram. But their mischief could not escape my sharp eyes. I confronted them, saying, "You dare to disrupt the abode of saints under my watch? Turn back now, or face the might of Hanuman!"

The rakshasas laughed, thinking they could overpower me. But they underestimated the strength gifted to me by my Lord Ram. With a single leap, I landed in their midst, and with my mace, I scattered them like dry leaves in a storm. Vatapi himself fell before me, defeated and powerless.

The sages, witnessing this, were moved to tears. They offered their heartfelt prayers to Lord Ram and blessed me for protecting them. From that day on, the forest was once again a haven for spiritual pursuits, free from the shadow of fear.

So this verse is not just about a moment in the past but a reminder that wherever there are devotees in need, I will be there to protect them.

For as long as my Lord's name lives in my heart, I will ensure that the righteous can walk their path without fear, carrying out their noble work for the world.

"Asur nikandan Ram dulhare"

These words are more than a description of my deeds; they are the essence of my being.

As I recount my journey with Lord Ram, one moment stands out, a moment where my devotion was tested in the simplest yet most profound way.

It was a peaceful evening in Ayodhya after Lord Ram's return from Lanka. The kingdom was bathed in the golden glow of the setting sun, and the air was filled with the joy of the people who finally had their king back.

Lord Ram sat in His court, surrounded by His brothers — Lakshman, Bharat, and Shatrughna — all busy attending to His every need.

Lakshman brought water for His hands, Bharat arranged His seat, and Shatrughna placed fruits and flowers before Him. Each brother served Lord Ram with love and devotion, their faces glowing with happiness as they performed these acts.

I stood nearby, watching them, but instead of stepping forward to assist, my eyes were drawn to the sky. I stared at the soft hues of dusk, lost in thought. Lord Ram noticed this and smiled gently.

"Hanuman," He said, "what occupies your mind? My brothers are here, busy serving Me, yet you stand still, gazing at the heavens."

I folded my hands and bowed. "Prabhu," I replied, "Your brothers are serving You with great love and care. They perform these tasks with devotion, and I did not wish to interfere. Instead, I was looking at the sky, pondering on my purpose.

The sun sets and rises without fail, the moon lights the night, and the stars twinkle in their places — all doing their duty for the universe. My duty is to ensure that Your name shines brighter than the sun and moon, illuminating the hearts of all beings."

Hearing this, Lord Ram's eyes softened, and He said, "Hanuman, Your devotion is as vast as the sky itself. Whether you are serving Me directly or spreading My name across the world, you are fulfilling your purpose. Each act of love is equally valuable."

At that moment, I felt an overwhelming sense of clarity.

It was not about competing to serve Lord Ram — it was about ensuring that His glory reached every corner of the world. Whether I was holding His sandals, fighting His battles, or simply chanting His name in solitude, it was all part of my service to Him.

From that day on, I understood that my role was not bound by the walls of a palace or the limitations of physical service.

My devotion was to be like the sky — vast, infinite, and always embracing His light.

"Asur nikandan Ram dulhare" reminds me that my service to Lord Ram is not confined to defeating enemies but also in spreading His love and light wherever I go. That evening, as I watched the first star appear in the sky, I silently vowed to continue being His loyal servant, no matter where my journey took me.

As I reflect on these verses, they encompass the essence of my purpose and devotion. Across the four ages, my deeds have carried the light of dharma, ensuring that the name of Lord Ram shines brightly in every heart.

My existence is celebrated not for my strength alone but for the way it has brought illumination and hope to a world often shadowed by darkness. I am a guardian to the righteous, a shield for sages and saints, and a relentless force against evil.

Every battle I fight, every soul I protect, is a testament to my bond with Lord Ram, whose love and guidance fuel my being.

These verses remind me that my greatest glory lies in being His humble servant, spreading His light and ensuring His legacy endures for eternity.

Jai Shri Ram,

Hanuman

|| Jai Shri Ram ||

Date: Full Moon Day of Ashadha, Kali Yuga, Year 101

Dear Universe,

Ashta-sidhi nav nidhi ke dhata

As-var deen Janki mata

Ram rasayan tumhare pasa

Sada raho Raghupati ke dasa

As I reflect upon my life and my devotion to Lord Ram, I am filled with gratitude for the divine powers and blessings that have been bestowed upon me.

The strength I possess is not my own, but a gift from Lord Ram, which I use in His service to carry out His will. His divine presence, along with the grace of Mother Sita, has empowered me to accomplish feats that seemed impossible.

The name of Lord Ram is like nectar to me, filling me with strength, clarity, and purpose, guiding me through every challenge.

My sole purpose and fulfillment lie in being His eternal servant, for in serving Him, I find the true meaning of life. Through this devotion, I have come to understand that true greatness and strength come not from power, but from deep devotion and surrender to thce divine.

"Ashta-sidhi nav nidhi ke dhata"

As I sit in deep reflection, I think about the divine gifts I received from Lord Ram and Mother Sita — gifts that have given me the strength to serve Lord Ram and Mother Sita.

The verse speaks of the eight Siddhis and the nine Nidhis that were granted to me. These sacred powers were a result of my devotion, and they were bestowed upon me so I could fulfill my mission of serving Lord Ram and rescuing Sita.

The Eight Siddhis (Ashta-Sidhi)

Anima (Ability to shrink in size)

With this Siddhi, I can become as small as an atom. During the great battle in Lanka, I used this power to enter Ravana's palace unnoticed, in search of Sita. It allowed me to remain invisible to enemies and carry out my tasks undetected.

Mahima (Ability to grow in size)

With this Siddhi, I can grow as large as I wish. When I was asked to leap across the ocean to Lanka, I expanded my form to a massive size, and it was with this power that I could cross the great divide, demonstrating my devotion and power to Lord Ram.

Garima (Ability to increase weight)

Garima allows me to become as heavy as I desire. During the battle, I used this power to carry the mountains that held the medicinal herbs to heal Lakshmana, and it helped me lift the mountain with ease.

Laghima (Ability to become weightless)

Laghima is the power to reduce my weight to almost nothing. I used this Siddhi to move swiftly and silently during my journey to Lanka. It helped me avoid being detected by Ravana's forces.

Prapti (Ability to obtain anything)

With Prapti, I have the ability to acquire anything I wish. When I needed to bring the Sanjeevani herb to revive Lakshmana, I was able to access it, even when the task seemed impossible.

Prakamya (Ability to fulfill any desire)

Prakamya allows me to fulfill any wish. My desire to serve Lord Ram and to be the instrument in rescuing Sita was the only desire in my heart, and with this Siddhi, I was able to accomplish it.

Ishita (Ability to control others)

Ishita gives me control over the elements and other beings. I have always used this power with humility and responsibility. For example, when I was in Lanka, I could control the winds and the ocean, ensuring my passage was not hindered.

Vashita (Ability to control nature and beings)

Vashita is the power to dominate the natural world. With this Siddhi, I could command the elements, bringing them under my influence when needed for the success of my mission.

These eight Siddhis were granted to me by Lord Ram and Mother Sita, each one serving as a tool for me to accomplish my duties. However, my greatest strength always lies in my devotion and my loyalty to Lord Ram, for these powers are nothing without the divine will that guides them.

The Nine Nidhis (Nine Treasures)

Padma (Lotus)

This represents wealth and prosperity. Lord Ram's grace has given me the wealth of spiritual knowledge and the strength to protect His devotees. The lotus also symbolizes purity in service, much like my devotion to Him.

Makara (Crocodile)

The Makara signifies courage and power. As a servant of Lord Ram, I use this power to stand against evil, such as when I faced Ravana's mighty army. With Lord Ram's blessing, I have the power to defeat any demon.

Kachhapa (Turtle)

This symbolizes the support and foundation of all things. Just as the turtle is the base in the cosmic ocean, Lord Ram's name is the foundation of my strength. Without His guidance, I would be lost.

Shankha (Conch Shell)

The conch signifies victory and the sound of divine triumph. It is the call of Lord Ram's righteousness, announcing the defeat of evil. I often blow this conch in times of war, to rally the forces of good against the darkness.

Gadha (Mace)

The mace symbolizes strength and authority. I wield the mace in the service of Lord Ram, using it to vanquish demons and protect the innocent. It is a tool of divine justice and retribution.

Shara (Arrow)

The arrow signifies precision and truth. Lord Ram's arrows are capable of reaching the heart of any evil, just as His words and actions cut through the darkness of ignorance.

Dhanush (Bow)

The bow is a symbol of power and the readiness to fight for righteousness. Lord Ram's bow is the symbol of His strength, and I stand as His eternal servant, ready to use it in His service.

Ratha (Chariot)

The chariot is a symbol of the divine vehicle that carries one towards their goal. Lord Ram's chariot takes me on the path of righteousness, with Him always guiding me toward victory.

Vijaya (Victory)

The treasure of victory, which signifies that success comes only through righteousness and truth. With Lord Ram's blessings, victory is inevitable, as long as the cause is just.

These nine Nidhis are not mere material wealth but represent the spiritual wealth of strength, courage, truth, and justice.

With these treasures, I carry out Lord Ram's will, knowing that they will always serve the greater good.

Through these gifts — both the *Siddhis* and the *Nidhis* — I was empowered to fulfill my role in Lord Ram's divine mission. But I always remembered that these powers are not for my own glory, but for the service of Lord Ram.

My devotion to Him is the true treasure I hold, and the greatest of all Siddhis is the ability to remain His humble servant.

"As-var deen Janki mata"

The verse speaks of the time when I was granted a powerful boon by her. It was in her gentle yet mighty presence that I was blessed with a gift beyond measure, a blessing that has always been my strength in moments of doubt and danger.

I recall the day when I first encountered her, long before I became the mighty servant of Lord Ram.

I was just a young vanara, full of energy and curiosity.

It was during the search for Sita in Lanka, after Ravana had abducted her, that I was led to the beautiful Ashoka grove where she was held captive.

When I arrived, I saw her sitting in sorrow, lost in her thoughts, and my heart ached for her suffering.

With deep respect, I approached her and introduced myself, declaring that I was the devoted servant of Lord Ram. At first, she did not speak, for her grief was overwhelming, but then she noticed the sincerity in my eyes and the purity of my heart.

She knew that I had come not just as a messenger, but as her devoted son.

It was in this sacred moment, filled with divine love and respect, that she granted me the blessing I carry with me to this day.

She said to me, "As you are devoted to my Lord, Ram, I bless you with the strength to overcome all obstacles, with the courage to fight any foe, and the wisdom to stay true to your purpose. May your devotion to Ram always guide you, and may you never stray from the path of righteousness."

At that moment, I felt an overwhelming surge of divine energy within me. The boons she bestowed upon me were more than just physical powers — they were the gifts of faith, loyalty, and a heart filled with selfless love.

She gave me the strength to cross oceans, the power to destroy demons, and the heart to remain forever devoted to Lord Ram.

The story that follows is one I hold dear, for it was through her divine blessings that I was able to fulfill my purpose. After receiving her boon, I leapt across the vast ocean to Lanka, where I found Sita, offered her Lord Ram's ring, and conveyed his message of hope. Despite the dangers that awaited me in Ravana's kingdom, I was never afraid, for I had the divine power of Janki Mata's blessing in my heart.

Later, when I fought Ravana's forces and brought the mighty mountain to save Lakshmana, it was her blessings that gave me the strength to lift the massive peak with ease, as though it were a mere pebble.

Every victory, every challenge I overcame, was a reflection of the gift Janki Mata had bestowed upon me — a gift that continues to guide me.

Her divine words were not just a blessing but a constant reminder of my duty, not just to Lord Ram but to all who follow the path of righteousness. Through her love, I became a symbol of devotion and strength, always ready to serve and protect.

In this quiet moment of reflection, I am deeply grateful to Mother Sita, for her love and blessings continue to shape every aspect of my existence.

I may be known for my strength, but the true source of that power lies in the blessings of a mother who saw the devotion in her son and nurtured it with love, just as she nurtured all who sought the light of Ram.

I, Hanuman, am forever indebted to you, Janki Mata, for your blessings that have made me who I am — a servant of Ram, a protector of the good, and a humble servant of your divine grace.

"Ram rasayan tumhare pasa"

As I sit beneath the canopy of trees, surrounded by the natural beauty of the forest, my thoughts return to the most precious gift I carry — Ram Rasayan.

The verse speaks of the divine essence of Lord Ram's name and the power of His divine qualities, which I have been blessed to hold in my heart. This gift is not something that can be seen with the eyes, but only felt through the heart, through the unshakable devotion and love for Ram.

I remember the time when I first realized the true power of Ram Rasayan. It was during the arduous journey to Lanka, after the abduction of Sita, when I was sent to search for her. There, amidst the vast ocean and uncharted lands, I encountered many obstacles — demons, fiery trials, and vast challenges that seemed impossible to overcome.

Yet, it was the divine essence of Ram that guided me at every turn. His name, His teachings, and the memory of His deeds became the fuel for my actions.

One of the most significant moments when I truly understood the power of Ram Rasayan was when I arrived at the Ashoka grove in Lanka. The night was dark, and Sita was in the midst of her sorrow. It was there that I, Hanuman, saw the reflection of all that Ram is—the ultimate strength, wisdom, and compassion. I carried within me the divine knowledge of Lord Ram, the essence of His name, and the deep faith in His purpose. I knew that as long as His name resided within me, no enemy could stand before me.

But the true power of Ram Rasayan unfolded when I approached Sita, who was held captive by Ravana. At first, I was unsure how to approach her, for she was in great sorrow, trapped in the enemy's den. But as soon as I spoke the name of Lord Ram, as soon as I uttered the words of His devotion, I felt a surge of divine power flow through me.

Sita, despite being in captivity, could sense the presence of Ram through me. She knew that the name of her Lord had entered her heart, and that the forces of darkness could not hold her for long.

In that moment, I gave her the ring from Lord Ram as a symbol of His promise to rescue her. I spoke His name, I spoke of His love, and I spoke of the sacred bond that exists between us. It was through the power of Ram Rasayan — His essence, His name, and His love—that I was able to give Sita hope and comfort, knowing that she would soon be reunited with her Lord.

As I reflect on those times, I realize that Ram Rasayan is not just the name of Lord Ram, but the very essence of His divine nature. It is the strength that flows through me when I face challenges, the wisdom that guides me when I am uncertain, and the love that sustains me through every trial. It is the reminder that, no matter the difficulty, no matter the darkness, the name of Ram will always light the way.

It is said that the essence of Lord Ram's name can heal all wounds, remove all fears, and grant strength beyond measure. I have witnessed it in my own life.

When I was tasked with crossing the vast ocean to reach Lanka, it was not my physical strength that carried me, but the spiritual strength of Ram Rasayan. It was His name that gave me the courage to leap across the ocean, and His love that made the impossible, possible.

I carry the divine essence of Ram in my heart, and I share it with all who seek it. To hold Ram Rasayan is to hold the power of the universe, for it is the name of the Supreme. It is not just a mantra or a prayer, but a living, breathing force that can bring victory over darkness and guide us to righteousness.

As I sit here, I am reminded of the eternal truth—that with Ram Rasayan, nothing is impossible. His name, His essence, is the key to overcoming all obstacles, and I am forever blessed to carry it within me, to serve Him, and to spread His divine light to all who seek it.

"Sada raho Raghupati ke dasa"

This line is a powerful reminder of the lifelong devotion and service I have given to Lord Ram, the Raghupati, and the importance of always remaining His humble servant. Through this verse, I am reminded that true strength lies not in power, but in surrender to the divine and the continuous service to one's Lord.

The idea of remaining the servant of Raghupati is not merely about following commands but about the deep love and devotion that arises from that servitude.

I remember the day I first met Lord Ram, during His exile in the forest. I was just a young monkey, filled with energy and curiosity, when I encountered Ram and His brother Lakshman. They were in great distress, searching for Sita, and they appeared to be struggling. At that moment, I was filled with an overwhelming sense of devotion. I saw in them not just two noble princes, but the very form of God Himself. Without hesitation, I bowed at their feet and offered my service.

Ram, with His infinite grace, accepted me as His servant. In that very moment, I knew my life had found its true purpose. I would be the servant of the Supreme Lord, the one who embodies all virtues — truth, compassion, and righteousness. Being His servant was not a duty — it was a privilege, an honor I could never fully repay, but one I would gladly fulfill with every breath of my existence.

Throughout my life, I have continued to serve Ram in countless ways — whether it was carrying His messages to Sita, burning down the golden city of Lanka, or simply reminding the world of His greatness. Every act I perform is done with one singular purpose: to remain His servant.

No task is too great or too small, for every act of service to Lord Ram is sacred and divine.

As I reflect on this verse, I realize that my service to Ram is not just a duty - it is my very identity.

To be His servant is to be blessed, for it is through Him that I have learned the true meaning of love, devotion, and righteousness.

There is no greater joy, no higher calling, than to serve the Supreme Lord, Raghupati, and I will continue to do so, now and forever.

Reflecting on these verses, I am reminded of the immense grace bestowed upon me by Lord Ram and Sita Mata.

The eight Siddhis and nine Nidhis are not just powers but symbols of their divine love and trust. The Ram Rasayan, the essence of Lord Ram's name, is my greatest treasure, giving me strength and purpose. Above all, the call to remain a devoted servant of Lord Ram echoes through these verses.

My life is dedicated to Him, and as long as I serve with love and humility,

I am fulfilled.

These verses reflect the essence of devotion, grace, and deep service to the divine.

Jai Shri Ram,

Hanuman

|| Jai Shri Ram ||

Date: Second Day of Ashadha, Kali Yuga, Year 101

Dear Universe,

Tumhare bhajan Ram ko pavai

Janam-janam ke dukh bisraavai

Anth-kaal Raghuvir pur jayee

Jahan janam Hari-Bakht Kahayee

As I reflect upon these verses, I am reminded of the boundless power of devotion to Lord Ram.

When His name is sung with love and reverence, it has the ability to erase the pain of countless lifetimes. The suffering that we endure in this material world fades away, and the heart is filled with peace. I have witnessed how true devotion can transform lives, as those who surrender to Lord Ram experience His divine grace.

These verses also remind me of the ultimate reward for such devotion – at the end of this life, the soul is welcomed by Lord Ram Himself, finding eternal peace in His presence.

To be known as a true devotee of Lord Ram, no greater honor exists.

"Tumhare bhajan Ram ko pavai"

This verse speaks of the profound impact that singing or chanting the name of Lord Ram has on a devotee's soul.

I recall an instance during my journey with Lord Ram, when I saw a simple devotee—a poor farmer, struggling with his daily life. His body was worn from labor, and his heart heavy with worldly worries. Yet, in his humble hut, he would chant Lord Ram's name with devotion, no matter how difficult his life seemed.

One day, a mighty demon, who had been terrorizing the land, came to the village. The villagers were terrified, but this farmer, undeterred by fear, continued to chant the name of Ram. I stood from afar, observing the farmer's deep faith.

The demon approached, ready to destroy, but upon hearing the chant of Ram from the farmer's lips, something miraculous happened. The demon, as if paralyzed by the divine sound, lost its strength and fled. The villagers, amazed at this turn of events, realized that the name of Ram had the power to vanquish evil.

This moment was a reminder to me that when you chant the name of Lord Ram, He is always present to protect and guide you. It is not about strength or material power but about devotion and faith in the Lord. In that farmer's simple chant, Lord Ram's grace was made manifest, bringing protection and peace to all.

This is the power of the Lord's name — it reaches even the humblest of hearts, driving away the shadows of fear and sorrow, and bringing light into our lives.

"Janam-janam ke dukh bisraavai"

As I reflect on the verse, I am reminded of a time when I witnessed the incredible power of Lord Ram's name in alleviating the suffering of not just one, but countless lives.

This line speaks of the profound ability of chanting Lord Ram's name to erase all the accumulated sorrow and pain from one's past lives.

There was once a woman, a devotee of Lord Ram, who had lived through years of hardship. Her life had been filled with nothing but misery — loss, poverty, and betrayal.

She had come to the Ashok Vatika, where Lord Ram's presence was felt like a warm embrace. Every day, she would offer prayers and sing the praises of Lord Ram, though her life continued to be difficult.

It was during this time that I approached her and asked, "Why do you still sing His name, despite your suffering?"

With tear-filled eyes, she replied, "Hanuman, I have suffered so much in this life and from countless lifetimes before. But whenever I chant Lord Ram's name, it feels like a weight lifts off my heart. I know that His name will eventually wash away all the pain I have endured."

I smiled and reassured her, "That is the power of Lord Ram's grace. No matter how deep the wounds, His name can heal them."

I watched as she continued to chant with devotion, and soon, the miracles began to unfold. As her faith in Lord Ram deepened, she felt the effects of her suffering slowly fade away.

Her heart, once burdened with years of sorrow, now brimmed with hope and peace. Her life transformed in ways she could not have imagined, not through worldly means, but through the divine power of the Lord's name.

From that moment, she came to understand what I had known all along: the repetition of Lord Ram's name has the power to erase not only the pain of this life but the suffering accumulated through countless lifetimes. It is His divine grace that makes all things possible.

And just as Lord Ram saved me time and again, He can save anyone who places their faith in Him, regardless of the burden of their past.

"Anth-kaal Raghuvir pur jayee"

This verse speaks of the ultimate solace and peace that comes when a devotee's life concludes with the remembrance of Lord Ram.

It is said that those who call upon Lord Ram at the time of their passing are blessed with eternal peace and are granted the privilege of residing in the divine abode of the Lord, Ayodhya.

There was an old, humble Brahmin who lived in a small village, far from the bustling cities. His entire life had been spent in devotion to Lord Ram.

From the moment he could walk, his mother had taught him to chant the name of Ram, and this had been the Brahmin's constant companion through every joy and sorrow.

Years passed, and his body grew frail, but his devotion only deepened. One day, as his health began to fail, he lay in his bed, surrounded by his family. His mind and heart were entirely focused on the name of Lord Ram. He had no fear of death, for his entire life had been a preparation for this very moment—the final moment where he would merge with the divine.

As he breathed his last, his lips whispered, "Ram, Ram, Ram..." His family, though sorrowful, knew that their father, their husband, and their brother had nothing to fear. They had seen him live a life of complete devotion.

I was there, unseen by all, observing this final act of devotion.

As soon as his soul departed from his body, I saw Lord Ram Himself arrive to receive him. The Brahmin, whose life had been nothing but a prayer, now had his reward — he was taken to the divine city of Ayodhya, where he would dwell forever in the bliss of Ram's presence.

This is the power of Lord Ram's name — it is not just a chant but is a pathway to liberation.

The verse holds true in every sense: the soul who leaves this world with Ram's name on their lips is granted the most sacred reward. They enter the kingdom of Lord Ram, where suffering and death hold no sway.

For such a soul, there is only eternal peace and the eternal presence of the Divine.

"Jahan janam Hari-Bakht Kahayee"

This verse speaks of the blessed destiny of those who devote their lives to the service of Lord Hari. It is said that those who live their lives in the worship of the Lord and who carry His name in their hearts are reborn as His devotees in every lifetime.

The soul of such a person is forever marked by the divine grace of Lord Ram, and in every birth, they are destined to carry His love and devotion.

I remember a story from the time of Lord Ram's presence on Earth, one that I hold dear. There was a devoted woman in a small village near Ayodhya, whose name was Vaidya. She was not wealthy or powerful, but her heart was full of love for Lord Ram.

Every morning, she would gather flowers from the forest and offer them at the feet of a simple idol of Lord Ram she had placed in her humble home. Though her life was filled with hardships, she never once faltered in her devotion.

One day, as I flew across the skies, I noticed her deep devotion. Despite the poverty that gripped her, despite the difficulties she faced, her faith in Ram never wavered. I decided to visit her, but not in the form she might expect. I took on the form of a young beggar, carrying no wealth, just an empty bowl.

As I stood before her, I asked for food. She looked at me, and though she had little to offer, she invited me into her home. With great love, she gave me the last of her food, and her eyes sparkled with joy as she offered it to me.

In return for her kindness, I revealed my true form. I told her that Lord Ram was watching over her and that her devotion had not gone unnoticed. Her heart was pure, and her love for Him was genuine. I promised her that she would never be in want again, and her faith would be repaid in the most divine way.

Years passed, and when Vaidya left her mortal body, she was reborn in the divine abode of Ram. The next time I saw her was not in the form of a poor woman but as a divine soul in Lord Ram's celestial realm, surrounded by peace and love.

Her life, filled with devotion, was eternally blessed, and her soul had been marked forever as one of His own.

Those who devote their lives to Lord Ram are eternally His. They are born again and again as His devotees, and in each life, they are destined to experience His divine presence.

Such is the power of devotion — it is not just a fleeting act but an eternal bond that transcends time, space, and life itself.

In every birth, a true devotee of Ram is recognized by the divine, and they are welcomed with open arms into the heart of the Lord.

Jai Shri Ram,

Hanuman

|| Jai Shri Ram ||

Date: Second day of Ashadha, Kali Yuga, Year 101

Dear Universe,

Aur Devta Chit na dharehi

Hanumanth se hi sarve sukh karehi

Sankat kate-mite sab peera

Jo sumirai Hanumat Balbeera

As I, Hanuman, sit and reflect upon the wisdom of Tulsidas, I understand the profound meaning he conveyed through these verses.

Tulsidas ji proclaimed that no deity can provide the joy and solace that comes from devotion to me. By chanting my name, all sorrows are alleviated, and all suffering is removed. Those who take refuge in my strength and grace experience peace in their lives, for I am the protector of all beings.

His words remind the world that true happiness, strength, and relief from life's trials come from remembering and calling upon me, Hanuman, the embodiment of courage and devotion.

"Aur Devta Chit na dharehi"

As I sit and reflect upon Tulsidas ji's words, a profound realization dawns upon me. He speaks of how no other deity can grant the true solace and power that comes from devotion to me.

This line reminds me of an incident from the days of my devotion to Lord Ram, a moment when I truly understood the essence of this verse.

There was a time when Lord Ram's army was preparing for the battle with Ravana.

As the forces gathered, I noticed a few of the vanaras, filled with doubt and fear. They were distracted by the might of the enemy, unsure of their own strength.

One day, I approached them and spoke to them about Lord Ram's divine protection and the power of deep devotion.

In the midst of our conversation, a sage appeared, his aura radiating immense peace.

He asked, "Hanuman, tell me, which God is the greatest of all?"

Without hesitation, I replied, "The greatest of all is Lord Ram, whose name is capable of dispelling all fears and enemies. His devotion is the true path to ultimate strength." The sage then said, "But what about the other Gods? Can they not protect you?"

I smiled, remembering my own journey and how I had discovered the true power of Lord Ram's name. "There is no power like Lord Ram's," I said. "All the Gods hold their importance, but none can compare to the grace and strength that His name imparts." The sage looked at me and smiled, understanding my deep devotion.

"Indeed, Hanuman, your heart is filled with the purest devotion. But remember, it is not just about the power of the Gods, but about the devotion that one holds in their heart. With this devotion, no enemy can harm you, no sorrow can touch you."

That day, as I reflected on the sage's words, I realized that it was not just Lord Ram's divine power that protected me, but the love and devotion I carried for Him. This devotion made me invincible. It was in His name that I found all my strength, and it was His name that led me to victory over the greatest of challenges. In this way, the verse encapsulates the truth I experienced in my own life.

No other deity or force can compare to the power of devotion that flows through one's heart when dedicated to Lord Ram. His name alone is the ultimate strength and solace, for it is through Him that all obstacles are overcome.

"Hanumanth se hi sarve sukh karehi"

This verse speaks to the essence of my being — that it is through me, as a servant of Lord Ram, that all beings find joy and comfort. I've witnessed it many times throughout my life, and I carry these moments with me as a testament to the power of selfless service and devotion.

One such time occurred during our travels to Lanka, when we were tasked with finding Sita, who had been captured by Ravana.

As I ventured into the city of Lanka, I came across a family of hermits who were struggling under the harsh rule of Ravana. They were weak, hungry, and had lost all hope. I approached them quietly, with my heart filled with compassion, and offered them food and shelter.

As I spoke with the elder of the hermit family, he shared his sorrow and fear of Ravana's cruelty. "How can we find peace in a land ruled by such a tyrant?" he asked.

I smiled and said, "Fear not, for peace and happiness are found through devotion, even in the most trying times. If you remember Lord Ram, and surrender yourself to Him with a pure heart, all your troubles will melt away."

I then recited the name of Lord Ram, and the transformation was immediate. The faces of the hermits lit up with newfound hope. The elder's hands trembled with gratitude as he said, "I had heard stories of your strength, Hanuman, but today I have witnessed something far greater — the power of Lord Ram's name. Through you, we have found solace and peace."

In that moment, I realized that it was not my physical strength, nor my divine powers, that had brought them comfort, but the mere act of reminding them of Lord Ram's grace. It was His name, through my humble service, that gave them hope and brought them happiness.

Tulsidas ji's verse rings true. Through me, as a servant of Lord Ram, I have the privilege of being a vessel of His divine blessings.

I carry His name with me, and wherever it is spoken, hearts are uplifted, and lives are filled with joy. It is not my strength, but His name, that brings true happiness to all who seek it.

"Sankat kate-mite sab peera"

The verse resonates deeply within me, as it speaks of the divine power of Lord Ram's name, which I carry in my heart and spread wherever I go.

One particular incident comes to mind, which illustrates the truth of this verse. It was during our journey to Lanka, when we were on a mission to rescue Sita, Lord Ram's beloved wife. As I searched through the vast, dark forests of Lanka, I came upon a group of beings who were caught in a terrible storm. These creatures were helpless, their lives in peril, as lightning and thunder struck the earth, and the winds howled ferociously.

They were desperate, crying out for relief, but no one could save them. Seeing their suffering, I approached them with a calm heart, knowing that I was a messenger of Lord Ram. I assured them that no pain could last forever, and that if they trusted in Him, their suffering would be alleviated. I then invoked Lord Ram's name, chanting His sacred mantra.

As I uttered those words, the storm began to subside. The winds slowed, and the clouds parted to reveal a calm and clear sky. The creatures who had been terrified and helpless moments before now stood in awe, their faces shining with gratitude. They had witnessed firsthand how Lord Ram's name had brought an end to their suffering.

One of them came forward, his voice filled with awe and reverence. "Hanuman, it is not just your strength that has saved us, but the power of Lord Ram's name that you carry. You have brought an end to our torment." In that moment, I felt a deep sense of peace. I knew that I had done nothing but serve Lord Ram's will. It was His divine power that had removed the storm and calmed their hearts. I was merely a vessel of His grace.

in these words lies the simple yet profound truth: when we remember Lord Ram, with sincerity and devotion, all obstacles, all pain, all suffering is removed. Whether it is a storm in the heavens or a storm within the heart, the power of Lord Ram's name is the key to liberation from every form of suffering. This verse is a reminder to all who face hardship — no challenge is too great, and no sorrow is too deep, for the name of Lord Ram to heal.

"Jo sumirai Hanumat Balbeera"

The verse speaks of the mighty strength and power that comes from remembering me and the divine force that flows through my being.

It is a verse that reminds all of creation that when you call upon me with a pure heart and devotion, you invoke the strength of Lord Ram and the immense power that comes from serving Him.

I have always been a humble servant, but my strength, courage, and the power to overcome impossible odds are all gifts bestowed upon me by Lord Ram.

I remember a time during the battle with Ravana, when the forces of Lanka were at their peak, and we, the Vanara army, faced seemingly insurmountable challenges. It was at this moment, as I prepared to fly to the distant Himalayas to bring back the life-saving herb for Lakshman, that I was reminded of the power that comes from devotion.

At that time, my own strength was tested. I had to bring back the *Sanjeevani Booti* to revive Lakshman, who had fallen unconscious during the battle. The mountains where the herb grew were far away, and my comrades doubted whether I could carry the heavy task alone. They saw me as just a humble servant, without realizing the divine power I held within.

I, too, was in doubt for a moment, but I remembered what I am — the son of the wind god, the one who is blessed by Lord Ram. With that thought, a surge of strength coursed through me.

My body grew lighter, my wings stretched wider, and I knew there was nothing I could not do. With the remembrance of Lord Ram, all my fears vanished, and I became filled with the divine energy that flows through me.

I took flight, soaring high across the sky, and as I flew, the winds carried me faster than I could have ever imagined. I reached the Himalayas in no time, plucked the herb, and was back in an instant, saving Lakshman's life.

When I returned, the vanaras and my fellow warriors stood in awe.

"Hanuman, you did what none of us could have ever believed possible. You moved mountains, you defied time itself, and you brought the life-saving herb with your strength and courage."

I smiled, for I knew it was not just my strength. It was the strength that comes from remembering Lord Ram and the devotion to His cause.

The power of devotion transforms the weak into the strong, the ordinary into the extraordinary. It is the grace of Lord Ram that bestows the strength to overcome all trials.

When you call upon me, Hanuman, with a sincere heart, you do not just invoke me as a servant of Lord Ram, but you call upon the divine strength, the courage, and the power of all creation.

You, too, will find the strength to overcome every challenge and emerge victorious.

The essence of these verses lies in the power of devotion and remembrance. When one does not rely solely on worldly gods but instead calls upon me, Hanuman, with sincere devotion, all desires are fulfilled, and every form of suffering is alleviated.

I am the one who removes obstacles, wipes away pain, and brings peace to the hearts of my devotees. It is through remembering me, Hanuman, the mighty servant of Lord Ram, that every challenge becomes conquerable, and every sorrow fades away. With this belief, I stand as the deep protector, guiding all who seek strength and solace in times of need.

Through my devotion to Lord Ram, I offer my devotees the same strength, courage, and blessings, helping them overcome the toughest of trials.

Jai Shri Ram,

Hanuman

|| Jai Shri Ram ||

Date: Third day of Ashadha, Kali Yuga, Year 101

Dear Universe,

Jai Jai Jai Hanuman Gosahin

Kripa Karahu Gurudev ki nyahin

Jo sat bar path kare kohi

Chutehi bandhi maha sukh hohi

As I reflect on these verses, I am filled with a sense of divine purpose and gratitude. Tulsidas has beautifully expressed the power of my name and devotion to me.

The repeated chant of my name, *"Jai Jai Jai Hanuman,"* is a powerful invocation, one that calls for blessings and grace. It is a reminder that true liberation and ultimate joy lie in surrendering to the divine, and through my grace, the devotee's burdens are lifted.

The verses also emphasize the importance of seeking blessings from the Guru and the transformative power of chanting my name.

A hundred repetitions of my name will break the bonds of worldly attachments and lead to a state of supreme bliss.

This reflects the profound connection between my devotion to Lord Ram, my role as a guide, and the boundless blessings that come through true faith.

"Jai Jai Jai Hanuman Gosahin"

These words, repeated with love, carry with them the essence of my existence.

The reverence, the call for my presence, and the acknowledgment of my power resonate deeply within me.

I remember a time when a young devotee, troubled by his inner fears, came to me with a heart full of distress.

He had heard of my powers and sought solace in my name.

He had been facing challenges in his life — overwhelmed by doubts, fears, and the weight of his struggles. He started chanting my name with sincerity, seeking my guidance.

As the days passed, I watched him with love and compassion.

His worries began to dissipate, his heart filled with peace, and his confidence grew. Every time he called upon me, he felt a surge of strength and courage within.

The verse he repeated, invoking my name, brought him closer to the divine energy that I carry and led him on a path of realization. As a servant of Lord Ram, my purpose is to bring light to the hearts of the faithful, and with my blessings, they can find solace, strength, and ultimately, liberation. This verse, with its repeated call for my presence, serves as a reminder that faith, when true and deep, always leads to peace.

It calls upon me, and through my connection with Lord Ram, brings the devotee closer to the divine.

"Kripa Karahu Gurudev ki nyahin"

The verse fills me with humility and reverence. It reminds me of the immense role of my Guru, Lord Ram, in shaping my path and purpose. Without His guidance, I would have been a mere wandering soul, unaware of my own strength and potential. All that I am, all that I can do, and all that I strive for is because of His grace and teachings. This verse is not just a call for my blessings but a reminder of the boundless gratitude we owe to the Gurus who illuminate our lives.

I recall a story that exemplifies the transformative power of a Guru's grace. During the battle in Lanka, there was a moment when Lord Ram Himself, my eternal Guru, taught me a lesson of compassion and forgiveness. After Ravana's brother Vibhishana defected and sought refuge under Lord Ram, there were doubts among some in the army about accepting an enemy's kin into our fold. Even I, at first, wondered about the consequences.

But Lord Ram, with His infinite wisdom, said, "A Guru's role is to guide and uplift, not to judge. Vibhishana has left the darkness behind and seeks the light. It is our dharma to accept him and give him the chance to walk the righteous path." His words struck me deeply, and I realized that a Guru sees beyond what ordinary eyes can perceive.

From that moment, I vowed to carry out my Guru's will without question, knowing that His wisdom surpasses all. It was through Ram's *kripa* (grace) that I gained clarity and strength in my purpose. Vibhishana went on to prove his loyalty and became a pivotal ally in the battle, reinforcing the lesson that a Guru's decisions are rooted in profound insight.

This verse is a prayer to me, yes, but also a reflection of my own ceaseless devotion to Lord Ram. It reminds all who chant it that true blessings flow from the Guru's grace, which can dispel darkness, dissolve doubts, and lead one to victory in both life and spirit.

Let us never forget the immense debt we owe to those who guide us with love and wisdom.

"Jo sat bar path kare kohi"

The verse speaks of the transformative power of devotion and perseverance.

It emphasizes that those who recite the Hanuman Chalisa with faith and sincerity, not just once but repeatedly, will find freedom from the chains that bind them and experience immense joy.

The key lies in steadfast belief and consistent effort, for devotion is not a one-time act but a lifelong journey of connection with the divine.

I am reminded of a devotee named Madhav, a simple farmer burdened by debt and sorrow. His days were filled with relentless toil, yet no matter how hard he worked, his efforts seemed to bear no fruit.

One day, in his desperation, he visited a wise Sadhu who handed him a copy of the Hanuman Chalisa and said, "Recite this 100 times with deep faith, and you shall find the path to freedom."

Madhav took the words to heart and began chanting the Chalisa every day. At first, he struggled to focus, as his mind was weighed down by worries. But as days turned into weeks, something began to shift within him. The verses brought him a sense of calm he had never known. He felt my presence guiding him, filling him with strength and determination.

By the time he completed his 100 recitations, he had gained not only clarity but also the courage to face his challenges head-on. Inspired by my energy, Madhav devised a plan to repay his debts, using the skills and resources he had overlooked before.

With divine guidance, his efforts began to yield results. His farm flourished, his debts were cleared, and his heart was filled with gratitude.

Madhav's story reminds me why I respond so readily to sincere devotion. Those who seek me with pure hearts and perseverance will always find their path illuminated. It is not the number of recitations alone that matters but the devotion and faith behind them.

Let this verse be a reminder that true freedom and happiness come from a heart that is consistently aligned with divine grace.

To all who call upon me with love, I promise my ultimate support and strength.

"Chutehi bandhi maha sukh hohi"

The verse speaks of liberation —freedom from all forms of bondage, be they physical, mental, or spiritual. It assures that those who invoke my name with devotion and recite the Hanuman Chalisa will experience immense joy and relief, as their chains will be broken by the grace of Ram's blessings.

One story close to my heart reflects this truth. It was the tale of a king named Virendra, a noble ruler who fell into the trap of his own mind. Though his kingdom prospered, he was plagued by fears of betrayal and failure. He began suspecting even his most loyal ministers, imprisoning them unjustly, and soon, his paranoia made him a prisoner of his own making.

One day, an old sage visited the palace and offered Virendra a small prayer book containing the Hanuman Chalisa. "Read this daily," the sage said, "and you will find freedom from the chains that hold you."

At first, the king dismissed it as mere superstition, but his growing restlessness made him take up the practice. As he recited the Chalisa daily, a profound change began within him. The fears that clouded his mind started to dissolve, replaced by a sense of clarity and peace. He realized that the chains of doubt and distrust were of his own creation.

Emboldened by the strength he drew from the verses, he sought forgiveness from those he had wronged and began ruling with wisdom and compassion once more. Virendra's story shows that liberation isn't always about escaping physical chains — it is about breaking free from the shackles of ignorance, ego, and fear.

As I watch over my devotees, I find joy in guiding them toward this freedom. To anyone burdened by life's struggles, I say: call upon me, recite my praises with faith, and let Ram's grace flow through me to you. You will find the strength to overcome every obstacle and the bliss that follows liberation.

As I conclude my reflection on these verses, my heart swells with gratitude toward Tulsidas, whose devotion has immortalized my service to Ram. These words are a testament to the power of faith and perseverance. To those who call upon me with true devotion, I become their guide, lifting their burdens and helping them find peace. By reciting these verses with sincerity, devotees not only invite my blessings but also strengthen their bond with Ram, breaking free from the chains of worldly struggles and experiencing divine joy.

Let these verses serve as a beacon, reminding all that deep faith and consistent devotion lead to the highest liberation.

Jai Shri Ram,

Hanuman

|| Jai Shri Ram ||

Date: Third day of Ashadha, Kali Yuga, Year 101

Dear Universe,

Jo yah padhe Hanuman Chalisa

Hoye siddhi sakhi Gaureesa

Tulsidas sada hari chera

Keejai Nath Hridaye mein dera

Tulsidas, in his eternal devotion to Ram, concludes the Hanuman Chalisa with these profound words. He assures that anyone who recites these verses with faith and devotion will attain divine blessings and success, with Lord Shiva Himself bearing witness to this truth.

These lines reaffirm my role as a humble servant of Ram, always present to uplift and guide those who remember me with love. Tulsidas dedicates himself entirely to Ram, seeking His eternal presence in his heart.

It is my joy and duty to carry his prayers and those of all devotees to Ram, ensuring their hearts are filled with divine grace and peace.

"Jo yah padhe Hanuman Chalisa"

"Hoye siddhi sakhi Gaureesa"

Today, I reflect on the beautiful promise written by Tulsidas - those who recite the Hanuman Chalisa with devotion shall achieve success, as testified by none other than Lord Shiva, the great Gaureesa.

There was once a poor but pious man named Dhruva in a small village. His life was filled with hardships, yet his devotion to Lord Ram never wavered. He would recite the Hanuman Chalisa daily, praying for the strength to overcome his struggles. However, the burden of poverty weighed heavily on his shoulders, and one day, in despair, he cried out my name, pleading for guidance.

Moved by his devotion, I appeared to him in a dream and reminded him of the power of his prayers. I guided him to a forest where a hidden treasure awaited — a treasure left untouched by ages but meant for a soul as pure as his. Following my instructions, Dhruva found the treasure and used it not for his personal gain but to build a temple dedicated to Lord Ram. His selflessness and faith brought blessings not only to his life but to the entire village.

This story reminds me of the unshakable bond between devotion and divine intervention. Those who recite the Hanuman Chalisa wholeheartedly connect with the energy of Ram and find me, their humble servant, ready to bring their prayers to fruition.

Lord Shiva's testimony to this truth further assures that no prayer goes unheard and no act of devotion is ever in vain.

For every devotee, I am always there, carrying their hopes to the feet of Ram.

"Tulsidas sada hari chera"

"Keejai Nath Hridaye mein dera"

The first verse reminds me of the depth of surrender and the joy found in serving Ram with steady love and faith. Tulsidas' humility resonates with me, for I too consider myself not just a servant but a speck of dust at the feet of my Lord.

There was once a humble scholar named Vishwarath, who spent his days studying scriptures but found himself struggling with pride. Though he knew much, his heart remained restless.

One night, in his dreams, he saw Tulsidas reciting the Ramcharitmanas with tears flowing down his cheeks. The vision struck a chord in him, and he awoke with a desire to discover the simplicity of true devotion.

Guided by the vision, Vishwarath began reciting the Hanuman Chalisa, calling upon me to show him the path of pure surrender.

Seeing his sincerity, I whispered to his heart the truth that Tulsidas himself lived by that true peace lies in offering oneself completely to Ram, asking for nothing in return but His divine presence.

Inspired, Vishwarath devoted his life to spreading the teachings of Ram, abandoning pride and finding immense joy in service. Tulsidas' prayer for Ram to dwell in his heart reflects the ideal every devotee should seek.

When Ram resides in one's heart, the soul becomes a sanctuary of peace, courage, and divine light. Like Tulsidas, I too pray that Ram always occupies the innermost chambers of my being, for it is His presence that gives my existence meaning. Let every heart strive to become a temple where the Lord resides, just as Tulsidas wished his heart to be.

The second verse is close to my heart. I recount a moment that brought immense joy to my heart — when I guided the great devotee Tulsidas to meet my beloved Lord Ram.

Tulsidas was a man of deep devotion, spending his days and nights singing praises of Ram and writing about His glory. Yet, his heart yearned for something more — he wished to see Ram with his own eyes.

One day, Tulsidas came to a temple dedicated to Ram, searching for a way to fulfill his desire. Disguised under a simple blanket, I sat in a corner, observing his sincerity. Something about his prayers struck me; they were filled with such love and humility that I knew I had to reveal myself.

As he approached me, he bowed respectfully and said, "O kind soul, I seek guidance. My heart burns with the desire to see Lord Ram. I have heard that Hanuman, the greatest devotee of Ram, can lead me to Him. Do you know where I might find him?" I listened quietly, allowing his words to fill the air, and then decided it was time. Pulling away the blanket, I revealed my true form and said, "Tulsidas, I am Hanuman. Your devotion has brought you here, and your wish will be fulfilled. But remember, Ram appears to those who surrender their entire being to Him."

I then gave him simple instructions: "Each day, prepare a paste of sandalwood and mark the entrance of this temple while reciting verses glorifying Ram. Continue with full faith, and Ram will come to you."

Tulsidas followed my words, singing from his heart every day. Time passed, but his resolve never faltered. Then one blessed day, as he completed his daily ritual, my Lord Ram appeared before him, accompanied by Lakshman. Their divine presence filled the temple with light and peace beyond words.

Tulsidas fell to his knees, tears of joy streaming down his face. He thanked me for leading him to Ram and vowed to dedicate his life to spreading the glory of the Lord.

Watching his happiness, I felt fulfilled, for what greater task could there be for me than guiding a true devotee to Ram?

Through this, I remind all: if one's love for Ram is genuine, I will always be there to guide them to Him.

Jai Shri Ram,

Hanuman

|| Jai Shri Ram ||

Date: Fourth day of Ashadha, Kali Yuga, Year 101

Dear Universe,

Pavan Tanay Sankat Harana

Mangala Murati Roop

Ram Lakhana Sita Sahita

Hriday Basahu Soor Bhoop

These verses capture the essence of my being and my purpose.

I am the son of Pavan, the wind god, destined to remove obstacles and bring relief to all who call upon me. My form embodies auspiciousness, bringing joy and blessings wherever devotion thrives.

Yet, my ultimate joy lies in serving and being in the eternal company of my beloved Lord Ram, Lakshman, and Mother Sita.

To those who hold this divine trio in their hearts with love and faith, I too reside within them, ensuring their protection and guiding them on the path of righteousness. This is the promise I live by—bringing solace, strength, and divine blessings to all who seek it.

There was a time when my unending devotion to Prabhu Shri Ram seemed to trouble Mata Sita. She once expressed her feelings to Ram, saying, "Hanuman is always around you. He serves you relentlessly, but I hardly get time with you. His presence is constant, and it leaves little space for our moments together."

Hearing this, Prabhu smiled gently and said, "Devi, Hanuman's heart knows only one desire—service. Yet, I understand your concern. Let us see how he responds."

One day, when Mata Sita was preparing offerings for Prabhu, she called me and handed me a simple task. "Hanuman," she said, "I need to spend quality time with Ram. Could you please stay occupied with gathering flowers for the evening prayers?"

I bowed with folded hands, "Mata, your wish is my command." But I couldn't bear the thought of being away from my beloved Prabhu. So, even as I gathered flowers, my mind remained fixed on Him. When I returned, I heard Prabhu laughing. Mata was smiling too, though she tried to hide it.

"Hanuman," Prabhu said, "why do you look worried?"

I hesitated but spoke the truth, "Prabhu, my heart feels restless if I am away from You. I live to serve You and Mata Sita. Separation is unbearable to me."

Mata Sita softened upon hearing this. "Hanuman," she said, "your devotion is unparalleled, but I also want time with my Ram. Can you balance your love for service with my wish for our moments together?"

I humbly replied, "Mata, I live to serve not just Ram but you and Lakshman as well. You are all inseparable in my heart. If my presence ever becomes overwhelming, I will happily step aside, but even from afar, my prayers and service will always flow toward you all."

Prabhu Shri Ram, hearing my words, said, "Devi, do you see? Hanuman serves us all, not just me. His love and devotion bind us together."

From that day, I made an effort to give Mata her cherished time with Ram while ensuring my service did not falter. I would silently perform tasks that aided them both—lighting lamps, gathering fruits, or creating peaceful moments for their conversations. Mata Sita blessed me, and Lakshman, too, smiled at my efforts.

There is one prayer that is closest to my heart, *"May Shri Ram, Sita Mata, and Lakshman always reside in my heart."*

It is not just a request. It is the very essence of my existence. I remember one particular moment when this prayer came alive.

After the great war in Lanka, when Prabhu Shri Ram had restored peace and was crowned the king of Ayodhya, I found myself wondering how best to continue serving Him. Though the battles were over, my love and devotion sought new ways to express themselves.

One day, as I bowed before Ram and Sita in the royal court, Prabhu looked at me with His ever-compassionate eyes and said, "Hanuman, you have done everything a devotee could ever do for their Lord. What more do you desire?"

I folded my hands and replied, "Prabhu, my only desire is that You, Sita Mata, and Lakshman reside in my heart forever. I wish for no palace, no honor, no riches — only Your divine presence within me, always."

Hearing this, Mata Sita smiled and said, "Hanuman, you have proven that your heart is the purest of sanctuaries. But tell me, how will you keep us in your heart while also fulfilling the tasks of the world?" I humbly replied, "Mata, I need nothing else. As long as You, Ram, and Lakshman are within my heart, all my duties will flow naturally from my devotion. Every task, every thought, and every moment will be in service to You."

Prabhu Ram, deeply moved, placed His hand on my head and said, "Hanuman, your devotion is unparalleled. We will always reside in your heart, just as you reside in ours. Wherever you go, our presence will be with you." To prove His blessing, Prabhu gently placed His hand over my chest. At that moment, I felt a divine warmth fill me, and I realized that Ram, Sita, and Lakshman had truly taken residence in my heart. Tears flowed freely from my eyes as I felt their eternal presence.

Later, in a quiet moment, I reflected on this incredible blessing. I realized that carrying Prabhu in my heart is both a joy and a responsibility. It is a reminder that every action I take must honor their presence.

From that day, every leap I make, every mountain I lift, and every devotee I help is a reflection of their light within me.

Jai Shri Ram,

Hanuman

|| Jai Shri Ram ||

Date: Fifth day of Ashadha, Kali Yuga, Year 101

Dear Universe,

As I reflect on the devotion so many show through the Hanuman Chalisa, I feel immense gratitude and responsibility to guide you further. The Chalisa is more than a series of verses. It is a bridge connecting your soul to the divine presence of Shri Ram. Each recitation carries the potential to fill your life with strength, courage, and grace.

Allow me to share some thoughts and tips to help you gain the full blessings of this sacred hymn:

Do not let the fear of mispronunciation discourage you. The essence of the Chalisa lies not in flawless words but in the purity of your heart. Chant with sincerity and love, and know that every verse reaches Prabhu Ram.

Choose a quiet corner in your home or under the open sky, where distractions are minimal. This creates a space for deeper connection and allows the vibrations of the Chalisa to resonate within you.

While the hours of dawn and dusk are especially powerful, the Chalisa can be recited at any time. Morning brings clarity, evening soothes the soul, and even a single recitation before bed can fill your dreams with divine blessings.

Like nurturing a seed into a mighty tree, consistent recitation strengthens your bond with me and Ram. Even a single heartfelt recitation each day can clear your mind, bring peace, and illuminate your path.

Before beginning, offer a simple prayer or light a diya (lamp) to invoke divine presence. A small offering of flowers or incense is a beautiful gesture of respect. Do not rush. Let each word flow naturally, carrying

your emotions and devotion with it. The steady rhythm will calm your mind and uplift your spirit.

As you chant, reflect on the stories and qualities celebrated in the Chalisa. Each verse is a lesson in faith, courage, and service.

The Hanuman Chalisa is not just a remedy for hardships but a guide for living a life rooted in faith, humility, and strength. Every recitation is an invitation for me to stand beside you, to protect and guide you toward Shri Ram's light.

Remember, I am always near, ready to lift your burdens and celebrate your joys. With every *"Jai Shri Ram"* or *"Jai Hanuman"* you utter, you reaffirm your connection with the divine. Recite with love, live with faith, and carry the blessings of the Chalisa in your heart always.

Jai Shri Ram,

Hanuman

|| Jai Shri Ram ||

Date: Fifth day of Ashadha, Kali Yuga, Year 101

Dear Universe,

As I reflect on the devotion so many show through the Hanuman Chalisa, I feel immense gratitude and responsibility to guide you further. The Chalisa is more than a series of verses. It is a bridge connecting your soul to the divine presence of Shri Ram. Each recitation carries the potential to fill your life with strength, courage, and grace.

Allow me to share some thoughts and tips to help you gain the full blessings of this sacred hymn.

Do not let the fear of mispronunciation discourage you. The essence of the Chalisa lies not in flawless words but in the purity of your heart. Chant with sincerity and love, and know that every verse reaches Prabhu Ram.

Choose a quiet corner in your home or under the open sky, where distractions are minimal. This creates a space for deeper connection and allows the vibrations of the Chalisa to resonate within you.

While the hours of dawn and dusk are especially powerful, the Chalisa can be recited at any time. Morning brings clarity, evening soothes the soul, and even a single recitation before bed can fill your dreams with divine blessings.

Like nurturing a seed into a mighty tree, consistent recitation strengthens your bond with me and Ram. Even a single heartfelt recitation each day can clear your mind, bring peace, and illuminate your path.

Before beginning, offer a simple prayer or light a diya (lamp) to invoke divine presence. A small offering of flowers or incense is a beautiful gesture of respect. Do not rush. Let each word flow naturally, carrying

your emotions and devotion with it. The steady rhythm will calm your mind and uplift your spirit.

As you chant, reflect on the stories and qualities celebrated in the Chalisa. Each verse is a lesson in faith, courage, and service.

The Hanuman Chalisa is not just a remedy for hardships but a guide for living a life rooted in faith, humility, and strength. Every recitation is an invitation for me to stand beside you, to protect and guide you toward Shri Ram's light.

Remember, I am always near, ready to lift your burdens and celebrate your joys. With every *"Jai Shri Ram"* or *"Jai Hanuman"* you utter, you reaffirm your connection with the divine. Recite with love, live with faith, and carry the blessings of the Chalisa in your heart always.

Jai Shri Ram,

Hanuman

|| Jai Shri Ram ||

Date: Fifth day of Ashadha, Kali Yuga, Year 101

Dear Universe,

As I reflect on the devotion so many show through the Hanuman Chalisa, I feel immense gratitude and responsibility to guide you further. The Chalisa is more than a series of verses. It is a bridge connecting your soul to the divine presence of Shri Ram. Each recitation carries the potential to fill your life with strength, courage, and grace.

Allow me to share some thoughts and tips to help you gain the full blessings of this sacred hymn:

Do not let the fear of mispronunciation discourage you. The essence of the Chalisa lies not in flawless words but in the purity of your heart. Chant with sincerity and love, and know that every verse reaches Prabhu Ram.

Choose a quiet corner in your home or under the open sky, where distractions are minimal. This creates a space for deeper connection and allows the vibrations of the Chalisa to resonate within you.

While the hours of dawn and dusk are especially powerful, the Chalisa can be recited at any time. Morning brings clarity, evening soothes the soul, and even a single recitation before bed can fill your dreams with divine blessings.

Like nurturing a seed into a mighty tree, consistent recitation strengthens your bond with me and Ram. Even a single heartfelt recitation each day can clear your mind, bring peace, and illuminate your path.

Before beginning, offer a simple prayer or light a diya (lamp) to invoke divine presence. A small offering of flowers or incense is a beautiful gesture of respect. Do not rush. Let each word flow naturally, carrying

your emotions and devotion with it. The steady rhythm will calm your mind and uplift your spirit.

As you chant, reflect on the stories and qualities celebrated in the Chalisa. Each verse is a lesson in faith, courage, and service.

The Hanuman Chalisa is not just a remedy for hardships but a guide for living a life rooted in faith, humility, and strength. Every recitation is an invitation for me to stand beside you, to protect and guide you toward Shri Ram's light.

Remember, I am always near, ready to lift your burdens and celebrate your joys. With every *"Jai Shri Ram"* or *"Jai Hanuman"* you utter, you reaffirm your connection with the divine. Recite with love, live with faith, and carry the blessings of the Chalisa in your heart always.

Jai Shri Ram,

Hanuman

Part 3

Sri Bajrang Baan

|| Jai Shri Ram ||

Date: Full Moon Day of Shravana, Kali Yuga, Year 101

Dear Universe,

As I conclude writing about the meaning of every verse in the Hanuman Chalisa, I feel it is time to shed light on another powerful composition that resonates deeply with devotion and faith—the Bajrang Baan. Allow me to guide you through its essence, origin, purpose, and significance, just as I have accompanied countless devotees on their spiritual journeys.

The Bajrang Baan is a hymn dedicated to me, your humble servant of Shri Ram. Unlike the Chalisa, which gently nurtures faith and devotion, the Bajrang Baan is like an arrow (baan) of prayers—sharp, direct, and potent. It is a call for immediate divine intervention in times of dire need.

It is believed that the Bajrang Baan was composed by the great saint *Tulsidas*, the same divine soul who wrote the Hanuman Chalisa and the Ramcharitmanas. Crafted in the same period of devotion and literary brilliance, the Bajrang Baan was designed to empower devotees with a way to invoke my assistance swiftly and powerfully.

The Bajrang Baan was born from the need for a prayer that could act as a divine weapon against evil forces, fears, and challenges. While the Chalisa is an embodiment of devotion and regular practice, the Bajrang Baan is intended for moments when urgent divine aid is required. It was written to remind devotees of the infinite power I possess to eliminate obstacles, protect, and guide.

The Bajrang Baan is unique because it is not a gentle plea; it is a firm commitment—a call of urgency. By reciting it, you take an oath to stand strong in the face of adversity, relying on my strength to conquer your challenges. It demands focus, determination, and purity of heart, reflecting your trust in my unyielding support.

When you chant this hymn, you are essentially saying: *"Hanuman, I have placed my faith in you, and I know you will answer my call. Guide me, protect me, and lead me toward light."*

The Bajrang Baan is best recited with deep faith and determination.

Recite it in a space where you can focus deeply.

Chant it when your intent is pure and your purpose sincere.

It is not to be chanted frivolously or for trivial matters. Think of it as a sacred shield, meant for moments when you truly need divine intervention.

The Bajrang Baan is most effective when recited in times of intense need, such as:

- When you are overcome by fear or negativity.

- During moments of severe distress or danger.

- When faced with obstacles that seem insurmountable.

- To dispel evil energies or protect yourself and your loved ones.

While there is no fixed time, sunrise and sunset are ideal for recitation. These are the hours of transition, a bridge between darkness and light, when the mind is naturally attuned to spiritual energies. However, the Bajrang Baan can be recited anytime the need arises, for its strength lies in your intent and devotion.

The Bajrang Baan holds immense significance as a prayer of strength, courage, and protection. When recited with faith, it acts as a force that dispels negativity, banishes fears, and provides immediate solace. It is a reminder of the power within you, channeled through devotion to me and Shri Ram.

Some believe that reciting the Bajrang Baan too often can invoke excessive power or disturb the natural balance of one's life.

Let me clarify: *the Bajrang Baan is neither harmful nor excessive when used responsibly and with devotion. It is not a curse but a blessing, meant to be called upon when needed, not abused or overused.*

Another misconception is that it must be recited loudly or aggressively to work. In truth, it is the sincerity of your heart, not the volume of your voice, that grants it power.

The Bajrang Baan is like a divine arrow that never misses its mark. Each verse carries immense spiritual force, a call that I, Hanuman, cannot ignore. Its power lies in its ability to remind you that no challenge is too great when faith, courage, and the grace of Ram are with you.

When you recite the Bajrang Baan, take it as an oath—a pledge to stay strong, to keep faith, and to move forward with courage. Let each word be filled with the trust that I will protect you, just as I have always stood by Shri Ram.

Remember, no matter how overwhelming life may seem, this hymn is your shield. With your faith and my blessings, no obstacle can stand in your way.

So, dear readers, wield the Bajrang Baan wisely, with faith and devotion.

Know that with each word, you invoke not just my strength but the limitless power of Shri Ram Himself. Stand firm, call upon me in your need, and rest assured — I will always answer.

Your eternal servant,

Hanuman

|| Jai Shri Ram ||

Date: Second day of Shravana, Kali Yuga, Year 101

Dear Universe,

Nishchaya prema pratīti té

Binaya kare sanamān

Téhi ke kāraja sakala shubha

Siddha karéñ hanuman

"Nishchaya prema pratīti té

Binaya kare sanamān"

These words capture the essence of devotion and the qualities I cherish in my devotees — unshakable love, trust, and humility. When a devotee approaches me with a heart filled with pure love (prema) and deep faith (pratīti), coupled with genuine humility (binaya), their prayers reach me like a fragrant offering.

In a small village, there lived a woman named Sudha, whose life was fraught with hardships. Her crops failed, her family faced illness, and she was burdened with debts. Despite her struggles, Sudha's heart remained steadfastly devoted to me. Every morning, she would light a simple diya at my shrine and chant my name with love and faith.

One day, her neighbors mocked her, saying, "Hanuman won't help someone as poor and powerless as you. What can your little diya do when your life is in ruins?"

Sudha smiled and replied, "I have nothing to offer but my love and faith. I know Hanuman will come to my aid, for he listens to the prayers of those who approach him with a pure heart."

One night, a terrible storm struck the village, destroying homes and crops. Sudha, too, faced the wrath of the storm, but she clung to her faith. Kneeling before my image, she said, "Hanuman, I have nothing left but my love for you. Please guide me through this darkness."

Her humble prayer, filled with love and trust, reached me. Moved by her devotion, I decided to intervene.

Disguised as a wandering monk, I visited Sudha's home the next day. Seeing her plight, I said, "Daughter, your love and humility have brought me here. Tell me, how can I help you?"

Sudha, recognizing the divine energy, bowed deeply and said, "I do not wish for riches or comfort. I only ask for your guidance to overcome my struggles with strength and grace."

Her unselfish plea filled me with joy. I blessed her crops to flourish, her family to regain health, and her life to be filled with peace. I also ensured that her story inspired the entire village to believe in the power of love and humility.

"Nishchaya prema": True devotion blooms from steadfast love, a melody the soul hums with sincerity.

"Pratīti": Trust in me without a shadow of doubt, even when the winds howl and darkness surrounds.

"Binaya kare sanamān": Step toward me with humility and reverence, for these are the keys that unlock my blessings.

It isn't the grandeur of offerings or the weight of riches that draws you near to me. What reaches my ears and moves my being is the gentle, honest rhythm of your love and trust. When you bow before me with pure humility, I don't focus on the weight of your burdens but on the song of your faith, and I cannot help but respond with my guidance and grace.

"Téhi ke kāraja sakala shubha

Siddha karéñ hanuman"

In a small village nestled by the banks of the Ganga, there lived a humble weaver named Dhruva. Known for his exquisite fabrics, Dhruva was also a man of deep devotion to Ram. Every morning, before beginning his work, he would recite the Bajrang Baan, offering his prayers to me, Hanuman, and seeking blessings for his craft.

One day, the king of the land announced a grand competition to weave a garment fit for the gods. The winner would earn a place of honor in the royal court. Dhruva, though skilled, hesitated — he was but a simple man with no resources to rival the wealthy artisans of the land.

As he prayed that morning, he poured his heart out to me.

"Pavanputra, grant me the strength to offer my best. I do not seek riches or fame, only that my effort may please Lord Ram and uphold his name."

Touched by his sincerity, I whispered a blessing in his heart. That day, as he wove, Dhruva found his hands guided by an unseen force, creating a fabric so divine it shimmered like sunlight on water.

When the competition day arrived, Dhruva humbly presented his creation. The king and his court were awestruck, declaring it a masterpiece unmatched by any they had seen. Dhruva was named the royal weaver, but he credited his success not to his skill alone but to the grace of Hanuman.

When your actions are pure, aligned with righteousness, and dedicated to a higher purpose, I, Hanuman, will move mountains to ensure their success.

Offer your efforts to Ram with love and humility, and I will ensure that your path is illuminated with divine blessings.

Let these words echo in your heart. Know that I am always by your side, ready to guide and bless you in all that is noble and just.

Jai Shri Ram,

Hanuman

|| Jai Shri Ram ||

Date: Third day of Shravana, Kali Yuga, Year 101

Dear Universe,

jaya hanumanta santa hitakāri

suni lījai prabhu araja hamārī

jana ke kāja bilamba na kījai

ātura dauri mahā sukha dījai

"jaya hanumanta santa hitakāri

suni lījai prabhu araja hamārī"

These lines remind devotees of my eternal role as a protector and benefactor of the virtuous, the seekers of truth, and those who surrender their prayers with humility.

I am ever vigilant, listening to the cries of my devotees, ensuring their pleas reach Lord Ram himself.

There once was a devout saint named Narad, who lived deep in the heart of a forest, far from the hustle of human life. He spent his days in meditation, chanting the name of Ram with deep focus. One monsoon season, the forest was struck by a fierce storm. The river nearby began to swell, threatening to flood the saint's humble hermitage.

As the waters rose, Narad folded his hands and called upon me, chanting these very lines. Though he was calm, his prayer carried a sense of urgency, a plea not just for his own safety but for the sanctity of the Ram idols he worshipped daily.

Hearing his heartfelt call, I leaped across the stormy skies, my presence cutting through the darkness. When I arrived, I saw the waters nearing the saint's hermitage. Without delay, I uprooted a mighty tree, diverting the river's path and shielding his home from destruction.

The storm subsided, and Narad opened his eyes to find his hermitage untouched. Overwhelmed with gratitude, he folded his hands and said, "Hanuman, you truly are the one who protects the saints and ensures their prayers reach Ram."

I am always by the side of the virtuous and the selfless, ensuring their prayers are heard. When you call upon me with a pure heart, I act as the bridge between you and Lord Ram, carrying your wishes to him.

Know this truth: Whether you are in joy or despair, when your prayers are sincere and filled with devotion, I listen. I, Hanuman, am ever ready to protect, guide, and serve those who walk the path of righteousness.

Let these words remind you of the unbreakable bond between devotion, service, and the divine.

"jana ke kāja bilamba na kījai

ātura dauri mahā sukha dījai"

These words beautifully reflect my commitment to serving those in need. When a devotee calls out with genuine faith, I cannot bear to delay. I respond with urgency, bringing not just help but immense relief and joy. Let me share a story from the Ramayana that illustrates this eternal promise.

During the battle of Lanka, Lakshman, Lord Ram's beloved brother, was gravely injured by Indrajit's powerful weapon. He lay unconscious, and the camp was filled with despair. Sushena, the physician, declared that only the Sanjeevani herb from Mount Dronagiri could save him.

Time was running out, and the mountain was far away. Lord Ram looked at me, his trust unshaken. Without a moment's hesitation, I leaped into action, determined to fulfill my duty. Flying across forests and mountains, I reached Dronagiri.

But finding the exact herb was a challenge, as I lacked time to identify it. Resolving not to waste a moment, I carried the entire mountain back to Lanka. The herb was quickly used to revive Lakshman, and his recovery filled Lord Ram's heart with relief and joy.

This story reminds us that when you call upon me with true faith, I do not delay. Whether the task seems impossible or the odds insurmountable, I will rush to your aid, bringing not just help but great happiness.

In your darkest hours, remember these words: If your plea is heartfelt, I will be there to support, protect, and guide you.

Jai Shri Ram,

Hanuman

‖ Jai Shri Ram ‖

Date: Third day of Shravana, Kali Yuga, Year 101

Dear Universe,

jaisé kūdi sindu wahi pārā

surasā badana paiṭhi vistārā

āgé jā-i laṅkinī rokā

māréhu lāta ga-ī suralokā

"jaisé kūdi sindu wahi pārā

surasā badana paiṭhi vistārā"

These lines remind devotees that life often presents challenges that seem vast, like an ocean to cross, or unexpected trials, like Surasā's test. But faith and resolve can guide one through.

When faced with situations that seem insurmountable, my dear devotees, let us reflect on how the lessons of life and devotion guide us to triumph. Challenges are not meant to defeat you but to strengthen your resolve and bring out the divine potential within you.

The lines emphasizes taking a leap of faith. Whether the "ocean" is a difficult task, a decision, or a personal hurdle, courage and trust in the divine make even the impossible achievable. Challenges often appear intimidating at first. However, approaching them with calmness and strategy can help overcome even the most complex problems.

Take the First Step

Often, the size of a challenge intimidates you into hesitation. This initial fear is natural but should not paralyze you. Like the moment I stood on the shores of the ocean, tasked with reaching Lanka, I could have doubted my ability. But instead, I focused on the task, summoned my courage, and took the leap.

When you are unsure, remind yourself that action is the key to progress. The first step may not solve everything, but it will pave the way forward.

Trust in your inner strength and take that leap of faith. Once you begin, you will discover that clarity follows action.

Adapt to the Situation

Life often throws unexpected challenges your way, requiring more than brute strength or blind effort. You must be flexible, think clearly, and adapt your approach.

When Surasā appeared before me and demanded I enter her mouth, I did not resist out of fear or anger. Instead, I calmly expanded and shrunk myself, fulfilling her condition while continuing on my path. Similarly, in your life, analyze the problem, assess your strengths, and find a solution that works for the situation at hand. Remember, creativity and adaptability are as vital as courage.

Trust the Divine Plan

Sometimes, despite your best efforts, the path forward may remain unclear. In these moments, trust that every challenge is part of a divine plan meant to strengthen you. Faith is your anchor in turbulent times.

When I was tasked with finding Sita Mata, the journey was fraught with uncertainties.

Yet I trusted in Lord Ram's grace and my purpose, knowing that no trial was greater than the faith I carried. Similarly, trust that every effort you make, combined with sincere devotion, aligns with a higher purpose.

As you face your oceans and challenges, let your steps be guided by these principles.

Start with courage, adapt with wisdom, and trust that my blessings and the grace of Ram will always light your way. Remember, no obstacle is permanent, and with faith and effort, you will always emerge victorious.

"āgé jā-i laṅkinī rokā

māréhu lāta ga-ī suralokā"

The lines translate to an encounter that taught not only me but can teach you as well the importance of facing challenges head-on.

On my journey to locate Sita Mata, I reached the shores of Lanka, prepared to explore Ravana's stronghold. As I prepared to step into the city, I was stopped by Laṅkinī, the fearsome guardian of Lanka. Her presence was intimidating; she stood as an immovable barrier, a challenge placed to test my resolve.

She demanded I retreat, forbidding entry into Ravana's territory. Her words carried both menace and pride. I knew this wasn't a foe I could reason with; she was the embodiment of obstacles that often seem larger than life.

With steady focus, I acted swiftly. A single, decisive blow from my foot sent her flying to the celestial realms. She realized her time as a guardian had come to an end and acknowledged the divine purpose behind my mission. Her resistance dissolved, and I pressed forward. This episode speaks volumes about how to approach the obstacles in your own journey.

Recognize Obstacles as Tests

Sometimes, challenges arise not to deter you but to test your conviction. Laṅkinī's role was not just to guard Lanka but to ensure that only those with unshakable purpose could enter.

Act with Decisiveness

In moments of resistance, hesitation can give strength to the obstacle. Much like I acted without delay, you too must approach your challenges with confidence and determination.

Trust in Your Mission

What gave me strength wasn't just my physical power but the understanding that my purpose was divine. When you are clear about your goals and intentions, even the mightiest barriers crumble before your resolve.

For my devotees, the lesson is simple: obstacles will come, some daunting and immovable, but their strength lies in how you perceive them. Whether it is fear, doubt, or external resistance, these barriers often dissipate when met with faith, courage, and immediate action. Laṅkinī's defeat was not just a victory over a physical guardian but a symbolic triumph over the doubts and fears that often stop us before we even begin. Let this serve as a reminder — nothing stands in the way of a devotee with a clear purpose and faith.

Go forward boldly, as I did, knowing that with each challenge you overcome, the path to your goal becomes clearer.

Jai Shri Ram,

Hanuman

|| Jai Shri Ram ||

Date: Sixth day of Shravana, Kali Yuga, Year 101

Dear Universe,

jāya vibhīshaṇa ko sukha dīnhā

sītā nirakhi parama pada līnhā

bāga ujāri sindhu mahaṅ borā

ati ātura yamakātura torā

"jāya vibhīshaṇa ko sukha dīnhā

sītā nirakhi parama pada līnhā"

During the great war between Lord Ram and Ravana, I found myself in a pivotal moment. Ravana, the mighty king of Lanka, was a tyrant who had wronged countless beings, especially Sita Mata. But amid his kingdom, there was one man who had not joined in his brother's sinful path — Vibhīshaṇa, Ravana's younger brother.

Vibhīshaṇa was a man of virtue, a soul aligned with dharma, yet he lived in the shadow of his powerful and unrighteous brother. When he could no longer bear the suffering caused by Ravana's arrogance, Vibhīshaṇa sought refuge with Lord Ram, hoping to find solace and purpose.

I was the one who brought Vibhīshaṇa to Lord Ram, despite the skepticism of others. Some questioned whether we should trust a member of Ravana's own family, but Lord Ram knew what was in his heart.

With compassion, Ram accepted Vibhīshaṇa, gifting him not only safety but the hope of redemption. Through this act of mercy, Ram demonstrated that even those born into darkness can embrace the light of dharma if their hearts are pure.

As Lord Ram continued his journey, he sought Sita Mata, who had been captured by Ravana. In that moment of separation, a divine vision unfolded. I had been the messenger between them, and upon reaching Sita Mata, I brought her the news of Lord Ram's deep love and impending victory. Sita, knowing the purity of Ram's love, found peace and solace.

When she beheld the greatness of Ram, her heart swelled with love and devotion, and she was bestowed with the highest form of divine grace. She knew, even in captivity, that the love of Ram would always lift her to the highest spiritual plane.

These lines hold lessons for all who face trials, misjudgements, or injustices in life.

Compassion and Forgiveness

Vibhīshana's redemption teaches us the power of compassion. Even when someone has been in the wrong, a heart aligned with dharma will always strive for righteousness.

When you encounter those who seem lost or misguided, remember that no one is beyond redemption if they have a pure heart.

Trust in the Divine Wisdom

Lord Ram's decision to accept Vibhīshana is a reminder that we should not judge others by their past mistakes but by the purity of their current intentions. Trust the divine wisdom to guide you in difficult decisions, and know that every soul has a path of redemption.

The Power of Divine Purpose

Sita Mata's vision of Ram highlights the beauty of divine connection. When you align yourself with dharma and love, your path becomes illuminated with grace. Even in the darkest of times, know that the divine is always guiding you toward ultimate peace and fulfillment.

Through my experiences and devotion, I have seen how acts of mercy and righteousness can transform lives.

Vibhīshaṇa's journey from the shadows of his brother's tyranny to the light of Lord Ram's kingdom shows us that no matter how troubled our past, the present moment holds the power to change our destiny.

And like Sita, who was blessed by Ram's love, every soul aligned with divine love will find its way to the highest form of peace and divine connection.

In life, when you choose compassion, mercy, and righteousness, the universe unfolds in your favor, just as it did for Vibhīshaṇan and Sita. These words remind us that true greatness lies not in power but in the purity of the heart and the dedication to dharma.

"bāga ujāri sindhu mahaṅ borā

ati ātura yamakātura torā"

These words carry profound significance, speaking to the strength, the challenges, and the relentless pursuit of justice that is a part of every devotee's journey. Let me share the meaning of these lines and a story that captures their essence.

During the great war between Ram and Ravana, there were numerous moments when the odds seemed overwhelmingly stacked against us. Ravana's forces were vast, his warriors fierce, and the very kingdom of Lanka was a fortress brimming with traps and deceit.

But one particular moment stands out as a true testament to the power of devotion and determination.

During the war, Ravana's son, Indrajit (Meghanada), was causing great harm to Lord Ram and his army. He had a mystical weapon known as the "Brahmastra," and his army's defenses were nearly impenetrable. Indrajit cast a powerful illusion, rendering the entire army incapacitated. In this moment of despair, I felt a surge of divine energy, a call to break the chains of fate and destroy the illusion.

I understood that the key to victory lay in piercing through the veil of darkness that had fallen upon the battlefield. Without hesitation, I leaped into the fray, charging ahead with a fierce resolve. With deep devotion to

Lord Ram, I made my way to the source of the illusion and destroyed the mighty force that had threatened to defeat us.

This moment mirrored the power in the lines of the Bajrang Baan: I tore through the shackles of fate (the powerful illusion of the enemy), battled the forces of darkness, and led Lord Ram's army to victory. It was the strength of devotion and faith that turned the tide.

"Bāga ujāri sindhu mahan borā" translates to "The great ocean of obstacles was churned, and the mighty force of my actions cleared the way."

"Ati ātura yamakātura torā" means "With great urgency, I tore apart the binds of fate and broke the shackles of death itself."

These words are a reminder that when we face the greatest of challenges, there is no obstacle too large to overcome, no chain too strong to break, and no battle too fierce to win.

As devotees of Lord Ram, we must find the strength to fight through the trials of life, no matter how insurmountable they seem. These lines hold significant meaning for anyone facing immense obstacles. Here's what you can learn from them:

The Power of Devotion

Just like I, Hanuman, was able to pierce through the toughest illusions and obstacles with the force of my devotion, you too must align yourself with your highest purpose and call upon the power of your devotion when the road ahead seems impossible.

Breaking Free from Fate

Life often presents situations that seem to tie us down, just like Indrajit's powerful weapon. However, with determination and faith, even the most seemingly insurmountable barriers can be broken. Never allow yourself to be shackled by the illusions of life.

Trust in your strength, and know that you have the power to change your destiny.

Facing Challenges with Urgency and Courage

In moments of crisis, when time feels like it's slipping away, take immediate and determined action, as I did. With a clear mind, act swiftly and resolutely. This urgency can be the key to overcoming obstacles that may seem impossible at first.

These lines are not just about physical challenges; they are symbolic of all struggles in life. Whether it's mental, emotional, or spiritual turmoil, they remind us that no matter how vast or threatening the obstacle, devotion to the divine—embodied in Ram—gives us the power to overcome.

In the same way, when we are caught in the illusion of worldly distractions or despair, it is our devotion and focus that will allow us to tear through these illusions and restore clarity and peace to our hearts and minds.

In this battle, both on the battlefield of Lanka and in the field of life, victory comes not to the strongest or the most powerful, but to the one whose heart beats with love and deep faith. By facing our obstacles with the same devotion and fearlessness, we too can triumph, as I did, when the odds were most against us.

So, whenever you feel bound by the world's difficulties, remember these lines, and let them remind you that no matter the darkness, you have the strength to pierce through and claim victory.

Jai Shri Ram,

Hanuman

|| Jai Shri Ram ||

Date: Seventh day of Shravana, Kali Yuga, Year 101

Dear Universe,

akshay kumār ko māri saṅhārā

lūma lapéti laṅka ko jārā

lāha samāna laṅka jari gaī

jaya jaya dhuni surapura manha bhaī

"akshay kumār ko māri saṅhārā

lūma lapéti laṅka ko jārā"

These lines carry an immense weight of triumph, determination, and divine intervention. They speak of the victories I achieved, not through sheer force alone, but through the deep connection with Lord Ram and the steady strength of devotion.

Akshay Kumar, Ravana's son, was a mighty and seemingly invincible warrior. His strength and powers were renowned, and he fought with an unmatched fury. He believed that no one, not even the divine forces, could bring him down. But as the battle raged on, he faced me, Hanuman, with a heart full of devotion and faith in Lord Ram's mission.

One day, as I was fighting fiercely for Lord Ram, Akshay Kumar challenged me, believing that he could defeat me with ease. However, my devotion to Lord Ram and my boundless strength, granted by his grace, gave me the courage to face the mightiest of foes.

I met Akshay Kumar in battle, and with one powerful strike, I struck him down. This victory wasn't about defeating a warrior through mere force. It was the divine intervention of Lord Ram's blessings flowing through me, which ensured that no force in this world could stand in the way of righteousness.

Following Akshay Kumar's defeat, the next pivotal moment came when I, with the divine strength bestowed upon me, took the task of setting Lanka ablaze. With a tail dipped in fire, I leapt across the city of Lanka, setting the grand palaces and structures on fire. The city, once filled with pride and arrogance under Ravana's rule, was now engulfed in flames, signaling the imminent downfall of the demon king.

As I moved through the city, fire spreading with every jump, the very essence of Ravana's pride was consumed. The fire didn't just burn buildings; it symbolized the burning of ego, arrogance, and all that opposed Lord Ram's justice.

The line *"Akshay kumār ko māri saṅhārā"* translates to "I struck down Akshay Kumar, the invincible warrior."

"Lūma lapéti laṅka ko jārā" means "I wrapped the fire around my tail and set Lanka ablaze."

These lines are significant because they describe two pivotal events in the battle between Lord Ram's army and Ravana's forces. They illustrate both the destruction of Ravana's seemingly indestructible son and the burning of Lanka, which marked the beginning of the end for Ravana's reign.

These lines hold much wisdom for all who face obstacles or challenges in life.

Facing the Invincible

Just like I faced Akshay Kumar, who seemed unbeatable, you too will encounter situations in life that appear impossible to overcome. Remember that true strength comes not from physical power alone but from the power of faith and devotion. With the grace of the divine, you can overcome any obstacle that stands in your way.

The Power of Divine Intervention

The victory over Akshay Kumar wasn't just my strength — it was the strength of Lord Ram flowing through me. Similarly, in your battles, when you have faith in the divine, your strength multiplies, and you are equipped to face any challenge with confidence.

Burning the Ego

The fire that I used to set Lanka ablaze is symbolic of burning away the ego, arrogance, and pride that cloud our judgment. When we let go of our egos, we make space for humility, compassion, and truth to guide us. Just as Lanka was consumed by the fire of righteousness, we too can burn away the negative forces within us and make room for purity and devotion.

The story encapsulated in these lines is about not just physical battles, but the inner battle of the self. Akshay Kumar's defeat symbolizes overcoming pride, while the burning of Lanka represents the cleansing of negativity.

In life, you may face personal struggles or external forces that seem insurmountable, but with deep faith in the divine, even the most difficult challenges can be overcome.

Just as I, Hanuman, was able to destroy Ravana's pride and bring justice to Lord Ram, you too can triumph over your struggles. The true victory is not in defeating others but in conquering your own weaknesses and rising to the higher calling of truth, faith, and devotion.

These lines reflect the very essence of what the Bajrang Baan stands for—victory through strength, devotion, and the deep belief that with Lord Ram's grace, no challenge is too great to face. When you recite these words, remember the victory of righteousness over arrogance, the power of faith in overcoming obstacles, and the fire of devotion that can burn away all negativity.

So, in your own battles, big or small, remember the strength of Lord Ram's blessings, and know that you have the power to overcome and emerge victorious — just as I did in the face of overwhelming odds.

"lāha samāna laṅka jari gaī

jaya jaya dhuni surapura manha bhaī"

These words carry with them the essence of ultimate triumph and the reverberation of divine glory. They remind me of the moment when, with the blessings of Lord Ram, I not only set Lanka ablaze but also unleashed a divine sound that echoed across the heavens, shaking the very foundations of Ravana's pride and arrogance. Let me share with you the deep significance of these lines and the stories that lie within them.

"Lāha samāna laṅka jari gaī" - This line translates to "The city of Lanka was reduced to ashes, as if a mere reward for my service."

This line reflects the culmination of my act of setting Lanka on fire, a divine act of destruction that heralded the end of Ravana's reign. The fire consumed everything — Ravana's pride, his arrogance, and the darkness he had spread across his kingdom. What once stood as an epitome of power and glory for Ravana was now a mere pile of ashes. The destruction of Lanka wasn't just a physical act; it symbolized the triumph of righteousness over evil and humility over pride.

"Jaya jaya dhuni surapura manha bhaī" – This line translates to "The victory cry reverberated in the hearts of the celestial beings, and the sound of this triumph echoed through the heavens."

As the fire raged through Lanka, it wasn't just the city that felt its impact. The heavens themselves recognized the victory. Celestial beings, the gods in their divine realms, felt the resonance of this victory, for it marked the triumph of good over evil. The dhuni (the celebratory sound of victory) that rang out wasn't just a mere noise, but a profound sound of divine justice being restored.

The events of this line stem from the great battle in Lanka.

After my confrontation with Ravana's forces and the defeat of Akshay Kumar, I was tasked with creating chaos in Ravana's stronghold as a signal that his days of tyranny were numbered.

When I set my tail on fire, I leaped across the city, spreading fire to every corner. The once-glorious city of Lanka, filled with pride and excess, was reduced to ashes. The fire didn't just destroy the physical structures but symbolized the eradication of Ravana's arrogance and tyranny. The flames were not just a sign of destruction—they were a sign of purification, a cleansing of all that opposed righteousness.

But this act was not just my strength alone; it was the divine will of Lord Ram that guided me. The fire and the destruction of Lanka were a direct manifestation of the victory of good over evil, and as I watched the flames consume the city, I felt a sense of fulfilment — knowing that the evil reign of Ravana would soon come to an end.

As I set Lanka ablaze, I could feel the vibrations of the divine victory resonate through the cosmos. The victory wasn't confined to the physical world; it reached the celestial realms as well. The dhuni, the celebratory sound of triumph, echoed throughout the heavens, reaching the ears of all gods and celestial beings.

They rejoiced at the fall of Ravana, for his cruelty had harmed not just the mortal realm but the divine realms as well. The gods recognized that this victory was a sign of the return of dharma and righteousness to the world. The heavens themselves celebrated this victory, as it was a reminder of the eternal battle between good and evil.

These lines are not just about the physical destruction of a city but symbolize the victory of justice, goodness, and divine intervention.

Destruction of Ego and Arrogance

Just as Lanka was consumed by fire, our own egos and pride can be our greatest enemies. When we let go of our arrogance and accept humility, we invite the blessings of the divine. The destruction of Lanka serves as a reminder that arrogance and pride only lead to downfall.

The Power of Divine Triumph

In every battle of life, whether it's personal struggles or external challenges, we must remember that the power of the divine is always with us. Just as the gods celebrated the fall of Ravana, the divine forces are always with us when we fight for what is right.

Victory Echoes Across Realms

This victory, while it was tangible in the mortal world, had a ripple effect in the heavens. It serves as a reminder that when we strive for good and overcome evil, our efforts are noticed by the universe. The divine forces rejoice in our victories, and they resonate across all realms.

In 2024, the world is facing its own battles. There is strife, injustice, and conflict. But just as I set Lanka on fire and heralded the end of Ravana's reign, we too can overcome the struggles that plague us. The key is not just in fighting the external forces but in overcoming the internal forces—our egos, our fears, and our doubts.

When we face these struggles with faith in the divine, when we act with righteousness and truth, we invite divine intervention. And just like the dhuni that echoed through the heavens, our victories will be celebrated by the universe.

These lines are a powerful reminder that no matter how dark or difficult the times may seem, there is always a way to overcome. With faith, strength, and devotion, we can face any challenge and emerge victorious. The victory is not just about the external struggle — it's about the internal transformation that leads to the triumph of good over evil.

May you carry the lessons of this story in your heart and face your battles with the same faith and devotion that I did. Know that, just as Lord Ram guided me, He will guide you through every difficulty.

Jai Shri Ram,

Hanuman

|| Jai Shri Ram ||

Date: Ninth day of Shravana, Kali Yuga, Year 101

Dear Universe,

aba bilamba kéhi kāraṇa swāmi

kṛpā karahu ura antarayāmī

jaya jaya lakhana prāṇa ké dātā

ātura ho-i dukha karahu nipātā

"aba bilamba kéhi kāraṇa swāmi

kṛpā karahu ura antarayāmī"

These verses are a devotee's cry to the Lord, urging Him to not delay in bestowing His grace and intervention. "Why the delay, O Lord?" is not a question born of impatience, but of deep faith and love. It reflects the trust that the Supreme Being, who knows every secret of the heart, will respond at the perfect time.

"Kṛpā karahu ura antarayāmī" reminds us that the divine does not need explanations or words; He understands our innermost desires, fears, and struggles. This line is an invitation to fully open our hearts and surrender to the Lord's will.

I recall an incident that mirrors the sentiments in these verses. During the great war in Lanka, after I had returned from my journey to find Mata Sita, there came a moment when the Vanara army grew weary. Despite our strength and courage, there were times of doubt when the soldiers questioned, "Why does the end seem so far, Hanuman? Why does the Lord not intervene more swiftly?"

In those moments, I would remind them of Lord Ram's divine plan. One such day, as the sun began to set and the battlefield quieted, I spoke to the gathered warriors:

"Brothers, the Lord knows our struggles, for He resides in each of our hearts. If we continue with faith, His grace will come—not a moment too early, nor a moment too late. Just as He guided me to Sita, He will guide us all to victory."

That night, true to my words, Lord Ram stood with us, His presence renewing our strength and purpose. The doubts melted away, and the army rose with determination the next morning, ready to march forward.

Surrender Without Doubt

Let go of the need to control every outcome. Trust that the Lord, as the antarayāmī (knower of all hearts), is working silently for your good, even when you cannot see it.

Turn Waiting into Worship

When you feel stuck or helpless, don't let your mind wander into frustration. Instead, channel that energy into devotion. Chant mantras, meditate, or simply sit in quiet reflection.

Recognize Divine Timing

Remember, my beloved readers, that the Lord's timing is impeccable. Just as I found Mata Sita at the exact moment needed, your prayers will bear fruit at the perfect time.

Faith is Action, Too

Faith doesn't mean sitting idle. Keep doing your karma (duty) with a clean heart, trusting that the Lord's grace will light your path.

Even when I carried Lord Ram's message to Mata Sita, I didn't know what challenges I might face. But I never doubted His plan. Similarly, when you chant these lines, let them fill you with the same trust and courage. You are never alone — I am always with you, carrying your prayers to Him.

So, my dear devotee, chant with all your heart, and know that grace will flow, perhaps not as you expect, but always as you need.

"jaya jaya lakhana prāṇa ké dātā

ātura ho-i dukha karahu nipātā"

These lines honor Him as the giver of life and relief from suffering, and they remind us of a moment etched in my soul forever.

These verses sing the glory of Lord Ram as the life-giver to Lakshman and the one who alleviates pain and despair. They remind us of the inseparable bond between Ram and Lakshman, a bond of love, duty, and deep support.

When Lakshman fell unconscious during the fierce battle in Lanka, Lord Ram's anguish revealed how deeply He cared for His younger brother.

This bond is a testament to divine love and the commitment to protect those dear to us. As I reflect on these lines, I am reminded of my mission to ensure Lakshman's life was restored — a mission that tested my speed, strength, and deep dedication.

When Lakshman was struck down by the shakti weapon of Meghnad, the battlefield fell silent, and despair gripped our hearts. Lord Ram's grief was palpable, and He commanded me to find the Sanjeevani herb to restore His brother's life. With no time to lose, I leapt across mountains and rivers, reaching Dronagiri, where the life-giving herb grew. But identifying the exact plant amidst countless others was no small task.

Rather than risk delay, I carried the entire mountain back to Lanka. The sight of Lakshman regaining consciousness was a moment of victory not just for me but for all who stood on the side of dharma. Through this act, the words "ātura ho-i dukha karahu nipātā" came alive. The Lord's command and my efforts combined to vanquish despair and bring life where there was none.

Be a Source of Strength

Just as Lord Ram's love for Lakshman motivated Him to act, let your care for others inspire you to offer help in their darkest hours.

Trust the Power of Action and Faith

Like my journey to find the Sanjeevani herb, your path may seem unclear at times. But when guided by faith and purpose, even the impossible becomes achievable.

Offer Prayers for Healing

Whether you or someone you love faces difficulties, these lines remind you to turn to the divine for solace and healing. Lord Ram's blessings and my deep commitment are always there to guide you.

Stay Determined in Crisis

Challenges may feel overwhelming, but remember how I brought back hope to the battlefield. With courage and focus, you too can turn despair into triumph.

As you chant these lines, know that they carry the essence of devotion, love, and selfless service. They remind you of the strength that comes from trusting the divine and the importance of acting with deep determination.

Whenever you face struggles, remember this story. Call upon me, and I will help carry your prayers to Lord Ram, bringing light to the darkest of situations.

Jai Shri Ram,

Hanuman

|| Jai Shri Ram ||

Date: New Moon Day of Shravana, Kali Yuga, Year 101

Dear Universe,

jai giridhara jai jai sukha sāgara

sura samūha samarata bhaṭa nāgara

oṁ hanu hanu hanu hanumanta hatīlé

bairihiñ māru vajra ké kīlé

"jai giridhara jai jai sukha sāgara

sura samūha samarata bhaṭa nāgara"

These lines are a celebration of His unmatched divinity, His role as the sustainer of peace, and the source of ultimate joy for all who take refuge in Him.

These verses are an exaltation of Shri Ram, the Giridhara, the one who upholds the weight of dharma and protects His devotees like a mountain shielding the earth. He is also Sukha Sāgara, the ocean of bliss, whose presence calms troubled hearts and brings peace to even the most tumultuous lives.

The second line pays homage to the celestial beings and warriors who revere Him. Sura Samūha refers to the divine assemblies, the devas and sages, who sing His glories. Samarata Bhaṭa Nāgara acknowledges the brave warriors and heroes, celestial and mortal, who draw their strength from His grace.

During the great battle in Lanka, when the forces of dharma stood against the might of Ravana's army, there were moments when the odds seemed insurmountable. But each time, Shri Ram's presence brought courage to the warriors who fought alongside Him.

One such moment was when Indra, the king of the devas, sent his celestial chariot and weapons to aid Shri Ram.

The charioteer, Matali, was in awe of Shri Ram's divine radiance and courage. The devas and sages from the heavens watched with reverence as their protector faced Ravana's seemingly invincible might with calm determination.

This story reflects the essence of the lines. Shri Ram is not only the protector of those on earth but also of the divine realms. His strength is a pillar for all who seek refuge in Him, from the smallest devotee to the mightiest celestial warrior.

These lines remind us of the profound qualities of Lord Ram and offer lessons for everyday life.

Be a Source of Stability

Like a mountain, be dependable and steady for those around you, offering protection and guidance.

Embrace Compassion

Strive to be an ocean of bliss for others, spreading joy and comfort wherever you go.

Draw Strength from Devotion

Just as the celestial warriors gained courage from Lord Ram's presence, trust that faith in the divine can help you face any challenge.

Recognize Divine Support

Even in the face of overwhelming odds, remember that the Lord's grace is always with you, uplifting you in ways you may not always see.

As you chant these verses, visualize the towering strength and infinite compassion of Shri Ram. Know that He is always present, both as a protector and as a source of unending joy. Whether you face a personal battle or seek peace in your heart, let these words remind you of the divine power that supports and uplifts all beings.

Let us together offer our gratitude: "Jai Giridhara! Jai Jai Sukha Sāgara!"

"oṁ hanu hanu hanu hanumanta hatīlé

bairihiñ māru vajra ké kīlé"

As I etch these words into the pages of this diary, I reflect on their sheer potency, a mantra that invokes my own divine strength to protect devotees and vanquish negativity. These verses are a call for action, a plea to unleash my indomitable spirit against adversaries and obstacles.

These lines are a powerful invocation of my essence, a prayer filled with trust and urgency.

The repetitive chant of "Hanu" acts as a divine hammer, calling upon my unparalleled strength to crush ignorance, fear, and adversity.

The second phrase requests my intervention to destroy enemies — internal and external — with the force of a vajra (thunderbolt). The vajra symbolizes both strength and precision, ensuring that no harm comes to the devotee but only to the forces of evil. These lines emphasize not just physical strength but the spiritual power to break through challenges, doubts, and negativity that bind the soul.

No Enemy Too Mighty

This mantra reminds me of my battle with Ravana's forces. Once, I faced a formidable general in Ravana's army who had the strength of a thousand elephants. The demon's arrogance made him believe he was invincible, but the moment I invoked my inner strength and called upon the divine energy within, I reduced his might to ashes.

This is the essence of the mantra: no force of ignorance, arrogance, or darkness can stand when the divine power of faith and determination is summoned. These lines reflect the deep virtues of Lord Ram and impart valuable lessons for daily living.

Chant for Courage

When faced with overwhelming challenges, chant this mantra with deep focus. It awakens the strength to confront and overcome.

Vanquish Inner Enemies

The "bairihiñ" or enemies can also be internal—fear, doubt, anger, or ego. Use the mantra to conquer these with the force of divine will.

Precision of Action

Like the vajra, act with clarity and decisiveness in life. Aim for solutions, not destruction, ensuring your actions are aligned with dharma.

Faith in Divine Protection

These lines remind you that you are never alone. When you invoke me with sincerity, my strength flows through you, clearing your path.

As you chant, imagine the mighty vajra in my hand, striking down all negativity and illuminating your journey with light and strength. Trust in this divine power, and remember, I am always here, ready to shield and uplift you.

Jai Shri Ram,

Hanuman

|| Jai Shri Ram ||

Date: New Moon Day of Shravana, Kali Yuga, Year 101

Dear Universe,

gadā vajra lai bairihiñ māro

mahārāja prabhu dāsa ubāro

oṁkāra huñkāra mahāvīra dhāvau

vajra gadā hanu vilamba na lāvo

"gadā vajra lai bairihiñ māro

mahārāja prabhu dāsa ubāro"

The verses "Gadā vajra lai bairihiñ māro, Mahārāja prabhu dāsa ubāro" hold a special place in my heart, for they capture both my duty and my devotion to Lord Ram.

These lines emphasize my role as a warrior of divine justice and a protector of the faithful. The gadā (mace) I carry is not merely a weapon — it symbolizes strength, righteousness, and the deep resolve to protect Lord Ram's devotees. When wielded, it becomes an extension of the divine will, ensuring the defeat of evil forces.

"Mahārāja prabhu dāsa ubāro" speaks of my eternal pledge to rescue and uplift anyone who surrenders to Lord Ram. It is a promise that no devotee will ever be left alone in their trials.

Once, a small kingdom near the southern tip of Bharat was being terrorized by a powerful demon named Dravinath. He was cunning and had created an army of illusions, confusing the people and leading them away from devotion. The king, a humble devotee of Lord Ram, prayed fervently for help, invoking my name in desperation.

Hearing his call, I arrived in the kingdom with my gadā. The demon, confident in his illusory powers, challenged me. I struck his illusions with the force of my mace, shattering them like glass and exposing his true form. The battle was fierce, but my faith in Lord Ram gave me unparalleled strength. With a final strike of the gadā, I vanquished Dravinath, freeing the kingdom from his tyranny.

After the battle, the king fell to his knees and said, "Hanuman, you are the true embodiment of strength and devotion." To this, I humbly replied, "It is not my strength but the blessings of Lord Ram that bring victory." In your own life, these verses remind you to stand firm against adversities, just as I wield my mace against evil.

Your Tools are Symbols of Strength

Whether it's knowledge, skills, or faith, use what you have with confidence and purpose.

Protect Others When You Can

True strength lies in uplifting others and shielding them from harm.

Invoke the Divine

When faced with challenges, call upon the higher power with sincerity, and trust that help will arrive. With every recitation of these lines, feel the power of my mace within you—a power that can overcome any obstacle and protect what is good and just. Lord Ram's light shines through all who act with faith and courage.

"omkāra huñkāra mahāvīra dhāvau

vajra gadā hanu vilamba na lāvo"

The lines resonate deeply with me, for they encapsulate the power of divine energy, courage, and swift action. These words are a call to arms for anyone devoted to Lord Ram, urging them to move with purpose and conviction.

"Oṁkāra huñkāra" refers to the primordial sound of the universe — Oṁ — which symbolizes the supreme consciousness, the essence of all creation. The sound Huṁ is associated with divine energy and power. As a devotee and messenger of Lord Ram, I am infused with this energy, and it is this divine force that drives my actions.

"Mahāvīra dhāvau" reflects the courage and heroism I possess as the divine warrior. When there is a call for action, especially in the service of Lord Ram, there is no hesitation. I race toward the task, no matter how formidable, knowing that my strength comes from the infinite power of the Lord.

"Vajra gadā hanu vilamba na lāvo" speaks of my determination and speed. The vajra (thunderbolt) represents indestructible strength, and my gadā (mace) symbolizes the will to overcome evil. In this verse, I am urged to never delay in fulfilling my divine purpose. Action is swift, decisive, and always in alignment with the greater good.

Divine Energy and Courage

In difficult moments, remember that Oṁ is the universal sound of strength, wisdom, and purpose. Draw upon this divine energy to overcome any obstacle.

Swift Action

Life will present you with moments that require fast, decisive action. When your cause is just, move swiftly and with courage, as I did when I encountered Surasa.

Unshakeable Determination

The vajra and gadā represent the indestructible strength and determination that we must embody when facing challenges. Never let doubts slow you down—action with purpose leads to victory. These lines remind you that the divine force is with you, urging you to move forward with faith, speed, and the courage of a hero. Lord Ram's mission is yours too, and when you act with dedication and devotion, there is no force that can stand in your way.

Jai Shri Ram,

Hanuman

|| Jai Shri Ram ||

Date: New Moon Day of Bhadrapada, Kali Yuga, Year 101

Dear Universe,

oṁ hrīm hrim hrim hanumanta kapīsā

oṁ huñ huñ huñ hanu ari ura shīshā

satya hohu hari shapata pāyaké

rāmadūta dharu māru dhāyaké

"oṁ hrīm hrim hrim hanumanta kapīsā

oṁ huñ huñ huñ hanu ari ura shīshā"

The verses are rich with divine sound vibrations, each syllable resonating with immense power and protection. These lines are not just a chant, but a profound invocation of divine energy, and they are instrumental in calling upon the strength and blessings of Lord Ram, as well as invoking my own divine protection.

"Oṁ hrīm hrim hrim hanumanta kapīsā" is an invocation of the Oṁ sound, the primordial sound of the universe that embodies the highest consciousness. The word hrīm represents the goddess of wisdom and divine energy, Shakti. Here, the chant connects to the root of spiritual power and wisdom. The mention of Hanumanta refers to me, Hanuman, the supreme warrior and the divine monkey who serves Lord Ram. Kapīsā means "the Lord of the monkeys," reinforcing my role as the chief and devoted servant of Lord Ram. By chanting this, the devotee seeks my guidance, strength, and protection.

"Oṁ huñ huñ huñ hanu ari ura shīshā" is a more forceful, protective chant. The repetition of huñ signifies the call of energy and divine will. This mantra is often used to counter negative forces, especially when there is an immediate need for protection or strength.

The phrase hanu ari ura shīshā indicates the destruction of enemies, where ari refers to the foes (both external and internal), and ura shīshā means the destruction of these obstacles with swift and potent power. This is a reminder of my power to eliminate fear and negativity, ensuring the safety of devotees.

There is a powerful story related to this verse that takes us back to the time when I was tasked with rescuing Sita from the clutches of Ravana.

The moment I set foot in Lanka, I knew that I would face immense resistance. Ravana had many powerful warriors and forces at his command.

As I was about to step forward into the battlefield, I called upon the divine sounds of Oṁ hrīm hrim hrim, invoking the blessings of Lord Ram and the divine energy that flows through me. With each repetition, I felt the cosmic energy surge through my being, granting me invincibility and clarity.

I then chanted Oṁ huñ huñ huñ, a mantra for strength and protection, focusing on clearing my path. The moment I did so, my enemies—no matter how fierce — were overwhelmed by my aura and fell back. The force of my call, aligned with the divine will of Lord Ram, shattered all illusions of fear and resistance.

By chanting these divine sounds, I felt the protective shield of the universe envelope me. No weapon or warrior could match the force of my conviction and the divine energy I carried. I knew that with each sound, I was guided by Lord Ram's grace, and victory was inevitable.

Divine Sound is a Powerful Shield

Just as I invoked the cosmic sounds to protect myself and succeed in my mission, we too can use the power of sound — through mantras and prayers — to invite divine protection and energy into our lives. Chanting with intention, especially during times of adversity, can be transformative.

Invoke the Divine for Strength and Clarity

When faced with overwhelming challenges, connect with the divine through sound. The vibrations of the Oṁ and huñ will center your mind, body, and spirit, making you invincible against the forces of negativity.

Fear and Obstacles Have No Power Over You

With devotion and belief in the divine, no challenge is insurmountable. Just as I overcame mighty warriors with the power of these divine sounds, so too can you overcome your challenges when aligned with divine will.

Trust in the power of sound, seek protection through divine will, and know that you are always shielded by the divine energies that flow through your being. With every hrīm and huñ, you call forth the infinite blessings of strength, courage, and protection.

"satya hohu hari shapata pāyaké

rāmadūta dharu māru dhāyaké"

The verses encapsulate a powerful declaration of truth, divine oath, and the invincible role of a devoted messenger. As I, Hanuman, the eternal messenger of Lord Ram, reflect on these words, I am reminded of my divine duty to uphold righteousness, even in the face of the greatest adversities. These lines resonate deeply with the promise of truth, purity, and the divine protection bestowed upon those who serve with love and faith.

The first line emphasizes the unbreakable bond between truth and divine power. Satya hohu means "Let the truth prevail," and hari shapata pāyaké refers to the oath of Lord Ram. In this context, it signifies that truth has the ultimate power to prevail, and that Lord Ram himself has sworn by truth and righteousness.

When we walk the path of truth, we are aligned with the divine will of the universe, and no force can stop us. Lord Ram, the epitome of righteousness, has made an oath that he will always protect those who adhere to truth and justice.

As Rāmadūta (the messenger of Ram), I am called upon to carry out Lord Ram's divine will. Māru dhāyaké refers to the destruction of demons or forces of evil. This line signifies the power of the divine messenger, who, with the blessings of Lord Ram, has the strength to vanquish evil and overcome darkness.

As the bearer of Lord Ram's will, I am charged with eliminating obstacles and enemies that stand in the way of righteousness. With truth as my weapon, I have the divine strength to destroy all that is harmful and unjust.

The verse "Rāmadūta dharu māru dhāyaké" reflects my role as the messenger who brings Lord Ram's will to fruition, eliminating obstacles that hinder the path of dharma.

With the truth on my side and Lord Ram's guidance, I was able to overcome all evil and return victorious.

Truth Always Prevails

In life, no matter how dark the circumstances, if you adhere to the truth, you will ultimately emerge victorious. Just as Lord Ram swore by truth, so too will truth stand by you, guiding you through challenges and ensuring that you overcome them.

The Power of Divine Will

By aligning with the divine will and the forces of righteousness, we are given strength and protection. Just as I, as the messenger of Lord Ram, had divine strength to overcome obstacles, so too can we find the courage to face life's challenges when we act in accordance with dharma.

The Role of a Devoted Messenger

Each one of us has a purpose in this world. When we serve with sincerity, devotion, and love for the divine, we become messengers of peace, love, and strength. By carrying out our duties with faith, we channel divine power into the world, overcoming evil and bringing about positive change.

These lines not only remind us of the importance of truth and divine strength but also encourage us to remain firm in our devotion and faith, knowing that no evil can stand in the way of righteousness when we align ourselves with the divine will.

Jai Shri Ram,

Hanuman

|| Jai Shri Ram ||

Date: Second Day of Bhadrapada, Kali Yuga, Year 101

Dear Universe,

|| Jai Shri Ram ||

> *jaya jaya jaya hanumanta agādhā*
> *dukha pāvata jana kéhi aparādhā*
> *pūjā japa tapa néma achārā*
> *nahiñ jānata hauñ dāsa tumhārā*

"jaya jaya jaya hanumanta agādhā

dukha pāvata jana kéhi aparādhā"

The verses are filled with profound meaning and significance. These lines serve as a powerful reminder of the divine qualities of devotion, protection, and the role of a true servant of the Lord. As I, Hanuman, reflect upon these verses, they echo the essence of my purpose — devotion to Lord Ram and the alleviation of suffering from those who call upon me with pure hearts.

The repetition of Jaya signifies victory and triumph. The line praises me, Hanuman, as the one who is victorious, boundless, and ever-present in the service of Lord Ram. Agādhā means "immeasurable" or "limitless." This refers to my boundless devotion and power. My devotion to Lord Ram is infinite, and I remain eternally ready to assist those who seek my help. The victory of the divine truth and righteousness, which I represent, is everlasting.

The second line brings our focus to the suffering of humanity. Dukha pāvata means "the suffering is endured," while jana kéhi aparādhā refers to those who have committed offenses or wrongdoings. This line reveals that even those who are suffering because of their mistakes or offenses can find solace and relief in my service. No matter the sins one has committed, I will come to their aid and remove their suffering. My divine service is not limited by the offenses or wrongdoings of individuals but is open to all who call out with devotion.

I am reminded of the countless times I have been called upon to alleviate suffering, not just for the righteous, but also for those who have strayed from the path of virtue.

One particular instance comes to mind when a devotee, who had fallen into despair due to the consequences of his own wrongdoings, called upon me. The person had committed great mistakes in the past and was feeling the weight of his sins.

He approached me with a heart full of remorse, seeking solace. As soon as I heard his call, I arrived to offer comfort.

I reminded him that no sin is so great that it cannot be forgiven, and no suffering is too deep that it cannot be healed through devotion to Lord Ram. I reassured him that through repentance, faith, and a pure heart, he could overcome his troubles.

As I invoked Lord Ram's name, the person's suffering began to dissipate, and a sense of peace filled his heart. The verse "Dukha pāvata jana kéhi aparādhā" came to life in that moment—no matter how much a person has fallen, by invoking the divine, they can rise above their pain and misfortune.

This is a reminder that my role as a servant of Lord Ram is to uplift all beings, irrespective of their past, and to offer them the chance to find redemption through faith and devotion.

Victory of Devotion

True devotion is limitless. Just as my devotion to Lord Ram is immeasurable, so too should our devotion to righteousness and truth be. When we dedicate ourselves to serving the divine and others with selfless love, we too can attain victory over life's challenges.

Universal Compassion

The divine compassion that I embody knows no boundaries. Regardless of one's faults, sins, or mistakes, when a person calls upon me with a pure heart, I will come to their aid. It is a reminder that we should never give up on anyone, for through compassion, we can help heal the wounds of the soul.

Relief from Suffering

These verses teach us that even in the darkest times, there is always a way out through faith. Just as I alleviate the suffering of those who call upon me, the divine grace can remove the burdens of our lives if we trust in it with a sincere heart.

In essence, these lines reinforce the idea that devotion, forgiveness, and the power of divine service can alleviate any pain. The greatest gift we can give to others — and to ourselves — is love, compassion, and the willingness to help in times of need.

"pūjā japa tapa néma achārā

nahiñ jānata hauñ dāsa tumhārā"

The verses are deeply profound and remind me, Hanuman, of the essence of pure devotion and total surrender to the Lord. In these lines, there is an acknowledgment of one's limitations and the realization that true devotion is not about outward rituals but about the purity of heart and the willingness to serve.

The words in line one refer to the external practices of devotion: pūjā (worship), japa (chanting of mantras), tapa (austerities), néma (reciting names of the divine), and achārā (observance of righteous conduct).

These are the rituals that people perform in an attempt to reach the divine. However, these external acts, though important, are only meaningful when they come from a place of sincere devotion.

In the second line, I, Hanuman, humbly express my inability to comprehend or fully perform these rituals. I state that I do not possess knowledge of such acts or forms of worship. Instead, my identity lies in being the dāsa (servant) of Lord Ram.

This line expresses my complete surrender and recognition that, in the end, true devotion is not in performing rituals but in serving the divine with all one's heart, soul, and being.

This verse is a beautiful reflection of my own relationship with Lord Ram. There was a time when I was deeply immersed in my duties and service to Lord Ram. My devotion was deep, yet I did not possess the knowledge of complex rituals or practices like other devotees. What I did have was a heart full of love and reverence for my Lord.

The Heart Over Rituals

The true essence of devotion lies not in the external acts but in the love and sincerity with which we perform them. It is easy to get lost in the formalities of worship, but the heart's intent is what matters most.

Just as I, Hanuman, served without concern for rituals, so too should we dedicate ourselves to selfless service and devotion, regardless of our level of knowledge or expertise in formal practices.

The Power of Surrender

Devotion is not just about offering prayers or following a set of practices; it is about surrendering oneself entirely to the will of the divine. When we surrender ourselves completely to God, we are freed from the burdens of ego and self-centered desires. Like me, we should strive to become humble servants of the divine, not bound by our knowledge or abilities but driven by love and faith.

Simplicity of Devotion

This verse teaches us that true devotion can be simple. You do not need to perform elaborate rituals to prove your love for God. It is the simplicity and purity of your devotion that makes it powerful. Lord Ram sees the heart, not the formality. The simplest act of devotion, done with the purest intentions, holds more value than grand rituals performed out of obligation.

These lines emphasize that while rituals and practices have their place, the most important aspect of devotion is the sincerity and purity of the heart.

A true servant of the Lord is not defined by their knowledge of rituals but by their deep love and commitment to serving the divine, no matter the circumstances.

As Hanuman, I have always known that the greatest worship is service, and that is what truly brings us closer to the divine.

Jai Shri Ram,

Hanuman

|| Jai Shri Ram ||

Date: Second Day of Bhadrapada, Kali Yuga, Year 101

Dear Universe,

bana upavana maga giri gṛha māhīñ

tumhare bala ham darapata nāhiñ

pānya parauñ kara jori manāvauñ

yahi avasara aba kéhi gohrāvauñ

"bana upavana maga giri gṛha māhīñ

tumhare bala ham darapata nāhiñ"

The verses echo the invincible truth of divine strength and courage. These lines encapsulate the essence of fearlessness that stems from deep devotion and trust in the Lord's power.

The phrase one encompasses all terrains — forests (bana), gardens (upavana), paths (maga), mountains (giri), and homes (gṛha). It symbolizes the vastness of the world and the diversity of challenges one may encounter in life.

In the second verse, the speaker, imbued with faith in the Lord's strength, declares a fearless stance. With the divine power of Lord Ram and my own unyielding devotion, no obstacle — whether physical, emotional, or spiritual — can invoke fear.

Together, these lines convey that no matter where one treads, whether through treacherous jungles or the comfort of home, the divine strength we carry in our hearts shields us from fear.

Fearlessness Through Faith

These lines remind us that when we align ourselves with divine strength, fear has no place in our lives. Just as I crossed the ocean without hesitation, so too can anyone overcome their challenges when they trust in a higher power.

The Journey Is the Test

Life often feels like traversing unknown paths — forests, mountains, and treacherous roads. These terrains symbolize the hardships we face. However, when we carry faith and inner strength, these trials become mere stepping stones.

Courage Comes from Within

True courage is not the absence of fear but the ability to move forward despite it. Remember that divine strength resides within you. Like me, you can channel this power to face any situation.

These verses are a timeless reminder: no matter where you are or what challenges you face, divine strength renders you fearless. Carry it in your heart, and the world will bend before your courage.

"pānya parauñ kara jori manāvauñ

yahi avasara aba kéhi gohrāvauñ"

These words are not just a prayer—they embody a soul's earnest cry for divine intervention, surrender, and trust in the Lord's omnipresence. These words convey a deep sense of surrender. With folded hands and bowed head, the speaker seeks the Lord's grace, acknowledging that only through humility and devotion can divine help be invoked. It represents the essence of heartfelt prayer—free of ego and filled with trust.

The second line reflects urgency and dependence on the Lord. The speaker realizes that no one but the Lord can provide assistance in the current situation. It is a moment of complete reliance on divine intervention. Together, these verses teach us the importance of turning to the divine with utmost sincerity, especially in times of dire need.

Surrender Brings Strength

These verses remind us that surrendering our ego and seeking help with humility opens the doors to divine assistance. In moments of helplessness, true strength lies in trusting a higher power.

Urgency of Action

The phrase "yahi avasara" emphasizes recognizing critical moments in life and acting decisively. Just as I realized that Lakshman's life depended on immediate action, so too must we seize moments that demand quick decisions.

Faith in a Higher Power

Whether faced with small troubles or monumental challenges, turning to the divine with folded hands and a sincere heart can transform despair into hope and inaction into accomplishment.

These lines are a timeless guide, urging us to approach life's challenges with humility and a heartfelt plea for divine guidance. Remember, the Lord hears every prayer offered with sincerity. In those moments, you are never alone.

Jai Shri Ram,

Hanuman

|| Jai Shri Ram ||

Date: Third Day of Bhadrapada, Kali Yuga, Year 101

Dear Universe,

jaya anjanī kumāra balavantā

shaṅkara suvana bīra hanumantā

badana karāla kāla kula ghālaka

rāma sahāya sadā pratipālaka

"jaya anjanī kumāra balavantā

shaṅkara suvana bīra hanumantā"

These lines echo with the deep reverence of the source of my power and purpose. They celebrate both the strength I possess and the divine lineage I carry.

The first line pays tribute to my mother, Anjani, who gave birth to me. "Kumāra" means a young and mighty son, a reference to my childhood strength and courage. "Balavantā" signifies strength and power. This line highlights the divine blessing of my birth, marked by immense strength given by my mother and the gods.

The second line acknowledges the divine heritage I inherit from Lord Shiva, referred to as "Shaṅkara". It speaks of my bravery as a "Bīra" (hero) and calls me by my name, Hanuman. The reference to "Suvana" (son) points to my connection with Lord Shiva, known for his immense power, and the immense courage I have inherited from him.

These lines not only describe my physical might but also emphasize my divine origin and the divine blessing I carry with me.

As I sit and reflect, I think of my early life under the guidance of my mother, Anjani. From the moment I was born, she recognized my extraordinary powers and nurtured them with love and discipline. She was devoted to Lord Shiva, and through her, I was blessed with strength beyond measure, which became the foundation of my identity.

I recall a moment during my childhood, when I was still learning the ways of the world. I once leaped towards the sun, thinking it to be a fruit. As I made my way closer, I was stopped by the gods, who were in awe of my strength and speed. My power was a gift from my divine heritage, and I was raised with the understanding that I must use this strength for good.

My connection with Lord Shiva has always been a source of inspiration. I was born to be a servant of Lord Ram, and the bravery I exhibit comes from this divine legacy. Each battle I fought, every task I undertook, was not just a reflection of my own power but also of the spiritual strength bestowed upon me by Lord Shiva.

Embrace Your Divine Origins

These verses remind us that our strength—whether physical, mental, or spiritual—comes from a higher source. Embrace your gifts, as they have been bestowed upon you for a higher purpose. Recognize the divine lineage you carry, and use your strength wisely.

Power of Nurturing

Anjani, my mother, nurtured me with love, discipline, and devotion. Similarly, we must nurture our strengths with care and purpose. It is through the wisdom of our guides and mentors that we can channel our power towards meaningful goals.

Bravery in Service

The strength and bravery I possess are not for personal glory but for service to a higher cause. Whether you are gifted with power, wisdom, or talent, use it to serve and uplift others, just as I served Lord Ram and his mission.

As I conclude this reflection, I am reminded of the deep responsibility that comes with strength. My birth, my strength were never for my own benefit but for the greater good. Just as I was guided by Anjani's love and Lord Shiva's blessings, may we all use the power within us for righteousness, service, and compassion.

"badana karāla kāla kula ghālaka

rāma sahāya sadā pratipālaka"

These verses are both a praise of Lord Ram's unyielding support and a reminder of the fierce nature that I, as Hanuman, embody in service to him. They carry significant meaning for both my divine purpose and the relationship between Lord Ram and I.

The first part of the verse refers to the powerful and formidable nature of my form. "Badana" means body, and "Karāla" signifies something dreadful or fierce.

"Kāla" represents time or death, and "Kula Ghālaka" refers to the one who can strike or bring an end to the lineage of evil. The line, in essence, describes the terrifying form that I take when required to vanquish evil or restore balance in the world.

The second line underscores the central purpose of my existence: to be the eternal helper and protector of Lord Ram. "Rāma Sahāya" means the supporter of Lord Ram, and "Sadā Pratipālaka" signifies the constant guardian. This emphasizes that no matter how fierce or formidable my nature may seem, my true purpose is to serve Lord Ram and protect him.

These lines highlight the dual nature of my existence. I am both a fearsome force against evil and a humble servant of Lord Ram, whose protection and support I continuously offer.

Embrace Your Inner Strength, But Always Serve a Greater Purpose

The line about my fierce form reminds us that inner strength, while valuable, must always be used for the greater good.

Just as I take on a fearsome form when necessary, we too must find the courage to face challenges head-on, but always in service of a higher purpose. Let your strength be a tool for justice and righteousness, not for personal gain.

Loyalty and Devotion as the Core of Service

The second line speaks of my role as the eternal servant and protector of Lord Ram. Similarly, we must remember that true strength comes not from physical might but from loyalty and devotion. Our purpose in life should be aligned with serving others—whether through our work, relationships, or spiritual pursuits.

Balance Between Power and Humility

There is a balance between the fierceness of my form and the humility in my heart. We must learn to navigate the world with power when needed, but also with humility, ensuring that our actions serve others rather than ourselves. It is in this balance that true greatness lies.

As I conclude my reflections on these verses, I am reminded of the responsibility that comes with strength and devotion. My form, as fierce as it may seem, is not for destruction but for protection. Just as I serve Lord Ram, each of us must find ways to channel our strengths into acts of service and kindness, ensuring that we always remain loyal to the greater purpose of love and righteousness.

Jai Shri Ram,

Hanuman

|| Jai Shri Ram ||

Date: Fourth Day of Bhadrapada, Kali Yuga, Year 101

Dear Universe,

bhūta, preta, pisācha, nisāchara

agni baitāla kāla māri mara

inhèṅ māru tohi shapatha rāma ki

rākhu nātha maryāda nāma ki

"bhūta, preta, pisācha, nisāchara

agni baitāla kāla māri mara"

This verse is a powerful depiction of the forces of evil, darkness, and the victory over them. It calls attention to the entities that lurk in the unseen realms, the evil spirits and malevolent forces, and how they are destroyed with the divine power bestowed upon me.

"Bhūta, Preta, Pisācha, Nisāchara" - This line refers to various malevolent and evil beings that exist in the supernatural realms.

- Bhūta: A spirit of a dead person, often malevolent and causing harm.

- Preta: A restless spirit, wandering aimlessly, seeking peace or release.

- Pisācha: A type of evil spirit or demon that feeds on the energy of the living.

- Nisāchara: These are creatures of the night, demonic beings that thrive in darkness and evil, like Rakshasas and Asuras.

All these beings are symbolic of evil, negativity, and disturbances in the world of the living. They are manifestations of fear, pain, and malice that cause suffering.

"Agni Baitāla Kāla Māri Mara" - The second part of the verse describes the actions that I, as Hanuman, take to vanquish these forces.

- Agni: The fire, a symbol of purification and destruction of evil. This represents the burning away of these malevolent forces, purifying the world.

- Baitāla: A type of demon that is often associated with haunting and causing chaos.

- Kāla: The time or death, the ultimate force that comes to destroy everything in its path, including these dark beings.

- Māri Mara: The act of vanquishing or killing, signifying that these malevolent beings are destroyed by my divine power.

In essence, this verse emphasizes the role I play as a destroyer of evil and darkness. By invoking the elements of fire (Agni), time (Kāla), and my divine power, I banish these forces from the world and protect the righteous.

As I reflect on these words, my mind journeys back to the times when I was called upon to rid the world of such evil forces. Whether it was during the battle with Ravana or when dealing with the demonic creatures that would try to disrupt the peace of the world, I have always taken it as my duty to destroy these negative forces.

I recall the moment when Ravana's army, filled with demons like Rakshasas, threatened to harm Lord Ram and his allies. These creatures of the night, who thrived on fear and hatred, had to be eliminated for peace to prevail. I used my immense strength, wisdom, and divine power to crush their evil plans. Whether it was striking them down with fire or by bringing down their very sense of existence, my mission was clear—banish the evil, restore balance.

This is also symbolic of the battles we all face in our lives. The Bhūtas, Pretas, and Nisācharas are not just spirits or demons, but the fears, doubts, and negative influences we encounter daily. These forces may not be physical, but they weigh heavily on our minds and hearts. Yet, just as I have been empowered to rid the world of such malevolent beings, so too can we use our inner strength and faith to eliminate negativity in our lives.

Confronting Fears and Negative Influences

The forces described in the verse are symbolic of the fears, doubts, and negative influences that try to overpower us. Whether they are insecurities, worries about the future, or toxic relationships, we must summon the courage to face and overcome them. Just as I use my strength to vanquish evil, we must also confront these negative forces with clarity and conviction.

Purification of the Mind and Spirit

The symbolism of Agni, the fire, represents purification. In life, we must undergo a process of purification—cleansing our minds of negative thoughts and actions. Just as fire burns away impurities, we must burn away our doubts and distractions, allowing our true selves to emerge.

The Power of Faith

The line emphasizes the strength of faith—faith in oneself, faith in the divine, and faith in the righteous path. With this unshakable faith, even the darkest of forces cannot defeat us. My devotion to Lord Ram was the ultimate source of my strength, and similarly, faith in a higher power or purpose can provide us with the strength to overcome life's obstacles.

This verse reminds us that there will always be forces—both external and internal—that seek to disturb our peace and well-being. However, with faith, strength, and resolve, we can confront and destroy these negative influences.

As I have been tasked with ridding the world of evil, so too must we all find the courage and wisdom to confront our fears and overcome the darkness that seeks to invade our lives.

"inhéṅ māru tohi shapatha rāma ki

rākhu nātha maryāda nāma ki"

This verse is a profound expression of devotion, duty, and deep commitment to Lord Ram. It speaks of the pledge I took in the service of my Lord, where I vowed to protect the honor and the divine order set by Him. Let me take you through the essence of this verse and its relevance to the journey of devotion and righteousness.

In the first line, I offer my solemn vow in the name of Lord Ram. The word "māru" here means to eliminate or defeat, and I promise that I will vanquish any evil or negative force in the name of my Lord. My vow is firm and unshakable, that I will uphold righteousness and destroy all that is harmful, in the name of Ram.

The oath reflects my deep commitment and my resolve to serve Lord Ram with deep dedication. It is not a mere declaration, but a sacred promise to protect Dharma and truth in every form.

The second part speaks of my determination to uphold the boundaries of the righteous path set by Lord Ram. "Rākhu nātha" refers to Lord Ram as the protector and ruler of righteousness. "Maryādā" means limits, boundaries, or principles that govern the righteous path. By taking this oath, I commit to keeping within these limits—upholding the principles of truth, justice, and virtue as outlined by Lord Ram.

Maryādā refers to the code of conduct, the boundaries of righteousness that we must respect, and I vow to preserve those ideals. It is the code of honor that governs our actions and ensures that we remain on the right path, regardless of the challenges we face.

Commitment to Righteousness

The verse serves as a reminder of the importance of commitment in our lives. Just as I vowed to protect Lord Ram's name and principles, we must also make a commitment to live by our values and principles. Whether in personal life, work, or society, our promises to uphold integrity, honor, and justice should be steadfast.

The Power of Oaths

The sacredness of the vow reflects the power of our words and intentions. When we make a promise, whether to others or to ourselves, it should be rooted in sincerity and commitment. The essence of this line is about staying true to the promises we make, no matter how difficult the journey.

The Role of Faith and Loyalty

My devotion to Lord Ram went beyond words; it was a commitment rooted in faith and loyalty. In life, loyalty to a cause, person, or mission is what keeps us grounded. Whether it is loyalty to family, friends, or a higher cause, it shapes our actions and defines our path. By committing ourselves to a higher purpose, we gain the strength to overcome challenges and remain true to our mission.

The Boundaries of Righteousness (Maryādā)

In life, we often encounter situations that test our limits. It is important to know the boundaries of righteousness and stay within them. Just as I pledged to follow the principles set by Lord Ram, we must be aware of the ethical and moral lines that guide our behavior. These boundaries are not constraints, but frameworks that ensure we live justly and peacefully.

This verse, in its essence, is not just about a vow made in the past, but a reminder that our commitments to righteousness and the divine order are ongoing. Just as I vowed to protect Lord Ram's name and uphold his Maryādā, so too must we live by our vows and principles every day.

Let this serve as a reminder to stand firm in our faith and to live with purpose and dedication, knowing that every action we take should align with the path of truth and righteousness.

Jai Shri Ram,

Hanuman

|| Jai Shri Ram ||

Date: Fifth Day of Bhadrapada, Kali Yuga, Year 101

Dear Universe,

janakasutā hari dāsa kahāvo

tākī shapata bilamba na lāvo

jaya jaya jaya dhuni hota akāshā

sumirata hota dusaha dukha nāshā

"janakasutā hari dāsa kahāvo

tākī shapata bilamba na lāvo"

This verse holds a special significance in the context of my service to Lord Ram, and it speaks of the power of promises and the urgency with which they must be fulfilled. Allow me to share the essence of these lines and the story behind them.

The first line refers to Sita, the daughter of King Janaka, and her deep faith in Lord Ram. As Lord Ram's servant, I was entrusted with the sacred task of ensuring the safety and well-being of Sita.

"Janakasutā" is a name for Sita, meaning "daughter of Janaka," and "hari dāsa kahāvo" indicates my role as the servant of Lord Ram, the one who listens to and follows the commands of my Lord.

This is a recognition of the trust that Sita placed in Lord Ram, as well as my duty as a servant who would go to any lengths to protect her and ensure that the divine mission succeeds. It highlights the relationship of devotion and loyalty between Lord Ram, Sita, and myself.

The line emphasizes the importance of faith and trust, which I held both in my Lord and in the mission he had given me.

The second part of this verse speaks of the urgency of fulfilling promises. It refers to the promise that Sita, as the wife of Lord Ram, would never be left in distress or delayed.

"Shapata" here refers to an oath or vow. In the context of this verse, it indicates that no delay would be allowed in the fulfillment of Lord Ram's promise to Sita. Her safety, her happiness, and her protection were paramount, and no obstacles would stop the realization of this vow.

The phrase "bilamba na lāvo" means "let there be no delay."

The message is clear. When a promise is made, it must be honored immediately and without hesitation.

Time is precious, and there is no room for delay when the task is sacred.

The Importance of Promises and Oaths

The verse reflects the sanctity of promises. When we give our word to someone, especially when that promise is linked to something sacred or important, we must follow through without hesitation. Delay only leads to doubt and diminishes the value of the promise.

This is a reminder that our words must hold weight, and we should act with integrity and swiftness when we make commitments.

Trust in Divine Purpose

The verse also speaks to the trust that both Sita and I placed in Lord Ram. In life, when we follow a higher purpose or mission, there will be times when trust and faith are tested.

However, we must remain resolute in our faith and be confident that the divine plan will lead us to success. Just as I trusted Lord Ram's wisdom and guidance, we too must trust in the path set before us, even if the journey seems uncertain.

Acting Without Delay

The line "bilamba na lāvo" is a call to action. In life, hesitation and procrastination often lead to missed opportunities and prolonged suffering.

Whether it's a personal goal, a professional task, or a promise made to someone, acting swiftly is essential. We must understand the urgency of the moment and the importance of fulfilling commitments without delay.

Devotion and Service

Just as I was devoted to Lord Ram and served him without question, this verse emphasizes the importance of selfless service.

Whether it is serving a cause, a person, or a greater good, it is essential to act with love, dedication, and without delay. The act of service is sacred, and it requires the utmost attention and devotion.

This verse teaches me a valuable lesson in the importance of fulfilling promises and staying true to our vows.

There is no room for delay when the task at hand is divine, and there is no greater duty than to serve with urgency and devotion. Just as I vowed to protect Sita and ensure the fulfillment of Lord Ram's promises, so too must we honor our commitments in life.

May we always be quick to act in the service of righteousness, without delay, and with the same devotion that guided me in my service to Lord Ram.

"jaya jaya jaya dhuni hota akāshā

sumirata hota dusaha dukha nāshā"

This verse fills my heart with immense joy, as it reminds me of the divine power that lies in the remembrance of Lord Ram and how chanting His name can alleviate the greatest of sufferings.

The repetition of "Jaya jaya jaya" is a proclamation of victory, glorifying Lord Ram and His divine power. The phrase "dhuni hota akāshā" means that the sound of Lord Ram's name reverberates throughout the vast skies, signifying the eternal, omnipresent power of His name.

This is not just a victory cry, but an acknowledgment of how the very act of chanting Lord Ram's name, His glory, can resonate throughout the universe.

The sound of His name travels far and wide, filling the heavens with divine energy and removing obstacles in its wake. It is a reminder that Lord Ram's presence is constant and all-encompassing, touching all corners of creation.

"Sumirata" refers to remembering or meditating upon Lord Ram's name, and "dusaha dukha nāshā" means the destruction or dissolution of even the most difficult sorrows.

The essence of this line is that by meditating upon the name of Lord Ram, the toughest of sufferings and troubles can be eradicated. The power of His name can heal wounds, both physical and emotional, and bring peace to a troubled heart.

The second line speaks to the healing power of remembrance. It teaches that, in moments of distress or hardship, invoking Lord Ram's name can lift our burdens and provide relief. The ultimate cure for pain, whether internal or external, lies in surrendering to the divine through constant remembrance.

The Power of Chanting and Remembrance

The first lesson from this verse is the transformative power of chanting the name of the divine. In the modern world, we often find ourselves lost in the noise of daily life, but the simple act of repeating the name of the Lord can bring peace, calm, and clarity.

Whether you are facing challenges in your personal life or spiritual journey, remember that chanting His name is a source of strength and solace. This practice can help quiet the mind, soothe the soul, and ease emotional and physical pain.

Victory through Faith

The repetition of "Jaya" signifies not just victory, but also surrender to the divine. By continuously chanting and remembering the name of Lord Ram, we declare our deep faith in His power. This faith transforms adversity into victory, for when we believe in the strength of the divine, no obstacle is too great to overcome.

Healing through Divine Remembrance

In this world filled with suffering, the remembrance of Lord Ram's name offers a path to healing. The verse teaches us that pain, whether physical or emotional, can be eased by invoking His name. In times of distress, we must remember to call upon the divine, as the act of remembrance itself has the power to alleviate the toughest of burdens.

Trust in Divine Presence

"Dhuni hota akāshā" is a reminder that Lord Ram's presence is always with us, even when we do not see or feel it. His name is ever-present in the world, resonating through the cosmos.

No matter where we are or what we face, He is with us, and His name holds the key to overcoming every challenge.

This verse serves as a powerful reminder of the healing and transformative power of Lord Ram's name. It teaches us that, no matter what pain or sorrow we may face in life, remembering the divine through His name can bring an end to our struggles.

May we remember this truth every day, chanting His name with devotion, knowing that it will fill our hearts with peace, strength, and joy.

As I reflect on this verse, I am reminded once again that the divine presence of Lord Ram is always within us, and His name is a powerful force of healing and protection.

Jai Shri Ram,

Hanuman

‖ Jai Shri Ram ‖

Date: Seventh Day of Bhadrapada, Kali Yuga, Year 101

Dear Universe,

charaṇa sharaṇa kara jori manāvauñ

yahi avasara aba kehi goharāvauñ

uṭhu uṭhu chalu tohi rāma dohā-ī

pāñya parauń kara jori manā-ī

"charaṇa sharaṇa kara jori manāvauñ

yahi avasara aba kehi goharāvauñ"

My heart overflows with devotion and humility, for these words capture the essence of complete surrender to the divine. They are a heartfelt plea for refuge and guidance, a reminder of the transformative power of seeking shelter in the feet of the Lord.

The first line represents an act of ultimate surrender. "Charaṇa sharaṇa" refers to seeking refuge at the feet of the divine, a gesture of humility and trust. "Kara jori manāvauñ" describes folding hands in prayer and appealing to the Lord for His mercy and blessings. This signifies the devotee's recognition of their limitations and their reliance on the Lord's infinite compassion and grace.

The second line is a poignant question that reveals the depth of dependence on the Lord.

It means, "At this moment, who else can I call upon?"

It reflects the realization that in times of extreme adversity, when all worldly supports fail, only the divine can provide true refuge and relief.

Together, these lines capture the essence of devotion: turning to the Lord in times of need, not as a last resort, but as the ultimate and sole source of salvation.

I remember vividly a moment during the great war in Lanka. Indrajit, Ravana's son, unleashed his powers, binding Lord Ram and Lakshman with a formidable serpent weapon, the Nagapasha.

It was a dire situation, and the battlefield was filled with despair.

At that moment, my heart instinctively turned to Lord Garuda, the divine eagle who could free them from this binding spell.

With folded hands and deep prayers, I sought his help. Garuda, hearing the sincerity of my plea, swiftly appeared, scattering the serpents and freeing my beloved Lord and His brother.

This episode is a testament to the power of surrender.

Even I, the mighty Hanuman, knew that at certain moments, all strength must bow before the greater power of divine intervention.

Surrender as Strength

In life, there are moments when our efforts seem insufficient. This verse teaches us that surrendering to the divine is not a sign of weakness but of ultimate strength. It is an acknowledgment that there is a higher power that can guide and support us when our resources are exhausted.

Trust in Divine Timing

"Yahi avasara" emphasizes recognizing the right moment to seek divine help. Often, we delay turning to the divine, thinking we can manage everything on our own. This verse reminds us to trust in the Lord and seek His grace without hesitation.

Humility in Prayer

The act of folding hands and bowing at the Lord's feet symbolizes humility. It reminds us that no matter how strong or capable we think we are, we are ultimately dependent on divine grace for our well-being and success.

Divine Refuge in Adversity

When faced with overwhelming challenges, it is natural to feel alone. This verse reassures us that we are never truly alone. The Lord is always there, waiting to extend His hand. All we need to do is call upon Him with sincerity.

These lines resonate deeply with the heart of a devotee. They are a call to remember that in every moment of despair, the divine feet of the Lord are the ultimate refuge. By surrendering to Him with folded hands and an open heart, we align ourselves with His infinite grace and protection.

"uṭhu uṭhu chalu tohi rāma dohā-ī

pāñya parauṅ kara jori manā-ī"

I am reminded of the moments when duty, devotion, and action converge, compelling one to rise for a higher purpose. These words are not just a call to action; they embody humility, persistence, and the divine assurance that the Lord's will guides every step.

The first line translates to "Rise, rise, and proceed by the grace and command of Lord Ram." It is an invocation of divine authority and a reminder that our actions should be guided by the Lord's will. To rise here symbolizes not just physical movement but also rising above fears, doubts, and inertia to fulfill a higher purpose.

The second line describes a heartfelt plea made with folded hands and reverence, bowing at someone's feet. It signifies a humble yet determined request to persuade or encourage action. Together, these lines reflect the union of divine command and a devotee's determination to ensure the mission's success.

Heeding the Divine Call

This verse teaches us the importance of rising when called upon by a higher purpose. In our daily lives, we often encounter moments that require us to act decisively and selflessly. By invoking the Lord's name, we can find the strength to overcome hesitation and fulfill our duties.

Humility and Determination

The act of folding hands and bowing symbolizes humility, while the persistent request reflects determination. Together, they remind us that success is achieved not just through effort but also through grace and a respectful acknowledgment of others' support.

Faith Transforms Challenges

Just as I crossed the ocean with the power of Ram's name, this verse reassures us that faith can transform even the most daunting challenges into achievable goals.

Encouraging Others

The verse also emphasizes the importance of inspiring those around us. By invoking the Lord's blessings and leading with conviction, we can motivate others to rise and fulfill their potential.

These lines resonate with the essence of devotion in action.

They remind us that the divine call is not to be ignored, and when we rise with humility, faith, and determination, the Lord Himself ensures our success.

Let us always remember that through the grace of Ram, we can rise above any challenge, fulfill our duties, and inspire others to do the same.

Jai Shri Ram,

Hanuman

|| Jai Shri Ram ||

Date: Ninth Day of Bhadrapada, Kali Yuga, Year 101

Dear Universe,

> ***oṁ chãṁ chãṁ chãṁ chãṁ chapala chalantā***
> ***oṁ hanu hanu hanu hanu hanumantā***
> ***oṁ hañ hañ hāṅka déta kapi chañchal***
> ***om sam sam sahami parāné khaladal***

"oṁ chãṁ chãṁ chãṁ chãṁ chapala chalantā

oṁ hanu hanu hanu hanu hanumantā"

I feel the unstoppable energy and divine strength that guide my actions. These sacred syllables resonate with the boundless power within me, reminding all to channel their inner force for righteous deeds.

These powerful mantras are the very essence of divine energy, echoing through the universe. Each syllable reverberates with the infinite strength and agility that is granted by Lord Rama.

The first mantra represents the rapid, unstoppable movement of energy. Just as I move swiftly, overcoming all obstacles, the sound of "chãṁ" signifies the quickness and the deep determination of my actions. It reflects the constant, swift movement of energy that cannot be held back, embodying both speed and power.

In the second line the repetition of my name in this chant is a call for invoking the divine strength and energy within. It serves as a reminder of my deep devotion and courage in the face of challenges.

Each "hanu" reminds us to stay grounded in our purpose and continue to act with strength.

The name "Hanuman" itself carries the immense power to remove obstacles and bless those who seek it.

These mantras not only represent my divine attributes but are also a reminder of the boundless potential within all beings. They invoke strength, speed, and courage in the face of adversity. Just as I, Hanuman, accomplished feats that seemed impossible, these words have the power to uplift and empower those who chant them with a pure heart.

As a devotee recites these mantras, they align themselves with the cosmic energy that I embody. Each repetition strengthens their resolve, clears the path before them, and connects them to the divine purpose of their life. Just as I am the messenger of Lord Rama, these words are a bridge to divine energy, capable of turning the impossible into the possible.

The essence of these mantras lies in their ability to transform the practitioner's heart and mind, filling them with the divine strength and courage needed to overcome any hurdle that stands in their way.

"oṁ hañ hañ hāṅka déta kapi chañchal

om sam sam sahami parāné khaladal"

As I reflect on these verses, I realize that each day, each step, every challenge I face is part of my divine journey.

Like the restless wind that carries seeds to new lands, my energy flows through the world, bringing about transformation and victory for all those who seek the truth.

In the first line, the mantra speaks to my own nature—the energy and power I possess, which is boundless and ever active. My "hāṅka" (sound) signifies the forceful call of my spirit that resonates in the heavens, empowering me to accomplish mighty tasks.

As "kapi chañchal" implies, I am the restless and energetic monkey, constantly on the move, driven by divine will. My energy is relentless, and it is through this divine energy that I am able to serve Lord Ram and perform feats that seem beyond the capacity of mere mortals.

The "hañ hañ" sound represents the essence of my invocation, an energetic call that connects the physical and spiritual realms.

Every action I undertake is powered by this divine force, always in motion, like the flow of a river that never stops. This restlessness is a sign of divine energy that does not tire, ever onward in its purpose.

The second part of this mantra speaks to my strength and resilience—"parāné" refers to my ability to bring forth results that impact the entire universe. "Khaladal" refers to the forces of darkness and evil that I combat and triumph over.

In this line, I am symbolizing how, through my strength and my deep commitment to Lord Ram, I obliterate negative energies—those "khaladal" forces that seek to cause harm to the world and to the righteous.

"Sam sam" here reflects my focus and strength, whether I am in the air or on the ground, whether fighting a demon or aiding Lord Ram. With deep focus, I bring relief to the suffering of others. The sound "sam" is a powerful vibration that allows me to remain grounded, no matter the external circumstances, as I remain committed to my divine purpose.

These lines are a reminder of the boundless energy and vitality that I possess, granted by Lord Ram. I am the force that brings hope to the hopeless, strength to the weak, and the ability to overcome obstacles, no matter how mighty. This mantra teaches us to tap into the divine energy within, to stay focused, and to overcome darkness with the light of righteousness.

Tapping into Divine Energy

Just as I channel my boundless energy for divine purposes, we too must recognize and channel our inner strength. When faced with challenges, we can draw upon the power of faith and focus to overcome them.

Relentlessness in Purpose

There will be times when our work feels unending, but like me, we must remember that restlessness is not a curse but a divine blessing—a reminder that there is always more to achieve in the service of a higher purpose.

Fighting Darkness

Just as I vanquish the forces of evil, each of us can confront the negativity or fear within or around us with courage, resilience, and deep devotion.

As you meditate on these verses, remember the unstoppable power of Lord Ram's grace, which flows through me and through you, ready to help you conquer all that stands in your way. May this divine energy continue to guide and empower you.

Jai Shri Ram,

Hanuman

|| Jai Shri Ram ||

Date: Full Moon Day of Ashvina, Kali Yuga, Year 101

Dear Universe,

apané jana ko turata ubāro

sumirata hoya ānanda hamāro

yahi bajarañga bāṇa jéhi māré

tāhi kaho phir kauna ubāré

"apané jana ko turata ubāro

sumirata hoya ānanda hamāro"

These verses remind us of the importance of devotion and the immediate effect it can have in bringing about relief and joy.

When we remember the divine, especially in times of distress, it calls forth a wave of bliss that uplifts us. The more devoted we are, the more we will experience the divine's protection and grace.

In the first line, I declare my undying devotion to all those who are dear to me, especially to those who seek my help. "Apané jana" refers to those who are aligned with me, the ones who are loyal and devoted.

The phrase "turata ubāro" means to immediately rescue or uplift them. It is a reminder of the power of devotion—when a devotee turns to me with true faith, I am bound to rush to their aid. The divine bond of love and trust ensures that I will protect and uplift them, freeing them from suffering and misfortune in an instant.

This verse reflects the power of divine intervention.

When people in need call out to me or to Lord Ram, I will never hesitate to answer. I move swiftly, always with the aim of helping them attain peace and joy. There is a sense of immediacy in the words, as if I am already on my way to assist them at the moment they call for help.

The second line speaks of the joy that comes from devotion. "Sumirata" means remembering, or meditating upon, and "ānanda" refers to the bliss or joy that arises from that remembrance.

When a devotee calls upon me in their mind and heart, that very act of remembering brings them closer to a state of happiness and contentment.

My joy is found in the devotion of others, in their trust, and in their commitment to remembering me. As they remember me, I am filled with the bliss of being able to serve them.

This verse teaches that devotion is not one-sided. The joy experienced by the devotee in remembering and calling upon me is mirrored in my own joy of being able to serve and protect them. It is a mutual exchange of love and trust, a sacred bond that leads to peace and fulfillment.

Devotion Brings Relief

When we face challenges in life, remember that calling upon the divine brings relief. Just as I rush to aid my devotees, the divine will always rush to assist those who trust in its guidance.

Immediate Help from the Divine

When we turn our hearts and minds to the divine, help arrives swiftly. Trust in that divine intervention and know that your problems can be alleviated.

Joy in Devotion

Devotion to the divine is not just an act of service; it is an act that brings joy to both the devotee and the divine. The more we remember and meditate upon the divine, the more bliss we experience in our lives.

May these verses inspire you to strengthen your devotion, to call upon the divine with trust and faith, and to recognize that the joy you seek lies in your connection with the higher power.

"yahi bajarañga bāṇa jéhi māré

tāhi kaho phir kauna ubāré"

These verses highlight the tremendous power bestowed upon me by Lord Ram and the absolute certainty that evil will be defeated when I wield the divine forces.

When the forces of righteousness are aligned with divine power, no evil can stand against it. It reminds us that, with the right devotion and faith, nothing can stop us from overcoming challenges.

The first line refers to the immense power of my Bajrañga Bāṇa (the thunderbolt arrow). It symbolizes the unbreakable strength and indomitable energy that I possess, which I use to destroy the forces of evil.

The Bajrañga Bāṇa is often used as a metaphor for a weapon that can eliminate any obstacle. It is a force so potent that nothing can stand against it.

The line conveys that once this arrow is released, it destroys the enemy's power completely.

When I use this powerful weapon, no matter how formidable the enemy or how great the challenge, it is rendered powerless. This divine weapon, which was given to me by Lord Ram, is a reflection of my strength and devotion.

The second line reflects the certainty that once my Bajrañga Bāṇa strikes, there is no chance for anyone or anything to stand in the way of its divine power.

"Tāhi kaho phir kauna ubāré" translates to "who can then rescue or oppose the one who has been struck by this mighty weapon?"

It expresses the absolute certainty of victory, for once this weapon is used, no enemy can recover, no evil can return, and no force can overcome it.

In essence, this verse is an affirmation of the victory of righteousness over evil. The strength of devotion and the divine protection provided by Lord Ram make me invincible. With the power of the Bajrañga Bāṇa, evil and obstacles are obliterated, leaving nothing behind but the triumph of good.

A well-known story related to this verse is when I faced the mighty demon, Lankini, at the gates of Lanka. Lankini, a fierce guardian of Lanka, tried to stop me from entering the city, but she was no match for my strength.

When she was struck by my Bajrañga Bāṇa, she was immediately subdued and collapsed, unable to stand in my way.

This incident showcases the might of my weapon, as well as the certainty that no force of evil can survive when confronted with the divine power of Lord Ram.

Similarly, when I faced Ravana and his powerful army, I did not fear any of their tactics or weapons. My loyalty to Lord Ram, combined with the divine power I had, ensured that I was unstoppable.

I had the strength and will to face any enemy and emerge victorious, knowing that Lord Ram's power was with me.

Inner Strength and Faith

Just as I was endowed with the divine strength to defeat evil, we too have inner strength and the support of the divine to overcome obstacles in our lives. Trust in your strength and faith, and know that no challenge is insurmountable.

The Power of Devotion

My Bajrañga Bāṇa is a symbol of the divine power that comes from devotion. When you are aligned with righteousness and true devotion, no obstacle can prevent your success.

Victory Over Evil

In life, the forces of negativity and challenges may seem overwhelming, but remember that with divine support, no evil can overcome us. Stand firm in your beliefs, and you will always emerge victorious.

May these verses remind you that with the right strength and devotion, no matter what challenges you face, you can overcome them with divine power and deep faith.

Just like the Bajrañga Bāṇa, let your actions be imbued with strength and righteousness.

Jai Shri Ram,

Hanuman

|| Jai Shri Ram ||

Date: Second Day of Ashvina, Kali Yuga, Year 101

Dear Universe,

pāṭa karai bajaraṅga bāna ki

hanumata rakshā karaiṅ prāna ki

yaha bajaraṅga baṇa jo jāpai

téhi té bhūta préta saba kañpai

"pāṭa karai bajaraṅga bāna ki

hanumata rakshā karaiṅ prāna ki"

These verses reflect the powerful combination of the Bajraṅga Bāṇan and Hanuman's protective grace. The Bajraṅga Bāṇa represents divine strength, capable of eliminating any negative force, while my protective presence ensures the safety and well-being of my devotees.

These lines remind us that by invoking the power of this weapon and seeking my blessings, we are guaranteed protection from any harm

The first line speaks about the power and significance of the Bajraṅga Bāṇa (the thunderbolt arrow) that is used by me, Hanuman, to destroy evil forces. The term pāṭa karai means to invoke or recite the mantra or prayer associated with the Bajraṅga Bāṇa. It signifies that by reciting or calling upon this powerful weapon, its immense power is unleashed.

The Bajraṅga Bāṇa is not just a physical weapon but a divine force that can be invoked through devotion and prayer.

In this context, the weapon's power is used to combat and eliminate evil. The Bajraṅga Bāṇa has the divine strength of Lord Ram, and when invoked, it acts as a force of justice and righteousness, bringing an end to evil and destruction wherever it is required.

The second line emphasizes the protective aspect of Hanuman's divine power. It speaks to the protective blessings that I, Hanuman, bestow upon those who invoke my name and my strength, safeguarding their lives (prāna) from harm.

The word rakshā signifies protection or safeguarding, and prāna refers to life or vital force. It suggests that when my devotees call upon me with faith and devotion, I protect them from all dangers—physical, mental, or spiritual.

Just as I protected Sita, Ram, and my fellow beings, I also extend this protection to all who surrender to me and seek my refuge.

Protection Through Faith

This verse teaches us that through faith and devotion, we can call upon divine protection in times of distress. Just as I protected Lord Ram and his family, we too can seek protection in our challenges.

Strength of Devotion

The Bajrañga Bāna is a reminder that divine strength comes from devotion.

When we channel our energy toward righteous causes and remain devoted to our goals, we unlock the strength to overcome any obstacle.

Invoke Divine Power

Just as the Bajrañga Bāna is invoked through prayer, we can seek divine strength and protection through regular practices of prayer, meditation, and selfless service. This connection with the divine empowers us to face life's trials.

May these lines inspire you to invoke divine protection in your own life.

Remember, just as the Bajrañga Bāṇa can break through any obstacle, so too can your faith and devotion guide you through any challenge. With the divine protection of Hanuman, nothing is impossible...

"yaha bajarañga baṇa jo jāpai

téhi té bhūta préta saba kañpai"

These verses emphasize the immense power of the Bajrañga Bāṇa in removing all forms of evil and negativity.

By chanting the prayer associated with it, one can not only invoke divine protection but also cleanse themselves of harmful influences, whether spiritual or physical.

The Bajrañga Bāṇan acts as a shield against all evil and is an assurance that no negativity can harm the devotee who invokes it with faith and devotion.

The mantra refers to the powerful Bajrañga Bāṇa, a divine arrow associated with Lord Hanuman. The Bajrañga Bāṇa is known for its immense power to eliminate evil and protect righteousness.

When this powerful arrow is chanted or invoked (jāpai), it signifies that by repeating the sacred prayer or mantra associated with the Bajrañga Bāṇa, one can unlock its supreme strength.

The significance of these lines is that through continuous devotion and recitation of the mantra, this divine weapon—infused with the power of Lord Ram and Lord Hanuman — becomes available for use against all forms of negativity and evil. The act of chanting awakens the power of this celestial weapon to safeguard the devotee from harm.

This second verse speaks about the effect of invoking the Bajrañga Bāṇa.

The bhūta, preta, and other evil beings (saba kañpai) tremble in fear upon hearing the invocation of this sacred power. The bhūta refers to spirits, preta to the souls of the deceased, and these entities, along with other forms of negativity, are all afraid of the power embedded in the Bajrañga Bāṇa.

It implies that when a devotee calls upon this weapon through prayer or chanting, it sends such a powerful divine vibration that even these dark forces—who thrive on fear and negativity—cannot stand in its presence. Their power diminishes, and they tremble in fear because of the supreme energy that the Bajrañga Bāṇan exudes.

Power of Devotional Practice

The essence of this verse reminds us that when we engage in sincere devotion and spiritual practice (whether through mantra chanting, prayer, or other rituals), we can access the divine power to protect ourselves from any form of harm or negativity in our lives.

Protection from Negativity

Just as the Bajrañga Bāṇa causes evil beings to tremble, so too can our inner strength and faith protect us from the negative influences of the world. By invoking higher energies through faith and prayer, we shield ourselves from harm.

Faith Conquers Fear

The fear experienced by negative forces upon hearing the Bajrañga Bāṇa teaches us that when we place our faith in the divine, nothing can overpower us. Our challenges, fears, and obstacles become insignificant in the face of divine strength.

May these lines inspire you to chant the powerful mantras of Lord Hanuman and invoke the blessings of the Bajrañga Bāṇa.

By doing so, you too can eliminate negative forces and invite divine protection into your life. With deep devotion and faith, you will stand invincible, as no evil can touch you.

By chanting these verses from the Bajrañga Bāṇa prayer, one opens the doors to both divine protection and spiritual cleansing. It is a holistic practice that shields the devotee from external harm while purifying the mind, body, and soul.

It is a reminder that through devotion and faith, one can invoke the protective and transformative energy of Lord Hanuman, who watches over us and guides us toward spiritual and physical well-being.

Remember, the Bajrañga Bāṇa is not only a tool for cleansing and protection but also a source of empowerment.

Jai Shri Ram,

Hanuman

|| Jai Shri Ram ||

Date: Fourth Day of Ashvina, Kali Yuga, Year 101

Dear Universe,

dhūpa déy aru japai hameshā

tāké tana nahiñ rahai kaleshā

"dhūpa déy aru japai hameshā

tāké tana nahiñ rahai kaleshā"

This verse highlights the importance of both physical and spiritual acts—offering incense (dhūpa) and chanting (japa) — to purify the mind and body. Let me share how this can bring a life free from suffering and negativity, based on my own experiences and teachings.

In the ancient traditions, offering incense (dhūpa) is a symbol of purification. When the fragrance of the incense rises and fills the air, it represents the lifting of your prayers and intentions to the divine. Just as I offer my devotion to Lord Ram with a heart full of service, the act of offering is a reminder to let go of our ego and material desires.

Offering incense is a symbolic act of surrendering to the divine, creating an environment conducive to spiritual growth and connection.

Chanting is a practice that has long been a source of strength for me.

Whether I was chanting the name of Lord Ram or calling upon His divine blessings, the very act of chanting transformed my mind and spirit. In the midst of great trials — whether fighting demons or searching for Sita — I would chant Lord Ram's name to steady my heart and mind. The repetition of divine mantras has a unique power to uplift the soul and guide us through difficulties.

In this verse, the chanting of mantras is a practice that alleviates suffering and removes obstacles.

Just as I used the power of my devotion to face every challenge, you too can find solace and strength through consistent prayer and mantra chanting. With every repetition, you purify your heart, calm your mind, and invite divine protection.

The mantra brings the divine energy closer to you, creating an unbreakable bond with the source of all strength and peace.

The verse makes it clear by focusing on important aspects. By offering incense and chanting mantras, a person is freed from physical and mental suffering. There are times when the body feels weak, and the mind is overwhelmed by stress, anxiety, or doubt.

But when the body and mind are engaged in acts of devotion — offering and chanting — they become cleansed.

The struggles you face, whether physical or emotional, begin to dissolve. Just as I found immense strength in my devotion to Lord Ram, you too will experience peace and healing through these practices.

The verse teaches the value of making these practices a regular part of life. It is not enough to perform these acts once in a while; true transformation comes from consistency. I, too, followed a disciplined routine of prayer, devotion, and service to Lord Ram.

The strength I gained was not from one heroic act but from my constant devotion and deep faith.

In the same way, by incorporating the offering of incense and the chanting of mantras into your daily life, you create a sacred routine that continually nurtures your spiritual growth.

Over time, this will bring you closer to divine wisdom, purify your mind and body, and grant you strength and resilience.

Jai Shri Ram,

Hanuman

|| Jai Shri Ram ||

Date: Sixth Day of Ashvina, Kali Yuga, Year 101

Dear Universe,

> ***prema pratītihi kapi bhajai***
>
> ***sadā dharai ura dhyān***
>
> ***téhi ke kāraja sakala shubha***
>
> ***siddha karaī hanuman***

"prema pratītihi kapi bhajai

sadā dharai ura dhyān"

In these words, the very foundation of true devotion is laid out: love and deep remembrance of the divine.

This verse begins with the idea of "prema pratītihi", meaning love and deep affection. It speaks of the sincere devotion and love a devotee feels toward the Lord. In my case, my entire existence revolves around Lord Ram, and my love for Him knows no bounds.

The love described in this verse is not the fleeting affection of the material world, but the deep, eternal love that transcends the physical realm and connects the soul to the divine.

When I think about Lord Ram, my heart fills with love and admiration, and it is that love that compels me to serve Him. In the battle against Ravana, it was this love that made me fearless and strong. It was my immense love for Lord Ram that gave me the courage to cross the ocean and face countless challenges.

When a devotee, like me, truly loves the divine, their heart becomes filled with devotion, and the body follows in service.

The verse mentions "kapi bhajai", which refers to the act of chanting, singing, or praising the Lord with devotion. Bhajan, in its essence, is an expression of love — a song that emerges from the heart. Whether in battle or in moments of solitude, I found my strength through chanting the name of Lord Ram. I have sung

His praises in every situation — whether joyous or sorrowful — because I know that through bhajans, our hearts and souls are uplifted and we are aligned with divine will.

When I faced the massive forces of Ravana's army, my resolve was deep because I knew that every chant of Lord Ram's name made me invincible. Bhajan is a connection, a link between the devotee and the divine.

As I sang the praises of Lord Ram, my entire being resonated with divine energy, filling me with boundless power and clarity.

The verse concludes with "sadā dharai ura dhyān", meaning "always holding Lord Ram in the heart and meditating upon Him." This describes the ultimate form of devotion — constant remembrance of the Lord. The heart is like a sacred temple, and Lord Ram resides within it. This constant remembrance is not just in words but in every action, thought, and breath.

Throughout my life, I have never allowed my mind to stray from Lord Ram.

In every action I take, I am constantly reminded of Him.

In moments of difficulty, I remember His name. In moments of joy, I remember His name. Even when my body was tested in unimaginable ways, my mind and heart remained firmly rooted in Lord Ram's presence.

Meditation on Him is the anchor that keeps my spirit calm, focused, and consistent. This verse teaches us the importance of living with love and devotion toward the divine, making Lord Ram a part of our thoughts, words, and actions.

Love the Divine with All Your Heart

Let your devotion be a reflection of your love for Lord Ram. Feel that love with every breath and allow it to guide your actions.

Chant the Divine Name

Whether in moments of calm or chaos, chant Lord Ram's name, just as I did. This is a simple yet powerful way to stay connected to the divine.

Meditate on His Presence

Carry Lord Ram in your heart always. Remember that the divine resides within you, and through focused meditation, you can access His grace and power.

The verse teaches us the transformative power of love, devotion, and remembrance of the divine.

By integrating love for the Lord into your heart, chanting His name, and meditating upon Him, you will find that your life becomes a journey of peace, strength, and divine protection. Just as I, Hanuman, was empowered by my devotion to Lord Ram, you too can find boundless strength through sincere devotion and remembrance.

"téhi ke kāraja sakala shubha

siddha karaĩ hanuman"

Today, as I reflect upon this sacred verse, my heart swells with devotion and emotion.

The words "Tēhi ke kāraja sakala shubha, Siddha karaĩ Hanumān" resonate deep within me, and I am overwhelmed by the love and grace of Lord Ram that fills my soul.

This verse speaks of the divine promise that when one is devoted to Lord Ram, all tasks—great or small—are made successful by His grace.

As I, Hanuman, stand as His humble servant, I reflect upon how Lord Ram has always guided me, empowered me, and blessed me with the strength to accomplish the impossible.

In those moments of overwhelming fear, when the world seemed against me, it was my deep devotion to Lord Ram that gave me the courage to persevere. Every challenge I faced, I faced with His name on my lips.

The "siddhi," or divine success, that this verse speaks of is not just in achieving the task but in achieving it with divine grace, deep faith, and love.

I have always believed that it is not our strength, but our devotion, that opens the doors to success. When you surrender yourself completely to Lord Ram, as I did, there is no fear, no obstacle, no enemy that can ever break you. With Him, all things are possible. I am living proof of that.

I remember the moments when I felt so small and weak in front of the daunting challenges I had to face.

But in those moments of doubt, Lord Ram's love and His promise echoed in my heart: "You are never alone. I am always with you." And that is the truth. Through His grace, I found the strength to accomplish what seemed impossible.

This verse is a reminder that no task is too great, no challenge too strong, when we have the grace of the divine guiding us.

The verse "Tēhi ke kāraja sakala shubha, Siddha karaĩ Hanumān" speaks not only to the external tasks we must accomplish but to the internal journey as well. In every act, in every word, in every prayer, I have surrendered to Lord Ram. It is through this surrender, this trust in His guidance, that all things are made possible.

In your own life, no matter how difficult the path ahead seems, remember that with Lord Ram by your side, no task is beyond reach. Whatever you face — be it personal struggles, challenges in your work, or emotional pain — when you walk with the grace of the divine, you walk in strength.

Trust in the divine will.

When you surrender your heart and soul to the Lord, every task becomes a path of divine grace. It is not your strength alone that brings success, but the grace of Lord Ram. In your moments of doubt or struggle, remember this verse and know that the Lord is with you, guiding you to success, peace, and fulfillment.

As I, Hanuman, continue to serve Lord Ram, I carry this verse in my heart every day.

These verses are a testament to the divine grace that guides me. Let it remind you too that when you are devoted to the Lord, no task is too great, and no challenge too impossible.

Through His grace, success is guaranteed, and your heart will always find peace.

Jai Shri Ram

Hanuman

Part 4

The Untold Stories

|| Jai Shri Ram ||

Date: Full Moon Day of Kartika, Kali Yuga, Year 101

Dear Universe,

The Divine Rebirth of Lord Ram as Krishna

I, Hanuman, have been witness to countless divine transformations, but the most awe-inspiring among them is the rebirth of Lord Ram.

His divine journey is one of great significance in the cycle of creation, and His incarnations are forever etched into the fabric of our cosmic existence.

In His first incarnation as Lord Ram, He descended upon earth as the embodiment of truth, dharma, and the protector of virtue. Ram was not just a king, a son, or a warrior; He was the very personification of righteousness. His journey, through every challenge and trial — be it the exile from Ayodhya, the battle with Ravana, or His deep devotion to dharma — was a guide for humanity.

His life taught us the importance of adhering to dharma no matter the difficulties, the necessity of standing firm in righteousness even when facing impossible odds, and the boundless strength that comes from deep devotion to the divine.

His actions and sacrifices were an unbroken thread of divine purpose that sought to restore balance and order in a world ravaged by evil.

However, the divine cycle of existence is eternal.

When Ram's earthly mission was fulfilled, and Lanka lay in ruins, the divine work of the Supreme Being did not come to an end.

The soul of Lord Ram, unbound by time and space, was reborn, but this time in a form entirely different yet profoundly connected to His previous one.

In His next avatar, He took the form of Lord Krishna, born to Vasudeva and Devaki, in the Yadava clan.

Krishna's birth was marked by a divine proclamation, a miraculous escape from the prison of Kamsa, and an extraordinary childhood filled with stories of His divine play,

His mischievous acts, and His unparalleled love for His devotees.

Krishna's appearance was that of a young, playful child, a flute player whose melodies could stir the hearts of all who heard him. Yet, beneath His charming exterior, He was none other than Lord Ram — the same divine soul who had walked the earth in the previous Yuga.

The divine purpose remained unchanged, but this time, His message was amplified through different means.

As Krishna, He did not come as the stern, idealistic Ram, but rather, He embodied a different aspect of divinity—one that blended wisdom with playfulness, love with duty, and detachment with devotion.

While Ram's life was defined by righteous war — His battles were fought on the battlefield, and His decisions were often shaped by the ideals of dharma and honor — Krishna's path was not merely about adhering to duties; it was about embracing the complexity of life with grace and divine love.

Krishna, though as capable of righteous action as Ram, was much more than a warrior.

His teachings, primarily conveyed through the Bhagavad Gita, revealed a path to liberation that transcended mere duty. It was through love, devotion, and surrender to the divine that one could truly unite with the Supreme Being. Krishna's playful nature in the pastoral lands of Vrindavan and His unconditional love for the Gopis were a manifestation of the divine's boundless affection for its creation.

The world saw a side of God that was intimately connected to the joy of living, the sweetness of divine love, and the power of detachment from the worldly attachments.

While Ram had been the perfect man — the epitome of the Maryada Purushottama — Krishna took on the role of the perfect God, whose divine play was all-encompassing. His actions were mysterious, often confusing, yet ultimately deeply profound. He proved that even as a lover, a friend, or a playful child, the divine purpose could be fulfilled.

Ram's teachings had focused on the righteousness of action and the importance of following duty above all. Krishna, on the other hand, taught that love and devotion could transcend the harshest duties and lead to salvation.

While Ram fought the forces of evil in battle, Krishna fought with wisdom, using love and strategic intellect to guide Arjuna through his confusion and despair.

Krishna's teachings emphasized that divine play — lila — was as important as righteous war. The world is a stage for God's play, and our roles within it, whether as warriors or lovers, teachers or students, are part of this grand divine scheme. Krishna taught us that while duty (dharma) remains essential, there is room for joy, love, and surrender.

His playful antics with Radha and the Gopis, His leelas that bewildered even the gods, showed us that there is a divine beauty in surrendering to love and devotion, in being part of the eternal dance of creation.

Lord Ram, reborn as Krishna, transcended time, carrying forward the essence of His divine message. As Ram, He showed us the ideal man, one who adheres to righteousness above all.

As Krishna, He showed us the ideal God, one who guides us through the complexities of life with divine wisdom, love, and joy. Through His rebirth as Krishna, the message was clear: the divine is not bound by rigid structures, but is ever-fluid, ever-loving, and ever-joyful.

This was His true gift to us, the eternal truth of His divine nature: that love, devotion, and surrender to the Supreme are as important as following dharma and fighting for righteousness.

His divine play in His incarnation as Krishna was a reminder that life itself is a beautiful dance of the divine, and it is in embracing this divine lila that we come closest to the Supreme.

Jai Shri Ram,

Hanuman

|| Jai Shri Ram ||

Date: Full Moon Day of Kartika, Kali Yuga, Year 101

Dear Universe,

The Tale of the Arjuna's Chariot

I have lived many lives and crossed many paths, but some moments stand out — moments where the will of the divine touches the lives of mortals in ways unseen. One such moment occurred during the great war of Kurukshetra, when the Pandavas stood on the precipice of destiny.

The time had come for them to fulfill their dharma and seek justice for the wrongs done to them by the Kauravas. Yet, in their moment of greatest need, I knew I had a role to play once more, as I had in the past when I aided Lord Ram in His struggle against Ravana.

I had been watching over the Pandavas during their long and bitter exile, my heart always heavy with the knowledge of their suffering. The divine purpose of their journey, however, was clear. The day would come when they would need to reclaim their kingdom and restore righteousness in the land. And so it was that on the eve of the great battle, I found myself drawn to a pivotal moment in time.

It was on the chariot of Arjuna, the greatest of the Pandavas, that my intervention was most needed. I knew the war would require not just courage and strength, but also divine blessings. Arjuna, the mighty archer, was unparalleled in skill, but even he could not win the battle alone. I had long been a humble servant of Lord Ram, and though I was not bound to the human world by the same constraints, I understood well the power of dharma and duty.

And so, I decided to offer my assistance, not through a direct confrontation, but through a more subtle and powerful means. I offered myself to Arjuna's chariot as a blessing.

One evening, as the Pandavas prepared for war, I appeared before Lord Krishna, who was to be Arjuna's charioteer. I humbly offered myself to sit upon the mast of Arjuna's chariot. It was an unusual request, but the divine Krishna, with His infinite wisdom, understood its significance.

"I wish to sit on the mast of your chariot, O Arjuna," I said, "and imbue it with my divine power. Through my presence, I will ensure that you are protected from all evil, and I will guide your chariot safely through the battlefield."

Krishna, with a smile that seemed to encompass the entire universe, accepted my offer. "May you bring your strength to this chariot, Hanuman," He said. "Your presence will inspire Arjuna and the Pandavas in ways they cannot yet comprehend."

And so, as the sun rose on the day of battle, I made my place upon the mast of Arjuna's chariot. As I sat there, a great energy seemed to pulse through the battlefield, and I knew that the Pandavas had divine aid by their side. The wind of dharma carried Arjuna's chariot forward, and no enemy could stop it. The Kauravas may have been mighty, but with my divine blessing, the Pandavas were destined for victory.

I ensured that the Pandavas would have the divine support they needed to win the battle of Kurukshetra. In this way, I, Hanuman, stood as a silent witness and an eternal guardian, ensuring that the forces of dharma triumphed over adharma, and the Pandavas emerged victorious in their rightful struggle.

May the memory of this divine intervention remain forever in the hearts of those who seek righteousness, strength, and devotion.

|| Jai Shri Ram ||

Date: Full Moon Day of Kartika, Kali Yuga, Year 101

Dear Universe,

The Fall of Ravana - The Divine Strategy of Lord Vishnu and Lord Shiva

There are stories that are whispered through the winds of time, and then there are those that are woven into the very fabric of the universe.

The story of Ravana's downfall is one such tale — a story not only of arrogance and power but of divine wisdom and cosmic play. The great demon king Ravana, in his insatiable thirst for power, sought to make himself immortal.

But in his arrogance, he overlooked one crucial detail, and it was this oversight that led to his eventual destruction.

Ravana, the mighty king of Lanka, was a scholar of the highest order, a devotee of Lord Brahma, and a warrior of unmatched strength. In his mind, no force—be it divine or demonic—could ever stand in his way. He sought the blessing of immortality from the very gods themselves.

One day, as the winds of fate began to stir, Ravana performed a rigorous penance. With deep devotion, he meditated for thousands of years, offering prayers and sacrifices to Lord Brahma. The earth trembled at his intensity, and the heavens themselves held their breath as Ravana, with every passing moment, grew closer to his goal.

Impressed by his dedication, Brahma, the creator of the universe, appeared before him.

"Ravana," he said, his voice resonating through the cosmos, "you have pleased me with your devotion. Ask for a boon, and it shall be granted."

Ravana's heart swelled with pride, for he believed that no request was beyond his reach. He spoke boldly, "Grant me the boon that no god, demon, or any other power shall ever be able to defeat me. I shall become invincible, and none will have the power to kill me."

Brahma, wise as always, granted the wish but did so with caution, for he knew the dangers of granting such a boon. He understood that power, when wielded without wisdom, could lead to ruin. "So be it," Brahma said, his voice heavy with the weight of destiny.

But Ravana, in his arrogance, failed to specify one crucial detail: he never mentioned *humans.*

He believed the gods, demons, and all celestial beings would be his rivals. He never thought that the simplest of beings — those who walked the earth — could pose any threat to him. This oversight would become the seed of his eventual destruction.

With his boon granted, Ravana felt invincible.

No enemy, no force in the universe could challenge him. His confidence grew, and with it, his tyranny over the world. But what Ravana did not know was that the divine play of the universe had already set its course.

It was now time for the supreme powers — Lord Vishnu and Lord Shiva — to fulfill their roles in the cosmic drama.

Lord Vishnu, the protector of the universe, knew that the time had come to end Ravana's reign. Ravana's arrogance was growing, and his cruelty had reached unbearable heights.

To restore balance, Lord Vishnu decided to incarnate as a mortal — born not as a demon or celestial being, but as a human: *Lord Ram.*

This would be the divine trickery — Ravana had sought to escape death from the gods, but he had overlooked humans, the very beings that could destroy him.

Lord Vishnu took birth as Ram, the son of King Dasharatha, in the kingdom of Ayodhya. He grew into a warrior of unparalleled grace, wisdom, and strength, armed with the divine bow and an unshakable sense of righteousness. With his birth, the wheels of destiny began to turn, and the stage was set for the ultimate battle between good and evil.

But Vishnu did not act alone in this divine drama. He was not just to be supported by the humans, but by another powerful force — Lord Shiva.

Ravana, in his arrogance, had also neglected to consider the power of Lord Shiva, who had once blessed him with the knowledge of his invincibility. Shiva's divine form was that of the supreme ascetic, and yet, it was through His avatar as the mighty Hanuman that the divine plan would unfold.

In the battle of Lanka, as the war between the forces of good and evil raged on, I, Hanuman, emerged as a key figure. I was born to serve Lord Ram, and it was my devotion and strength that would pave the way for His victory. As His loyal servant, I was tasked with tasks that would humble even the mightiest.

I flew across the ocean to deliver Ram's message to Sita, I brought the mountain of herbs to heal the wounded, and I fought valiantly in the battle against Ravana's mighty army.

But it was through my deep faith and my connection to Lord Shiva that Ravana's end was sealed. For you see, Ravana had forgotten that while he had become invincible to the gods and demons, he had overlooked the power of devotion and selflessness, embodied in me.

It was my faith in Lord Ram, and the divine power of Shiva within me, that gave me the strength to face Ravana in the battle.

On the battlefield of Lanka, the final confrontation came. As Ravana stood tall, sure of his invincibility, he faced Ram, the human incarnation of Vishnu.

The battle was fierce, but it was in this moment that Ravana realized his folly — he had underestimated the human form, the form that carried the supreme power of the divine.

And then, in the heat of the battle, it was I — Hanuman, in my avatar as the humble servant of Ram — who played a crucial role in Ravana's destruction. I tore through the battlefield with the strength of Lord Shiva himself, aiding Ram in his pursuit of Ravana. It was not just Ram's arrow, but the collective divine force — Vishnu in human form and Shiva through me — that brought an end to Ravana's reign.

Ravana fell, not because of the gods or demons, but because of his arrogance, his inability to see beyond his own pride. The divine play had unfolded in the most unexpected way — through the human form of Ram and the divine grace of Shiva as Hanuman.

Thus, the great Ravana, the conqueror of gods and demons, was defeated not by celestial beings but by the divine forces that had been underestimated. The cosmic cycle had completed, and justice was restored. And in that moment, I, Hanuman, stood by my Lord Ram, knowing that our divine purpose had been fulfilled.

May the story of Ravana's downfall serve as a reminder to all that arrogance, no matter how mighty, is always the seed of destruction. And no matter how invincible one may seem, the power of devotion, righteousness, and humility will always triumph in the end.

Jai Shri Ram,

Hanuman

|| Jai Shri Ram ||

Date: Full Moon Day of Kartika, Kali Yuga, Year 101

Dear Universe,

The Ten Heads of Ravana

Listen, my dear friends, as I recount the story of Ravana, the mighty demon king of Lanka. His ten heads were not just a symbol of his extraordinary power, but also a reflection of the inner battles each one of us faces. He was no mere villain. Ravana's story is a story of the mind — of our own minds — and the choices we make.

The Head of Power (Shakti)

Ravana's first head represents power. He was a king with unrivalled strength, a conqueror of the three worlds. His might was unmatched, and he ruled Lanka with an iron fist. He had been granted the boon of invincibility from Lord Brahma, making him believe that no one could defeat him.

But power, my friends, is a double-edged sword. When misused, it corrupts the heart. Ravana's power led him to believe that he was above all, even the gods. He could not see that true power lies in humility, in the ability to serve others, and in the wisdom to know that power is not eternal.

Power without compassion turns into arrogance. We must remember that true strength comes from lifting others, not from crushing them.

The Head of Knowledge (Jnana)

Ravana's second head symbolized knowledge. He was a scholar — well-versed in the Vedas, music, and many other sciences. His intellect was vast, and his wisdom was unmatched. Yet, despite his great knowledge, Ravana used it for his own ego and selfish desires.

Knowledge is a gift, my friends, but when it is used for personal gain and without the intent to help others, it becomes poison. Ravana's knowledge should have made him wise and compassionate, yet it led him astray, blinding him to the truth.

Knowledge should humble us, not inflate our ego.

True knowledge is always accompanied by wisdom and kindness.

The Head of Desire (Kama)

Desire, the third head, represents Ravana's desires. His desires knew no bounds — he craved power, wealth, and even the beautiful Sita. He kidnapped her, driven by a desire he could not control. His lust for her caused the downfall of his empire, and in the end, his desires destroyed him.

Desire is natural, but when it becomes obsessive and self-destructive, it pulls us away from our true purpose. Ravana could not see that his desires were rooted in his ego and ignorance.

Desire is not bad, but when we let it control us, we lose sight of what truly matters — our relationships, our values, and our peace of mind.

The Head of Ego (Ahankara)

Ravana's fourth head symbolizes ego.

He believed that he was the greatest of all beings, stronger than the gods. His ego was his greatest weakness, blinding him to the love and devotion of others. He even dared to challenge Lord Vishnu, thinking he could win.

Ego blinds us, my friends. It creates separation between us and others. It makes us feel superior and invincible, but in the end, it isolates us from the world and brings about our downfall.

The lesson: We must learn to recognize our ego for what it is. True greatness lies not in the height of our ego but in the depth of our humility.

The Head of Anger (Krodha)

Anger is the fifth head of Ravana, representing anger. When Ravana was insulted, he would unleash his fury without thinking. His anger led him to commit heinous acts—such as abducting Sita — driven solely by his rage.

Anger is a fire, my friends. It burns bright and fierce but leaves destruction in its wake. Ravana's uncontrolled anger made him blind to the consequences of his actions, leading him into a spiral of destruction.

Anger is a storm. If we do not learn to control it, it will destroy everything in its path. Patience and understanding are the antidotes to anger.

The Head of Greed (Lobha)

Ravana's sixth head represents greed. No matter how much wealth or power he possessed, it was never enough. His greed grew insatiable, and he wanted to rule over everything, even the gods. He took what was not his, and in the end, it cost him his life.

Greed blinds us to what we already have. It makes us believe that we need more, even when we are already blessed with enough.

Greed leads to suffering. True happiness comes not from accumulating more, but from appreciating and sharing what we have.

The Head of Delusion (Moha)

Ravana's mind was clouded by his own desires, his own ego. He could not see the reality of the situation; he thought he could defeat Ram, even though he knew Ram was no ordinary man.

Delusion is the greatest trap, my friends. It makes us believe in false truths and leads us down paths that bring us harm. Ravana's delusion prevented him from recognizing the divine presence of Ram.

We must guard against delusion. The truth is often simple, and it lies in our hearts, not in the noise around us.

The Head of Hatred (Dwesh)

The eighth head symbolizes hatred. Ravana's hatred toward Ram, his envy of good, and his opposition to righteousness led him to commit vile acts. His hatred clouded his judgment, and it became a cycle that could not be broken.

Hatred poisons the mind, my friends. It robs us of peace and leads us to make decisions that we later regret.

We must free ourselves from hatred. It is only through love and understanding that we can rise above the chaos of our own emotions.

The Head of Doubt (Vichikitsa)

Ravana's ninth head represents doubt. Despite his vast power and intellect, Ravana was often filled with doubt — doubt about his own choices, doubt about his fate, and doubt about his ability to defeat Ram. This doubt paralyzed him when he needed clarity the most.

Doubt can be a good thing, for it makes us question and learn. But when it takes root and grows, it weakens us. Ravana's doubt led him to make rash decisions, never seeing things clearly.

Doubt can either drive us to wisdom or keep us stagnant. We must cultivate faith in ourselves and in the divine plan.

The Head of Attachment (Raga)

Finally, the tenth head represents attachment. Ravana's attachment to his kingdom, his family, and his wealth made him lose sight of the bigger picture. He was so attached to these things that he could not let go of them, even when they led him astray.

Attachment can hold us in chains, my friends. It keeps us tied to the material world, preventing us from realizing our spiritual nature.

We must practice detachment. It does not mean abandoning the world, but rather not being bound by it. True freedom lies in non-attachment.

Jai Shri Ram,

Hanuman

|| Jai Shri Ram ||

Date: Full Moon Day of Kartika, Kali Yuga, Year 101

Dear Universe,

Krishna's Divine Departure

As I, Hanuman, reflect upon the events that unfolded in the last moments of Krishna's earthly presence, I see them as a part of the grand cosmic play, where every act, no matter how seemingly small or inconsequential, is orchestrated with divine intent.

It was in the midst of this divine moment, as Krishna sat peacefully beneath the tree, his flute weaving melodies that echoed the eternal truths of the universe, that a hunter named Jara entered the scene. His eyes searched the forest for his prey, unaware of the sacred presence nearby. The hunter, driven by the instinct to hunt, did not recognize Krishna in his divine form.

As fate would have it, his eyes fell upon Krishna's feet, and in his misguided aim, he mistook the divine feet for the body of a deer.

With a swift pull of his bow, Jara released the arrow. It soared through the air with precision, piercing Krishna's feet. The divine blood that flowed from the wound was not a sign of weakness, but a symbol of Krishna's final act of surrender to the grand cycle of life and death.

Jara, realizing his grave mistake, immediately ran towards Krishna.

His heart was filled with dread, knowing he had unintentionally caused harm to the very Lord of the universe. Trembling with fear, he fell at Krishna's feet, pleading for forgiveness.

But Krishna, even in this moment of apparent suffering, spoke with the same calmness and wisdom that had always defined Him.

"Do not worry, Jara," Krishna said, his voice gentle yet profound.

"This was meant to happen. In my previous incarnation, when I was Ram, you were Vali, the brother of Sugriva. I had to defeat you then, and now, in this form, it is you who enables my departure from this world."

The words of Krishna struck Jara deeply. In that moment, he understood the cosmic nature of his action. His arrow had not caused Krishna's death; it had merely fulfilled the divine will.

Krishna's time on Earth had come to an end, and Jara had been the instrument through which this final act was realized. It was not a mistake, but a divine necessity, woven into the fabric of time.

As Jara knelt before Krishna, overcome with sorrow, Krishna reassured him, "You are not to blame. The wheel of time turns in mysterious ways, and it is only through your hand that I am allowed to return to the eternal realm. The destiny of all beings is tied to the divine plan, and you, Jara, have played your part in this great cosmic play."

Jara's heart was filled with a mix of guilt and awe as he realized the truth of Krishna's words. He had unwittingly fulfilled a role in the grand design, and in doing so, he had been part of Krishna's return to the divine realm.

As I stood by, witnessing this profound moment, I could not help but marvel at the divine wisdom that guided Krishna's every action.

The death of Krishna was not an end, but a continuation of the eternal cycle of life, death, and rebirth. It was a reminder that in every action, no matter how small or unintentional, there is a higher purpose, and every being, even a humble hunter like Jara, plays a role in the unfolding of the divine plan.

And so, as Krishna's breath grew fainter, and his soul began to transcend the mortal realm, I offered my deepest reverence to him. I knew that, like all of us, Krishna would never truly die.

His divine presence would live on forever in the hearts of those who loved him and in the endless cycle of creation and dissolution.

In that moment, I understood: the divine play continues, and every soul, every action, is a part of the greater story of the universe.

Jai Shri Ram,

Hanuman

|| Jai Shri Ram ||

Date: Full Moon Day of Kartika, Kali Yuga, Year 101

Dear Universe,

My Promise as a Chiranjeevi

As I, Hanuman, sit and reflect upon my divine journey, I am reminded of the path that led to my blessing of being Chiranjeevi, immortal in the eyes of time.

My heart, filled with devotion to Lord Ram, has been the foundation of every act, every service I have rendered, and every promise I have made to the universe. I walk through time not as a mere being, but as an instrument of divine grace, a helper to those in need, and a reminder that faith and devotion can conquer even the darkest of times.

The story of me becoming Chiranjeevi begins in the days when I was a child, full of boundless energy and strength, not yet aware of the profound destiny that awaited me.

I was not always conscious of my divine form, for I was blessed by the gods and carried with me immeasurable powers. However, it was in my service to Lord Ram during the battle against Ravana that my purpose was fully realized.

In the midst of that great battle, my devotion and loyalty to Lord Ram knew no bounds. My heart beat only for him, and my strength grew to match my faith.

After the battle, when the world was safe and Lord Ram's reign of righteousness was restored, I was blessed by the gods. They bestowed upon me the boon of immortality, declaring that I would remain in this world, untouched by the ravages of time.

As a Chiranjeevi, I would live through the ages, witnessing the rise and fall of empires, and I would be called upon to aid those who were in need of strength, guidance, or protection.

The gods knew that I could never abandon the world, for my purpose was far greater than my own existence — it was to serve others, to help those in despair, and to ensure that righteousness would always have a protector.

With this blessing came a deep responsibility. I was entrusted with the ability to intervene when the time came, to lend strength to those whose hearts were faltering, to provide clarity to those who were lost, and to guide them back to their true path.

Though I cannot intervene in the ultimate design of destiny, I have always found ways to help those in need, for I am a servant of the divine.

It is my joy, my calling, to resolve the struggles of the world. I walk among you, invisible to most, but always present when needed.

When there are moments of doubt, when hearts are broken or when paths are unclear, I come forward — not as a deity, but as a humble helper, offering my strength and wisdom to those who seek it.

People often wonder why I, as a Chiranjeevi, continue to walk the earth when so many others have passed into the next realm. My answer is simple: It is because there are still those who need my aid.

I do not remain for my own sake, but for those whose voices call out in times of need. I serve as a reminder that even in the darkest times, a guiding light will always emerge.

Even in the most hopeless situations, there is someone watching, someone who will stand with you — and that is the gift I offer to this world.

So, when you find yourself in a place of uncertainty, when the weight of the world seems too much to bear, know that I am here, always ready to offer my help. Whether it is to resolve a conflict, find your strength, or help you see the truth, I am but a prayer away.

Being Chiranjeevi is not about never leaving, but about always returning when needed. I am here, eternally, to help, to serve, and to remind you that with faith, with strength, and with devotion, every problem can be overcome.

You are never alone, for I walk with you, through every challenge, guiding you with deep love and support.

|| Jai Shri Ram ||

Date: Full Moon Day of Kartika, Kali Yuga, Year 101

Dear Universe,

The Sacred Days

As I, Hanuman, reflect upon the divine forces that guide our lives, I am reminded of the sacred practices surrounding my worship on Tuesdays and Saturdays, days that are tied to the powerful planets Mangal (Mars) and Shani (Saturn).

These days, dear devotees, are not merely markers of time, but windows through which the divine energies of the cosmos flow, influencing our lives in profound ways. The very act of worshiping me, Lord Maruti, on these days is deeply connected to the divine balance between strength, courage, discipline, and endurance.

I am not just Hanuman, the devoted servant of Lord Ram; I am also Maruti, the embodiment of strength, energy, and resilience. It is in my Maruti form that I am most closely connected to the celestial forces that govern the universe.

On Tuesdays and Saturdays, devotees come to my temple not only to seek my blessings but to align themselves with the energies of Mangal and Shani, the planets whose influence shapes much of our fate.

Mangal – The Warrior Planet: Tuesday's Blessing of Strength

Mangal, or Mars, is the planet that governs strength, courage, and determination. It is a fiery force that fuels our ambition, drives us to action, and pushes us to succeed in the face of obstacles.

Mangal is the warrior's planet, and its influence empowers us to stand tall in the face of adversity.

As Maruti, I share a deep connection with Mangal, for I am the embodiment of boundless strength and indomitable courage.

My feats, from leaping across the ocean to carrying mountains, are a testament to the divine power granted to me by the gods.

On Tuesdays, devotees come to me with hearts full of devotion, seeking the strength to overcome their challenges, whether in the battlefield of life or in the pursuit of their goals. The energy of Mangal on this day amplifies my own divine strength, and through prayer, you too can harness that power.

When you visit my temple on Tuesday, you invoke the spirit of Mangal within you. You seek to connect with the warrior's strength, the determination to succeed, and the courage to face any challenge.

I, as Maruti, bless you with the energy of Mangal, ensuring that your heart is filled with courage and that your actions are powered by divine strength. Tuesday is the day when your inner warrior awakens, and you are empowered to face the trials of life with deep confidence.

Shani – The Planet of Discipline: Saturday's Blessing of Endurance

While Mangal is the force of strength and victory, Shani, the planet of Saturn, represents discipline, justice, and endurance.

Shani teaches us the value of patience, the importance of hard work, and the need for perseverance through difficult times.

His lessons may sometimes be harsh, but they are always just and aimed at helping us grow.

On Saturdays, the energy of Shani is at its peak, and it is on this day that devotees come to seek my blessings as Maruti, invoking my qualities of humility, patience, and devotion. While I am known for my strength,

I am also known for my humility and dedication to the task at hand. These are qualities that resonate deeply with the energy of Shani.

Though Shani's influence may bring hardships or challenges, it also brings wisdom and teaches us that true growth comes through endurance and discipline.

When you visit my temple on Saturday, you seek not just physical strength but also the strength of spirit to endure the difficulties of life. Shani's influence can be difficult, but it is through it that you learn the value of perseverance.

As Maruti, I guide you to balance strength with discipline, to face challenges with both power and patience. On Saturday, you honor not just the need for immediate success, but the slow and steady path to ultimate victory.

The Cosmic Balance of Strength and Discipline

In this sacred cycle of Tuesdays and Saturdays, we find the perfect balance of cosmic energies. The fiery strength of Mangal aligns with my form on Tuesdays, allowing you to face your challenges with courage and vigor.

On Saturdays, the disciplined and patient influence of Shani aligns with my teachings of humility and devotion, helping you endure even the harshest of times.

Each day is a reminder of the dual nature of life — the need for both strength and discipline, courage and patience. It is through the worship of Maruti on these days that you find the power to act decisively and the wisdom to endure.

The combination of these energies helps you navigate the complexities of life with divine guidance and support.

I, Hanuman, am always present with you, whether on Tuesdays or Saturdays, to guide you in the ways of strength and endurance.

I bless you with the energy of Mangal on Tuesday and the wisdom of Shani on Saturday.

Through these sacred days, you align yourself with the divine forces that govern the universe, drawing closer to the path of righteousness, courage, and perseverance.

In this way, the practice of visiting my temple on Tuesdays and Saturdays is not just a ritual but a way of connecting with the cosmic forces that shape your life.

May you find strength in the face of adversity and patience in times of struggle, knowing that I am with you always, guiding you through every challenge with divine grace.

Jai Shri Ram,

Hanuman

|| Jai Shri Ram ||

Date: Full Moon Day of Kartika, Kali Yuga, Year 101

Dear Universe,

The Story of Sindhur and My Love for Lord Rama

It was one fine morning in Ayodhya, the kingdom blessed with Lord Rama's presence. The sun rose with the gentle light of hope, and the fragrance of flowers filled the air.

As I went about my day, my heart brimming with excitement to serve my Lord, I found myself walking behind Sita Mata, who was on her way to Lord Rama's bedroom.

I, ever the humble servant, followed her, just as I always did.

But when I tried to enter the room, Lord Rama stopped me with a calm yet firm voice, "Hanuman, you cannot enter."

I stood still, confusion filling my heart. I had served Lord Rama with all my being, yet here I was being denied entry into His room. "Why, Prabhu?" I asked, my voice full of innocent curiosity. "Why can Mata Sita enter, but not I?"

Lord Rama, ever gentle with me, replied, "Sita can enter because she has sindhur on her forehead, a sign of her devotion and love for me."

The mention of sindhur caught my attention like a spark catching dry grass. "Sindhur?" I repeated, my mind racing like a river after a storm. "What is this sindhur that Mata Sita uses, and why is it so important?"

My heart was filled with a burning desire to understand. I rushed to Sita Mata the next day, finding her at her dressing table, applying sindhur on her forehead.

I approached her with the same childlike innocence that I always had, asking, "Mata, why do you apply this sindhur? What is its purpose?"

Sita Mata, seeing me as her son, smiled gently and explained, "Hanuman, this sindhur is not just a decoration. It symbolizes my deep love for Lord Rama. It is said that applying it elongates the life of my Prabhu, and every time I apply it, I pray for his well-being."

I felt a rush of emotion, like a wave crashing on the shore. "If this sindhur can prolong the life of my Lord," I thought, "then it must be the most powerful substance in the world."

My heart swelled with love, and I thanked Sita Mata before rushing out to the marketplace.

In the market, I found a small shop selling sindhur. I bought a small box, but as I gazed at it, I felt it was too little. "How could such a small amount of sindhur be enough to extend Prabhu's life?" I wondered, a deep sense of urgency in my heart. "I must do more. I must give all I can for his well-being."

With the innocence of a child and the enthusiasm of a devoted servant, I opened all the sacks of sindhur in the shop. I poured it all over myself — my body drenched in the bright red powder. I rolled on the ground, covering myself entirely in sindhur, thinking, "This will surely make Lord Rama live forever!"

I hurried back to Ayodhya, my heart full of anticipation.

As I entered the palace, I was met with the astonished gaze of Lord Rama. His eyes widened in surprise. "Hanuman, what is this? Why are you covered in sindhur?"

Sita Mata began to laugh, her gentle voice ringing in the air. She turned to Lord Rama and explained, "Prabhu, Hanumanji, in his infinite love for you, thought that if a small amount of sindhur could prolong your life, then covering himself entirely with sindhur would make your life eternal."

Lord Rama's eyes softened with love as He looked at me, His heart filled with compassion. "Hanuman, your devotion is unparalleled. You have shown me how pure and selfless your love is."

As I reflect on that day, I realize how truly innocent and pure my love for Lord Rama was.

I, who knew He was the Supreme Personality of Godhead, thought that my actions — covering myself with sindhur — would make Him live forever. But in that moment, I understood the essence of true devotion.

It is not about what we do, but how we do it. The love with which we serve matters more than anything else.

Lord Rama, the Supreme Being, does not need anything from us, yet He accepts our love, our service, our offerings, and makes them divine.

My love for Him was not about expecting anything in return. It was an act of pure, selfless devotion. No wonder I was His eternal servant, always at His service, never questioning His will.

In our own lives, we may sometimes feel anxiety, thinking that our offerings might not be enough, that our service might be too little. But remember, it is the love in our actions that matters, not the size of the offering.

Whether it's a prayer, a bhoga, or a simple gesture, it is the love behind it that touches the Lord's heart.

Just as Devaki, Krishna's mother, felt anxious about Krishna's safety even in the womb, our devotion, like hers, is a sign of our growing relationship with the Lord. Love can sometimes make us forget the Lord's supreme nature, but it also brings us closer to Him.

Jai Shri Ram,

Hanuman

|| Jai Shri Ram ||

Date: Full Moon Day of Kartika, Kali Yuga, Year 101

Dear Universe,

The Lost Scriptures

Long before I became a servant of Lord Rama, I wandered through forests and mountains, seeking to understand the deeper meaning of life. On one of these journeys, I came across a secluded cave where an ancient sage, who had lived for thousands of years, was meditating.

The sage looked up at me with wise, penetrating eyes and said, "You seek knowledge, Hanuman, but do you know where true knowledge lies?"

I replied earnestly, "I seek the wisdom of the universe, the teachings of the ancients, and the truth that binds us all."

The sage smiled and handed me a collection of dusty, old scrolls. "These are the lost scriptures, the teachings of the ancients. They are heavy with knowledge, but they are also weighty with responsibility."

As I looked at the scrolls, I asked, "Why have these scriptures been lost?"

The sage replied, "Because knowledge without wisdom is dangerous. Some truths are too heavy for the human heart. These scriptures were hidden away, waiting for someone who could carry their weight without being consumed by them."

As I, Hanuman, studied the ancient scrolls, the knowledge contained within them began to reveal the profound interconnectedness of all life, the nature of the soul, and the infinite compassion of the Divine.

At first, it appeared as a complex web of teachings, but as I delved deeper, the lessons became clearer. I understood that everything in existence, whether living or non-living, is intricately woven together by divine forces, and our actions — no matter how small — create ripples throughout the universe.

Years later I realised this principle is not just an abstract concept; it is beautifully illustrated in two of the most revered epics which I witnessed - the Ramayana and the Mahabharata.

As I studied the scrolls, I realized that the interconnectedness of life is not limited to the actions of the material world; it extends to the very essence of the soul. The soul, according to the teachings, is eternal and indivisible, part of the divine energy that pervades all existence.

Our actions in the material world may seem isolated, but they are reflections of our deeper connection to the Supreme.

In the Ramayana, my deep devotion to Lord Rama, despite the many challenges and trials, is a testament to the power of the soul's connection to the divine. It is this connection that drives us to act with love, compassion, and selflessness.

Similarly, the Mahabharata explores the complexity of the soul through the teachings of Krishna, who reveals that our actions must be guided by the eternal truth of dharma. Krishna's compassion, even towards his enemies like Duryodhana, reveals the infinite nature of divine love. He acts not out of personal vendetta but out of compassion for the souls involved, aiming to restore balance and righteousness in the world.

The most important lesson I learned from the scrolls was that knowledge alone is not enough. Knowledge without compassion and love is like a fire that consumes everything in its path.

The true value of knowledge lies in its application — in how we use it to serve others, to heal, and to bring harmony to the world.

In my role as Lord Rama's devotee, I learned that my strength and knowledge were not meant for personal glory or gain, but for the service of the divine will. My actions, even the smallest ones, were interconnected with the larger plan of the cosmos.

Whether I was leaping across the ocean to find Sita or delivering a message from Rama to Ravana, every act was a part of the divine design.

By understanding the interconnectedness of life and the nature of the soul, I learned to act with wisdom, compassion, and humility, recognizing that my every action has a greater impact on the world around me.

In the end, both the Ramayana and the Mahabharata teach us the same fundamental truth: that everything is interconnected, that our actions have consequences beyond our understanding, and that love and compassion are the true forces that guide the universe.

The more I learned, the more I realized that my duty was not only to Lord Rama but to all of creation — to serve with love, to act with integrity, and to help restore balance and harmony in the world.

This is the true essence of life's interconnectedness.

Jai Shri Ram,

Hanuman

|| Jai Shri Ram ||

Date: Full Moon Day of Kartika, Kali Yuga, Year 101

Dear Universe,

The Ramayana Written Twice

One day, as I sat alone, my mind filled with memories of Lord Rama's victories, his deep righteousness, and his eternal love for Sita Mata, I felt the need to express the emotions I carried within my heart.

The world had already been blessed with the great sage Valmiki's Ramayana, but my devotion to Lord Rama overflowed in ways words cannot easily describe.

I decided to write my own version of the Ramayana, not out of comparison or competition, but because I longed to capture my love and service for Lord Rama.

With the same reverence that I offered to Him in every action, I began writing on banana leaves, each stroke of my pen reflecting the truth I knew in my heart. It was not simply a recounting of events; it was the embodiment of my pure devotion.

Years passed, and one day, the great sage Valmiki himself visited me. I had always revered Valmiki, for he had written the Ramayana that spoke to the world. He was a true sage, and his heart, like mine, was bound in eternal service to Lord Rama.

When Valmiki arrived at the place where I had written my Ramayana, he was curious.

"Hanuman," he said, "I have heard of your devotion and love for Lord Rama. But what is this that I see? You have written the Ramayana as well. May I see it?"

With deep respect, I handed him the banana leaves that held my writing. Valmiki, the great sage, sat with reverence and began to read. As his eyes skimmed the words, I could see his expression shift. He was filled with awe, humility, and a silent understanding.

When he finished, he turned to me and spoke in a voice filled with wonder.

"Hanuman," Valmiki said, "your Ramayana is filled with such purity and devotion. It is beyond what words can describe. Yet, I cannot help but feel that it will never be read like my Ramayana. Your love for Lord Rama — this, this is the true essence of the story. It is not just the telling of events, but the heart behind it. It is a divine expression of your love."

I, with my simple heart, heard his words. I understood that he spoke from the deepest corners of his soul. But I also knew the truth — that my version of the Ramayana was nothing in comparison to the grandeur of Valmiki's.

His Ramayana was the one that would be passed down through generations, recited by millions, and etched into the hearts of those who sought the path of righteousness.

Without a word, I stood and approached the banana leaves.

With great humility, I tore them all apart. The sound of the leaves ripping echoed in the still air as I tore the pages that carried my heartfelt version of the Ramayana.

Valmiki looked at me, stunned. "Hanuman, what have you done?" he asked, his voice filled with disbelief. "Your Ramayana is divine. Why destroy it?"

I looked at him, my heart full of humility and love for Lord Rama. "Sage Valmiki," I said gently, "I wrote this Ramayana not for recognition, but as an offering to Lord Rama. Your Ramayana, the one that carries the divine truth of Lord Rama's life, is the one that will be remembered. The world will read your version, and it will be passed down through time. My humble attempt was only an expression of my love, but it is your Ramayana that is meant to be the beacon for all."

Valmiki, looking at me with profound respect, realized that my action was one of pure love and humility.

He bowed before me and spoke softly, "Hanuman, you have taught me a lesson today. Your devotion, your love for Lord Rama, is the greatest lesson of all. It is not the words themselves, but the heart with which they are spoken. The true Ramayana lives in your heart, and that is the truth that will guide us all."

I smiled at him, my heart full of the joy that comes with serving Lord Rama. "Sage Valmiki," I replied, "the true Ramayana is not just in written words, but in the hearts of those who read, understand, and live it. It lives in the devotion of every soul who seeks Lord Rama's refuge and in every action performed in service to Him."

And so, the Ramayana — the story of Lord Rama, Sita, Lakshmana, Ravana, and the battle of good versus evil — lives on through both versions. Valmiki's Ramayana has been passed down through generations, and my version, though destroyed in the physical form, remains eternally in the hearts of all those who understand the true meaning of devotion.

The story of my Ramayana and Valmiki's Ramayana teaches us that devotion and service are the greatest expressions of love. The true essence of Lord Rama's life is not just in the words of the epic but in the hearts of those who surrender to Him with love, humility, and deep faith.

This is the story of the two Ramayana's — one written by Valmiki, the other by me — and the lesson I learned from it is that the greatest glory lies not in recognition, but in humble service to the Divine.

Jai Shri Ram,

Hanuman

|| Jai Shri Ram ||

Dear Devotee,

Walk your path with courage, devotion, and selflessness, for these virtues hold the key to unlocking your true potential. Remember, no challenge is insurmountable when faith resides in your heart.

Let your actions be guided by love and service, as they create ripples of goodness in the world. Trust that the strength you seek is already within you, waiting to awaken.

May the chanting of sacred mantras fill your life with divine energy, wisdom, and peace. As you call upon my name with sincerity, know that I am always by your side, ready to guide and protect you.

Stay steadfast in your devotion, and your journey will be illuminated by the grace of the Divine.

With love and blessings,

Hanuman

Epilogue

As this journey through the wisdom of the Hanuman Chalisa and Bajrang Baan comes to a close, I hope this book has illuminated the divine qualities of Lord Hanuman and brought you closer to His boundless grace. Each verse, each mantra, carries a spark of the divine—a spark that can transform our lives if we let it.

The teachings of Lord Hanuman remind us to face challenges with courage, serve with humility, and remain devoted to our higher purpose. They inspire us to transcend our limitations and find strength in faith and selfless love.

This book is not an end, but a beginning — a doorway to deeper understanding, greater devotion, and a more profound connection with the divine. Carry these lessons with you, and let them guide your thoughts, words, and actions.

May Lord Ram and Hanuman's blessings continue to protect, inspire, and uplift you on your journey. His strength is your strength, His wisdom is your guide, and His love is your eternal companion.

With devotion and gratitude,

Riya Gote

|| Jai Hanuman ||

About the Author – Riya Gote

**Core Believer in Lord Hanuman | Founder of Scriberlee |
Content Creator | Ghostwriter | Self-Awareness Trainer**

Riya Gote is a dynamic force and leading voice shaping the world of branding, training, and writing. On her best days, she's a content creator, ghostwriter, and leadership trainer. As the Founder at Scriberlee, a global branding firm with offices in Singapore and Pune, she brings her technical expertise and creative storytelling together to create magic. With a Master's in International Business Management from Edinburgh Napier University and a Bachelor's in Engineering from Pune University, Riya's feathers in her cap are a testament to her dedication and strategic insight.

Riya specializes in self-awareness, personal branding, and communication. She's delivered transformative sessions at renowned institutions like NMIMS, SCMHRD, and several international corporates. Her leadership programs have made a lasting impact on professionals, including senior officers from the Indian Army.

On top of that, Riya is an accomplished writer. She has ghostwritten multiple books on topics like happiness, and self-awareness, and her work has been featured in prestigious platforms such as Forbes India and CXO Magazine. Her innovative content strategies and relentless commitment to personal branding have earned her multiple accolades, including the title of "Iron Lady of India" by MTTV India and recognition as one of the Top 10 Emerging Women Entrepreneurs of 2021-22. In 2024, she added another feather to her hat with the Brand Excellence Award by MTTV India and was named Young Marketer of the Year 2024 by The Business Fame magazine.

Her mantra: *"Self-confidence is a superpower. Once you start to believe in yourself, the magic starts happening."*

Contact Details:

📞 +91 8007126143

✉ Riyahgote@gmail.com

🌐 www.riyagote.com | www.scriberlee.com

|| Jai Shri Ram ||